Beginning Programming with Python®

for
dummies®
A Wiley Brand

Beginning Programming with Python®

3rd Edition

by John Paul Mueller

A Wiley Brand

Beginning Programming with Python® For Dummies®, 3rd Edition

Published by: **John Wiley & Sons, Inc.,** 111 River Street, Hoboken, NJ 07030-5774, www.wiley.com

LIMIT OF LIABILITY/DISCLAIMER OF WARRANTY: WHILE THE PUBLISHER AND AUTHORS HAVE USED THEIR BEST EFFORTS IN PREPARING THIS WORK, THEY MAKE NO REPRESENTATIONS OR WARRANTIES WITH RESPECT TO THE ACCURACY OR COMPLETENESS OF THE CONTENTS OF THIS WORK AND SPECIFICALLY DISCLAIM ALL WARRANTIES, INCLUDING WITHOUT LIMITATION ANY IMPLIED WARRANTIES OF MERCHANTABILITY OR FITNESS FOR A PARTICULAR PURPOSE. NO WARRANTY MAY BE CREATED OR EXTENDED BY SALES REPRESENTATIVES, WRITTEN SALES MATERIALS OR PROMOTIONAL STATEMENTS FOR THIS WORK. THE FACT THAT AN ORGANIZATION, WEBSITE, OR PRODUCT IS REFERRED TO IN THIS WORK AS A CITATION AND/OR POTENTIAL SOURCE OF FURTHER INFORMATION DOES NOT MEAN THAT THE PUBLISHER AND AUTHORS ENDORSE THE INFORMATION OR SERVICES THE ORGANIZATION, WEBSITE, OR PRODUCT MAY PROVIDE OR RECOMMENDATIONS IT MAY MAKE. THIS WORK IS SOLD WITH THE UNDERSTANDING THAT THE PUBLISHER IS NOT ENGAGED IN RENDERING PROFESSIONAL SERVICES. THE ADVICE AND STRATEGIES CONTAINED HEREIN MAY NOT BE SUITABLE FOR YOUR SITUATION. YOU SHOULD CONSULT WITH A SPECIALIST WHERE APPROPRIATE. FURTHER, READERS SHOULD BE AWARE THAT WEBSITES LISTED IN THIS WORK MAY HAVE CHANGED OR DISAPPEARED BETWEEN WHEN THIS WORK WAS WRITTEN AND WHEN IT IS READ. NEITHER THE PUBLISHER NOR AUTHORS SHALL BE LIABLE FOR ANY LOSS OF PROFIT OR ANY OTHER COMMERCIAL DAMAGES, INCLUDING BUT NOT LIMITED TO SPECIAL, INCIDENTAL, CONSEQUENTIAL, OR OTHER DAMAGES.

For general information on our other products and services, please contact our Customer Care Department within the U.S. at 877-762-2974, outside the U.S. at 317-572-3993, or fax 317-572-4002. For technical support, please visit https://hub.wiley.com/community/support/dummies.

Wiley publishes in a variety of print and electronic formats and by print-on-demand. Some material included with standard print versions of this book may not be included in e-books or in print-on-demand. If this book refers to media such as a CD or DVD that is not included in the version you purchased, you may download this material at http://booksupport.wiley.com. For more information about Wiley products, visit www.wiley.com.

Library of Congress Control Number: 2022948492

ISBN: 978-1-119-91377-1 (pbk); ISBN 978-1-119-91378-8 (ebk); ISBN 978-1-119-91379-5 (ebk)

SKY10036664_111822

Contents at a Glance

Table of Contents

Introduction

Python is an example of a language that does everything right within the domain of things that it's designed to do. This isn't just me saying it, either: Programmers have voted by using Python enough that it's now the first-ranked language in the world (see `https://www.tiobe.com/tiobe-index/` for details). The amazing thing about Python is that you really can write an application on one platform and use it on every other platform that you need to support. In contrast to other programming languages that promised to provide platform independence, Python really does make that independence possible. In this case, the promise is as good as the result you get.

Python emphasizes code readability and a concise syntax that lets you write applications using fewer lines of code than other programming languages require. You can also use a coding style that meets your needs, given that Python supports the functional, imperative, object-oriented, and procedural coding styles (see Chapter 3 for details). In addition, because of the way Python works, you find it used in all sorts of fields that are filled with nonprogrammers. *Beginning Programming with Python For Dummies*, 3rd Edition is designed to help everyone, including nonprogrammers, get up and running with Python quickly.

Some people view Python as a scripted language, but it really is so much more. (Chapter 19 gives you just an inkling of the occupations that rely on Python to make things work.) However, Python does lend itself to educational and other uses for which other programming languages can fall short. In fact, this book uses both Google Colab and Jupyter Notebook for examples, which rely on the highly readable literate programming paradigm advanced by Stanford computer scientist Donald Knuth (see Chapter 4 for details). Your examples end up looking like highly readable reports that almost anyone can understand with ease.

About This Book

Beginning Programming with Python For Dummies, 3rd Edition is all about getting up and running with Python quickly. You want to learn the language fast so that you can become productive in using it to perform your real job, which could be anything. With the goal in mind of making things simple in every environment, this book emphasizes a code anywhere approach. If you want to code on your smart phone (not really recommended unless you like to squint a lot), you can do so as long as your smart phone has a browser that can access Google Colab. Likewise, coding while watching a TV equipped with a keyboard is possible, but not necessarily recommended because of the distractions involved. Besides, trying to write code that you can see only in that small square in the corner of the screen would be very tough. Highly recommended is your desktop, laptop, or tablet.

Unlike most books on the topic, this one starts you right at the beginning by showing you what makes Python different from other languages and how it can help you perform useful work in a job other than programming. As a result, you gain an understanding of what you need to do from the start, using hands-on examples and spending a good deal of time performing actually useful tasks. By the time you finish working through the examples in this book, you'll be writing simple programs and performing tasks such as sending an email using Python. No, you won't be an expert, but you will be able to use Python to meet specific needs in the job environment. To make absorbing the concepts even easier, this book uses the following conventions:

>> Text that you're meant to type just as it appears in the book is **bold**. The exception is when you're working through a step list: Because each step is bold, the text to type is not bold.

>> When you see words in *italics* as part of a typing sequence, you need to replace that value with something that works for you. For example, if you see "Type **Your Name** and press Enter," you need to replace *Your Name* with your actual name.

>> Web addresses and programming code appear in monofont. If you're reading a digital version of this book on a device connected to the Internet, note that you can click the web address to visit that website, like this: www.dummies.com.

>> When you need to type command sequences, you see them separated by a special arrow, like this: File ⇨ New File. In this case, you go to the File menu first and then select the New File entry on that menu. The result is that you see a new file created.

Foolish Assumptions

You might find it difficult to believe that I've assumed anything about you — after all, I haven't even met you yet! Although most assumptions are indeed foolish, I made these assumptions to provide a starting point for the book.

Familiarity with the platform you want to use is important because the book doesn't provide any guidance in this regard. To provide you with maximum information about Python, this book doesn't discuss any platform-specific issues. You really do need to know how to install applications (when working with a desktop system), use applications, work with your browser, and generally work with your chosen platform before you begin working with this book.

This book also assumes that you can locate information on the Internet. Sprinkled throughout are numerous references to online material that will enhance your learning experience. However, these added sources are useful only if you actually find and use them.

Icons Used in This Book

As you read this book, you see icons in the margins that indicate material of interest (or not, as the case may be). This section briefly describes each icon in this book.

Tips are nice because they help you save time or perform some task without a lot of extra work. The tips in this book are time-saving techniques or pointers to resources that you should try in order to get the maximum benefit from Python.

I don't want to sound like an angry parent or some kind of maniac, but you should avoid doing anything marked with a Warning icon. Otherwise, you could find that your program only serves to confuse users, who will then refuse to work with it.

Whenever you see this icon, think advanced tip or technique. You might find these tidbits of useful information just too boring for words, or they could contain the solution you need to get a program running. Skip these bits of information whenever you like.

If you don't get anything else out of a particular chapter or section, remember the material marked by this icon. This text usually contains an essential process or a bit of information that you must know to write Python programs successfully.

Beyond the Book

This book isn't the end of your Python programming experience — it's really just the beginning. I provide online content to make this book more flexible and better able to meet your needs. That way, as I receive email from you, I can do things like address questions and tell you how updates to either Python or its associated libraries affect book content. In fact, you gain access to all these cool additions:

>> **Cheat sheet:** You remember using crib notes in school to make a better mark on a test, don't you? You do? Well, a cheat sheet is sort of like that. It provides you with some special notes about tasks that you can do with Python that not every other developer knows. You can find the cheat sheet for this book by going to www.dummies.com and searching for *Beginning Programming with Python For Dummies,* 3rd Edition Cheat Sheet. It contains really neat information like how to perform magic when using Python.

>> **Updates:** Sometimes changes happen. For example, I might not have seen an upcoming change when I looked into my crystal ball during the writing of this book. In the past, that simply meant the book would become outdated and less useful, but you can now find updates to the book by going to www.dummies.com and searching for this book's title.

In addition to these updates, check out the blog posts with answers to reader questions and demonstrations of useful book-related techniques at http://blog.johnmuellerbooks.com/.

>> **Companion files:** Hey! Who really wants to type all the code in the book? Most readers would prefer to spend their time actually working through coding examples, rather than typing. Fortunately for you, the source code is available for download, so all you need to do is read the book to learn Python coding techniques. Each of the book examples even tells you precisely which example project to use. You can find these files by going to www.dummies.com and searching for this book's title. You can also find the downloadable source on my website at http://www.johnmuellerbooks.com/source-code/; just click the Download button for *Beginning Programming with Python For Dummies,* 3rd Edition. Be sure to unzip the file using the instructions at https://support.microsoft.com/en-us/windows/zip-and-unzip-files-8d28fa72-f2f9-712f-67df-f80cf89fd4e5 before attempting to use the source code, even if you can see it in Windows Explorer.

Where to Go from Here

It's time to start your Programming with Python adventure! If you're a complete programming novice, you should start with Chapter 1 and progress through the book at a pace that allows you to absorb as much of the material as possible.

If you're a novice who's in an absolute rush to get going with Python as quickly as possible, you could skip to Chapter 2 with the understanding that you may find some topics a bit confusing later. Skipping to Chapter 3 is possible if you want to start working with Python immediately and have access to Google Colab or a Jupyter Notebook installation.

Readers who have some exposure to Python can save time by moving directly to Chapter 4. This chapter gets you started working with notebooks so that you have a better idea of how to work with Google Colab or Jupyter Notebook for the examples in the remainder of the book. Make sure you also read through Chapter 5, which tells you how to perform magic in notebooks.

Assuming that you already have access to either Google Colab or Jupyter Notebook and know how to use your IDE of choice, you can move directly to Chapter 6. You can always go back to earlier chapters as necessary when you have questions. However, it's important that you understand how each example works before moving to the next one. Every example has important lessons for you, and you could miss vital content if you start skipping too much information.

1

Getting Started with Python

Chapter **1**

Talking to Your Computer

aving a conversation with your computer might sound like the script of a science fiction movie. After all, the members of the *Enterprise* on *Star Trek* regularly talked with their computer. In fact, the computer often talked back. However, with the rise of Apple's Siri (https://www.apple.com/siri/), Amazon's Echo (https://www.amazon.com/dp/B07XKF5RM3/) and other interactive software (https://windowsreport.com/talking-pc-software/), perhaps you really don't find a conversation so unbelievable.

REMEMBER

Asking the computer for information is one thing, but providing it with instructions is quite another. This chapter considers why you want to instruct your computer about anything and what benefit you gain from it. You also discover the need for a special language when performing this kind of communication and why you want to use Python to accomplish it. However, the main thing to get out of this chapter is that programming is simply a kind of communication that is akin to other forms of communication you already have with your computer.

Understanding Why You Want to Talk to Your Computer

Talking to a machine may seem quite odd at first (then again, people do talk to cats, dogs, cars, toasters, and other odd assorted things), but it's necessary because a computer can't read your mind — yet. Mind-reading computers are getting closer, as described in the article at `https://www.psychnewsdaily.com/this-computer-can-read-your-mind-and-render-your-thoughts-as-pictures/`. Even if the computer did read your mind, it would still be communicating with you. Nothing can occur without an exchange of information between the machine and you. Activities such as

>> Reading your email

>> Writing about your vacation

>> Finding the greatest gift in the world

are all examples of communication that occurs between a computer and you. That the computer further communicates with other machines or people to address requests that you make simply extends the basic idea that communication is necessary to produce any result.

In most cases, the communication takes place in a manner that is nearly invisible to you unless you really think about it. For example, when you visit a chat room (sometimes called *spaces* now; see `https://workspaceupdates.googleblog.com/2021/09/google-chat-rooms-are-now-spaces.html`) online, you might think that you're communicating with another person. However, you're communicating with your computer, your computer is communicating with the other person's computer through the chat room (whatever it consists of), and the other person's computer is communicating with that person (or possibly an AI). Figure 1-1 gives you an idea of what is actually taking place.

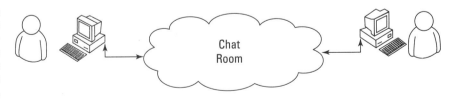

FIGURE 1-1: Communication with your computer may be invisible unless you really think about it.

Notice the cloud in the center of Figure 1-1. The cloud could contain anything, but you know that it at least contains other computers running other applications. These computers make it possible for your friend and you to chat. Now, think about how easy the whole process seems when you're using the chat application. Even though all these things are going on in the background, it seems as if you're simply chatting with your friend, and the process itself is invisible.

Knowing that an Application Is a Form of Communication

Computer communication occurs through the use of applications. You use one application to answer your email, another to purchase goods, and still another to create a presentation. An *application* (sometimes called an *app*) provides the means to express human ideas to the computer in a manner the computer can understand and defines the tools needed to shape the data used for the communication in specific ways. Data used to express the content of a presentation is different from data used to purchase a present for your mother. The way you view, use, and understand the data is different for each task, so you must use different applications to interact with the data in a manner that both the computer and you can understand.

You can obtain applications to meet just about any general need you can conceive of today. In fact, you probably have access to applications for which you haven't even thought about a purpose yet. Programmers have been busy creating millions of applications of all types for many years now, so it may be hard to understand what you can accomplish by creating some new method for talking with your computer through an application. The answer comes down to thinking about the data and how you want to interact with it. Some data simply isn't common enough to have attracted the attention of a programmer, or you may need the data in a format that no application currently supports, so you don't have any way to tell the computer about it unless you create a custom application to do it. The following sections describe applications from the perspective of working with unique data in a manner that is special in some way.

Thinking about procedures you use daily

A *procedure* is simply a set of steps you follow to perform a task. For example, when making toast, you might use a procedure like this:

1. Get the bread and butter from the refrigerator.
2. Open the bread bag and take out two pieces of bread.
3. Remove the cover from the toaster.

4. Place each piece of bread in its own slot.

5. Push the toaster lever down to start toasting the bread.

6. Wait for the toasting process to complete.

7. Remove toast from the toaster.

8. Place toast on a plate.

9. Butter the toast.

Your procedure might vary from the one presented here, but it's unlikely that you'd butter the toast before placing it in the toaster. Of course, you do actually have to remove the bread from the wrapper before you toast it (placing the bread, wrapper and all, into the toaster would likely produce undesirable results). Most people never actually think about the procedure for making toast. However, you use a procedure like this one even though you don't think about it.

REMEMBER

Computers can't perform tasks without a procedure. You must tell the computer which steps to perform, the order in which to perform them, and any exceptions to the rule that could cause failure. All this information (and more) appears within an application. In short, an application is simply a written procedure that you use to tell the computer what to do, when to do it, and how to do it. Because you've been using procedures all your life, all you really need to do is apply the knowledge you already possess to what a computer needs to know about specific tasks.

Writing procedures down

When I was in grade school, our teacher asked us to write a paper about making toast. After we turned in our papers, she brought in a toaster and some loaves of bread. Each paper was read and demonstrated. None of our procedures worked as expected, but they all produced humorous results. In my case, I forgot to tell the teacher to remove the bread from the wrapper, so she dutifully tried to stuff the piece of bread, wrapper and all, into the toaster. The lesson stuck with me. Writing about procedures can be quite hard because we know precisely want we want to do, but often we leave steps out — we assume that the other person also knows precisely what we want to do.

Writing procedures down isn't really sufficient, though — you also need to test the procedure by asking someone who isn't familiar with the task to perform it using your procedure. When working with computers, the computer is your perfect test subject.

Seeing applications as being like any other procedure

A computer acts like the grade school teacher in my example in the previous section. When you write an application, you're writing a procedure that defines a series of steps that the computer should perform to accomplish whatever task you have in mind. If you leave out a step, the results won't be what you expected. The computer won't know what you mean or that you intended for it to perform certain tasks automatically. The only thing the computer knows is that you have provided it with a specific procedure and it needs to perform that procedure.

Making your computer do funny things

People eventually get used to the procedures you create. They automatically compensate for deficiencies in the procedure or make notes about things that were left out. In other words, people compensate for problems with the procedures that you write.

REMEMBER

When you begin writing computer programs, you'll get frustrated because computers perform tasks precisely and read your instructions literally. For example, if you tell the computer that a certain value should equal 5, the computer will look for a value of exactly 5. A human might see 4.9 and know that the value is good enough, but a computer doesn't see things that way. It sees a value of 4.9 and decides that it doesn't equal 5 exactly. In short, computers are inflexible, unintuitive, and unimaginative. When you write a procedure for a computer, the computer will do precisely as you ask absolutely every time and never modify your procedure or decide that you really meant for it to do something else. In some cases (not many), the results can actually be quite humorous (such as that time the computer began reciting a limerick that you meant to keep private). A sense of humor is helpful in computer programming.

Defining What an Application Is

As previously mentioned, applications provide the means to define and express human ideas in a manner that a computer can understand. To accomplish this goal, the application relies on one or more procedures that tell the computer how to perform the tasks related to the manipulation of data and its presentation. What you see onscreen is the text from your word processor, but to see that information, the computer requires procedures for retrieving the data from disk, putting it into a form you can understand, and then presenting it to you. The following sections define the specifics of an application in more detail.

Understanding that computers use a special language

Human language is complex and difficult to understand. Even applications such as Siri and Alexa have serious limits in understanding what you're saying. Over the years, computers have gained the capability to input human speech as data and to interpret certain spoken words as commands, but computers still don't understand human speech. What the computer does is match voice patterns to data it understands and then match that data to specific commands.

Given what you know from previous sections of this chapter, computers could never rely on human speech to understand the procedures you write. Computers always take things literally, so you'd end up with completely unpredictable results if you were to use human language to write applications. That's why humans use special languages, called *programming languages*, to communicate with computers. These special languages make it possible to write procedures that are both specific and completely understandable by both humans and computers.

TECHNICAL STUFF

Computers don't actually speak any language. They use binary codes to flip switches internally and to perform math calculations. Computers don't even understand letters — they understand only numbers. A special application turns the computer-specific language you use to write a procedure into binary codes. For the purposes of this book, you really don't need to worry too much about the low-level specifics of how computers work at the binary level. However, it's interesting to know that computers speak math and numbers, not really a language at all.

Helping humans speak to the computer

It's important to keep the purpose of an application in mind as you write it. An application is there to help humans speak to the computer in a certain way. Every application works with some type of data that is input, stored, manipulated, and output so that the humans using the application obtain a desired result. Whether the application is a game or a spreadsheet, the basic idea is the same. Computers work with data provided by humans to obtain a desired result.

When you create an application, you're providing a new method for humans to speak to the computer. The new approach you create will make it possible for other humans to view data in new ways. The communication between human and computer should be easy enough that the application actually disappears from view. Think about the kinds of applications you've used in the past. The best applications are the ones that let you focus on whatever data you're interacting with. For example, a game application is considered immersive only if you can focus on the planet you're trying to save or the ship you're trying to fly, rather than the application that lets you do these things.

TIP

One of the best ways to start thinking about how you want to create an application is to look at other applications. Writing down what you like and dislike about other applications is a useful way to start discovering how you want your applications to look and work. Here are some questions you can ask yourself as you work with the applications:

>> What do I find distracting about the application?

>> Which features were easy to use?

>> Which features were hard to use?

>> How did the application make it easy to interact with my data?

>> How would I make the data easier to work with?

>> What do I hope to achieve with my application that this application doesn't provide?

Professional developers ask many other questions as part of creating an application, but these are good starter questions because they begin to help you think about applications as a means to help humans speak with computers. If you've ever found yourself frustrated by an application you used, you already know how other people will feel if you don't ask the appropriate questions when you create your application. Communication is the most important element of any application you create.

You can also start to think about the ways in which you work. Start writing procedures for the things you do. It's a good idea to take the process one step at a time and write everything you can think of about that step. When you get finished, ask someone else to try your procedure to see how it actually works. You might be surprised to learn that even with a lot of effort, you can easily forget to include steps.

WARNING

The world's worst application usually begins with a programmer who doesn't know what the application is supposed to do, why it's special, what need it addresses, or whom it is for. When you decide to create an application, make sure that you know why you're creating it and what you hope to achieve. Just having a plan in place really helps make programming fun. You can work on your new application and see your goals accomplished one at a time until you have a completed application to use and show off to your friends (all of whom will think you're really cool for creating it).

Understanding Why Python Is So Cool

Many programming languages are available today. In fact, a student can spend an entire semester in college studying computer languages and still not hear about them all. (I did just that during my college days.) You'd think that programmers would be happy with all these programming languages and just choose one to talk to the computer, but they keep inventing more.

REMEMBER

Programmers keep creating new languages for good reason. Each language has something special to offer — something it does exceptionally well. In addition, as computer technology evolves, so do the programming languages in order to keep up. Because creating an application is all about efficient communication, many programmers know multiple programming languages so that they can choose just the right language for a particular task. One language might work better to obtain data from a database, and another might create user interface elements especially well.

As with every other programming language, Python does some things exceptionally well, and you need to know what they are before you begin using it. You might be amazed by the really cool things you can do with Python. Knowing a programming language's strengths and weaknesses helps you use it better as well as avoid frustration by not using the language for things it doesn't do well. The following sections help you make these sorts of decisions about Python.

Unearthing the reasons for using Python

When Guido van Rossum (`https://gvanrossum.github.io/`) decided to create Python, the main objective was to develop a programming language that would make programmers efficient and productive. With that in mind, here are the reasons that you want to use Python when creating an application:

>> **Less application development time:** Python code is usually 2–10 times shorter than comparable code written in languages like C/C++ and Java, which means that you spend less time writing your application and more time using it.

>> **Ease of reading:** A programming language is like any other language — you need to be able to read it to understand what it does. Python code tends to be easier to read than the code written in other languages, which means you spend less time interpreting it and more time making essential changes.

>> **Reduced learning time:** The creators of Python wanted to make a programming language with fewer odd rules that make the language hard to learn. After all, programmers want to create applications, not learn obscure and difficult languages.

TIP

Although Python is a popular language, it's not always the most popular language out there (depending on the site you use for comparison). However, it currently ranks first on sites such as TIOBE (`https://www.tiobe.com/tiobe-index/`), an organization that tracks usage statistics (among other things). Another good place to look is Statistics Times (`https://statisticstimes.com/tech/top-computer-languages.php`), which also ranks Python as the number one language today.

If you're looking for a language solely for the purpose of obtaining a job, Python is a great choice, but Java, C/C++, or C# might be better choices, depending on the kind of job you want to get. Visual Basic is also a great choice, even if it isn't currently quite as popular as Python. Make sure to choose a language you like and one that will address your application-development needs, but also choose on the basis of what you intend to accomplish. You may be surprised to learn that many colleges use Python to teach coding, and it has become the most popular language in that venue (see `https://www.pythoncentral.io/how-is-python-used-in-education/` for details).

Deciding how you can personally benefit from Python

Ultimately, you can use any programming language to write any sort of application you want. If you use the wrong programming language for the job, the process will be slow, error prone, bug ridden, and you'll absolutely hate it — but you can get the job done. Of course, most of us would rather avoid horribly painful experiences, so you need to know what sorts of applications people typically use Python to create. Here's a list of the most common uses for Python (although people do use it for other purposes):

>> **Creating rough application examples:** Developers often need to create a *prototype,* a rough example of an application, before getting the resources to create the actual application. Python emphasizes productivity, so you can use it to create prototypes of an application quickly.

>> **Scripting browser-based applications:** Even though JavaScript is probably the most popular language used for browser-based application scripting, Python is a close second. Python offers functionality that JavaScript doesn't provide (see the comparison at `https://www.educba.com/python-vs-javascript/` for details) and its high efficiency makes it possible to create browser-based applications faster (a real plus in today's fast-paced world).

>> **Designing mathematic, scientific, and engineering applications:** Interestingly enough, Python provides access to some really cool libraries that make it easier to create math, scientific, and engineering applications. The two most popular libraries are NumPy (`https://numpy.org/`) and SciPy

(`https://scipy.org/`). These libraries greatly reduce the time you spend writing specialized code to perform common math, scientific, and engineering tasks.

» **Working with XML:** The eXtensible Markup Language (XML) is the basis of most data storage needs on the Internet and many desktop applications today. Unlike most languages, where XML is just sort of bolted on, Python makes it a first-class citizen. If you need to work with a web service, the main method for exchanging information on the Internet (or any other XML-intensive application), Python is a great choice.

» **Interacting with databases:** Business relies heavily on databases. Python isn't quite a query language, like the Structured Query Language (SQL) or Language INtegrated Query (LINQ), but it does do a great job of interacting with databases. It makes creating connections and manipulating data relatively painless.

» **Developing user interfaces:** Python isn't like some languages like C# where you have a built-in designer and can drag and drop items from a toolbox onto the user interface. However, it does have an extensive array of graphical user interface (GUI) frameworks — extensions that make graphics a lot easier to create (see `https://wiki.python.org/moin/GuiProgramming` for details). Some of these frameworks do come with designers that make the user interface creation process easier. The point is that Python isn't devoted to just one method of creating a user interface — you can use the method that best suits your needs.

Discovering which organizations use Python

Python really is quite good at the tasks that it was designed to perform. In fact, that's why a lot of large organizations use Python to perform at least some application-creation (development) tasks. You want a programming language that has good support from these large organizations because these organizations tend to spend money to make the language better. Table 1-1 lists some of the large organizations that use Python the most.

TIP

These are just a few of the many organizations that use Python extensively. You can find a more complete list of organizations at `https://www.python.org/about/success/`. The number of success stories has become so large that even this list probably isn't complete and the people supporting it have had to create categories to better organize it.

TABLE 1-1   Large Organizations That Use Python

Vendor	URL	Uses Python For . . .
Alice Educational Software – Carnegie Mellon University	`https://www.alice.org/`	Educational applications
Fermilab	`https://www.fnal.gov/`	Scientific applications
Go.com	`http://go.com/`	Browser-based applications
Google	`https://www.google.com/`	Search engine
Industrial Light & Magic	`https://www.ilm.com/`	Just about every programming need
Lawrence Livermore National Library	`https://www.llnl.gov/`	Scientific applications
National Space and Aeronautics Administration (NASA)	`(https://www.nasa.gov/)`	Scientific applications
New York Stock Exchange	`https://www.nyse.com/index`	Browser-based applications
Redhat	`https://www.redhat.com/en`	Linux installation tools
Yahoo!	`https://www.yahoo.com/`	Parts of Yahoo! Mail
YouTube	`https://www.youtube.com/`	Graphics engine

Finding useful Python applications

You might have an application written in Python sitting on your machine right now and not even know it. Python is used in a vast array of applications on the market today. The applications range from utilities that run at the console to full-fledged CAD/CAM suites. Some applications run on mobile devices, while others run on the large services employed by enterprises. In short, there is no limit to what you can do with Python, but it really does help to see what others have done. You can find a number of places online that list applications written in Python, but the best place to look is `https://wiki.python.org/moin/Applications`.

As a Python programmer, you'll also want to know that Python development tools are available to make your life easier. A *development tool* provides some level of automation in writing the procedures needed to tell the computer what to do. Having more development tools means that you have to perform less work in order to obtain a working application. Developers love to share their lists of favorite tools, but you can find a great list of tools broken into categories at `https://www.python.org/about/apps/`.

Comparing Python to other languages

Comparing one language to another is somewhat dangerous because the selection of a language is just as much a matter of taste and personal preference as it is any sort of quantifiable scientific fact. So before I'm attacked by the rabid protectors of the languages that follow, it's important to realize that I also use a number of languages and find at least some level of overlap among them all. There is no best language in the world, simply the language that works best for a particular application. With this idea in mind, the following sections provide an overview comparison of Python to other languages. (You can find comparisons to other languages at https://wiki.python.org/moin/LanguageComparisons.)

C#

A lot of people claim that Microsoft simply copied Java to create C#. That said, C# does have some advantages (and disadvantages) when compared to Java. The main (undisputed) intent behind C# is to create a better kind of C/C++ language — one that is easier to learn and use. However, we're here to talk about C# and Python. When compared to C#, Python has these advantages:

>> Significantly easier to learn

>> Smaller (more concise) code

>> Supported fully as open source

>> Better multiplatform support

>> Easily allows use of multiple development environments

>> Easier to extend using Java and C/C++

>> Enhanced scientific and engineering support

Java

For years, programmers looked for a language that they could use to write an application just once and have it run anywhere. Java is designed to work well on any platform. It relies on some tricks that you'll discover later in the book to accomplish this magic. For now, all you really need to know is that Java was so successful at running well everywhere that other languages have sought to emulate it (with varying levels of success). Even so, Python has some important advantages over Java, as shown in the following list:

>> Significantly easier to learn

>> Smaller (more concise) code

>> Enhanced variables (storage boxes in computer memory) that can hold different kinds of data based on the application's needs while running (dynamic typing)

>> Faster development times

Perl

Perl was originally an acronym for Practical Extraction and Report Language. Today, people simply call it Perl and let it go at that. However, Perl still shows its roots in that it excels at obtaining data from a database and presenting it in report format. Of course, Perl has been extended to do a lot more than that — you can use it to write all sorts of applications. (I've even used it for a web service application.) In a comparison with Python, you'll find that Python has these advantages over Perl:

>> Simpler to learn

>> Easier to read

>> Enhanced protection for data

>> Better Java integration

>> Fewer platform-specific biases

R

Data scientists often have a tough time choosing between R and Python because both languages are adept at statistical analysis and the sorts of graphing that data scientists need to understand data patterns. Both languages are also open source and support a large range of platforms. However, R is a bit more specialized than Python and tends to cater to the academic market. Consequently, Python has these advantages over R:

>> Emphasizes productivity and code readability

>> Is designed for use by enterprises

>> Offers easier debugging

>> Uses consistent coding techniques

>> Has greater flexibility

>> Is easier to learn

Haskell

Pure functional languages, such as Haskell, have some significant advantages because they work extremely well in multithreaded application due to the fact that pure functions always return the same value for the same inputs. There are no side effects. Many developers also see functional languages as easier to debug and less likely to produce bugs. Python is an impure functional language, which means it doesn't strictly adhere to all of the functional language requisites. However, Python has these advantages over Haskell:

- » Is easier to learn
- » Greater selection of libraries
- » Easier to use for prototyping and modeling
- » Viewed as a better server-side language
- » Has greater flexibility

Chapter **2**

Working with Google Colab

B ack in the Stone Age of computing, developers used punch cards to write their applications and then waited, sometimes a week, to get time on the computer to run an application that might instantly fail with an error. Programmers in that age were a frustrated bunch, prone to grimacing a lot. So moving to Integrated Development Environments (IDEs) (special editors that you use to write and run code) on large desktop machines seemed like a real achievement, but things became even better with time. Now you can write your applications anywhere and at any time with browser-based IDEs like Colabortory. Colaboratory (`https://colab.research.google.com/notebooks/welcome.ipynb`), or Colab for short, is a Google cloud-based service that lets you write Python code using a notebook-like environment, rather than the usual desktop IDE. (Jupyter Notebook, `https://jupyter.org/`, provides an environment similar to Colab on the desktop if you don't have an Internet connection.)

You don't have to install anything on your system to use Colab. The benefit of this approach is that you can work with code in small pieces and obtain nearly instant results from any work you do (no more frustrated grimacing). A notebook format also lends itself to output in a report format that works well for presentations and reports. The first section of this chapter helps you work through some Colab basics and understand how Colab differs from a standard IDE (and why this difference imparts significant benefit when learning how to program).

You can use Colab to perform specific tasks in a cell-oriented paradigm. The next sections of the chapter present a range of task-related topics that start with the use of notebooks. Of course, you also want to perform other sorts of tasks, such as creating various cell types and use them to create notebooks that have a report-like appearance with functional code.

Part of working with Colab is knowing how to run the example code, making it run as quickly as possible. Two sections of the chapter are dedicated to using hardware acceleration and running the example code in various ways.

Finally, this chapter can't address every aspect of Colab, so the last section of the chapter serves as a handy resource for locating the most reliable information about Colab.

REMEMBER

You don't have to type the source code for this chapter manually. In fact, using the downloadable source is a lot easier. You can find the source for this chapter in the BPP4D3E; 02; Colab Examples.ipynb file of the downloadable source. See the Introduction for details on how to find these source files.

Defining Google Colab

Colab helps you write, document, and test Python code using a single application. It's designed to mimic a desktop application called Jupyter Notebook (https://jupyter.org/), so you can use Jupyter Notebook in place of Colab to run the applications in this book. In fact, it's somewhat difficult to tell the two applications apart in the functionality they provide. Google Colab is the cloud version of Notebook, and the Welcome page makes this fact apparent. It even uses IPython (the previous name for Jupyter) Notebook (.ipynb) files for the site.

Even though the two applications are similar and both use .ipynb files, they do have some differences that you need to know about. The previous edition of this book used Jupyter Notebook, but Colab offers the ability to compute anywhere on any device that sports a browser, so this edition of the book focuses on Colab instead. The following sections help you understand the Colab differences.

Understanding what Google Colab does

You can use Colab to perform many tasks, but for the purpose of this book, you use it to write and run code, create its associated documentation, and display graphics. The downloadable source for this book is designed to run on Colab, but you can also use it with Jupyter Notebook if you want.

Jupyter Notebook is a localized application in that you use local resources with it. You could potentially use other sources, but doing so could prove inconvenient or impossible in some cases. For example, according to https://docs.github.com/repositories/working-with-files/using-files/working-with-non-code-files, your Notebook files will appear as static HTML pages when you use a GitHub repository. (*GitHub* is a cloud-based storage technology specifically oriented to working with code.) In fact, some features won't work at all.

TIP

Colab enables you to fully interact with your Notebook files using GitHub as a repository, and Colab supports a number of other online storage options as well, so you can regard Colab as your online partner in creating Python code. The GitHub repository for this book is at https://github.com/JohnPaulMueller/BPP4D3E.

The other reason you really need to know about Colab is that you can use it with your alternative device. During the writing process, some of the example code was tested on an Android-based tablet (an ASUS ZenPad 3S 10). The target tablet has Chrome installed and executes the code well enough to follow the examples. All this said, you likely won't want to try to write code using a tablet of that size (it has a 9.7-inch diagonal screen) — the text was incredibly small, for one thing, and the lack of a keyboard could be a problem, too. The point is that you don't absolutely have to have a Windows, Linux, or macOS system to try the code, but the alternatives might not provide quite the performance you expect.

REMEMBER

Google Colab generally doesn't work with browsers other than Chrome (the browser used in this chapter), Firefox, or Safari (although initial tests with Microsoft Edge have also been encouraging). In most cases, you see an error message, such as This site may not work in your browser. Please use a supported browser, and no other display if you try to start Colab in a browser that it doesn't support. The included More Info link takes you to https://research.google.com/colaboratory/faq.html#browsers, where you can learn more information.

Working with Google Colab features

Google Colab provides access to a number of features through the menu system. One of these features, hardware acceleration, appears in the "Using Hardware Acceleration" section, later in this chapter. The features in this section all appear on the Tools menu.

Locating commands

The Tools ⇨ Command Palette option displays a list of commands you can execute, as shown in Figure 2-1. Some of these commands also have shortcut keys, such as Ctrl+Alt+M for adding a comment to a cell. All these commands help you to perform tasks associated with Notebook content, such as adding forms.

SOME FIREFOX ODDITIES

Even with online help, you may still find that your copy of Firefox displays a `SecurityError: The operation is insecure.` error message. The initial error dialog box points to some unrelated issue, such as cookies, but you see this error message when you click Details. Simply dismissing the dialog box by clicking OK makes Colab appear to be working because it displays your code, but you won't see results from running the code.

As a first step toward fixing this problem, make sure that your copy of Firefox is current; older versions don't provide the required support. After you've updated your copy, setting the `network.websocket.allowInsecureFromHTTPS` preference using `About:Config` to `True` should resolve the problem, but sometimes it doesn't. In this case, verify that Firefox actually does allow third-party cookies by selecting both the Always option for Accept Third Party Cookies and Site Data entry and the Remember History option in the History section on the Privacy & Security tab of the Options dialog box. Restart Firefox after each change and then try Colab again. If none of these fixes works, you must use Chrome to work with Colab on your system.

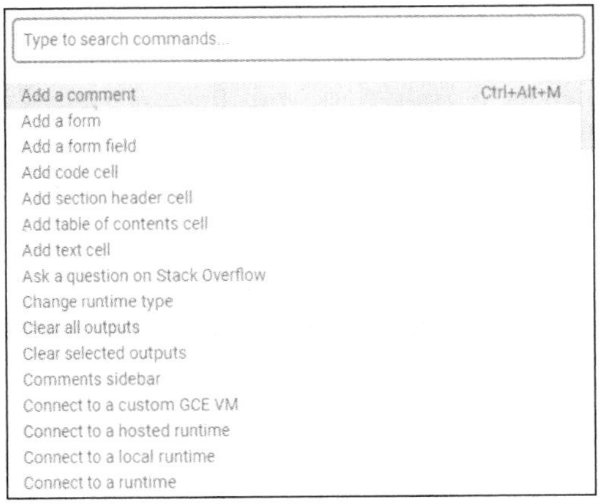

FIGURE 2-1: Using Colab commands makes configuring your Notebook easy.

Configuring settings

The Tools ⇨ Settings option displays the Settings dialog box, shown in Figure 2-2. The four common and one optional (not shown) settings tabs perform these tasks:

> » **Site:** Configures how the site works. The most interesting setting is the theme. Selecting Adaptive lets Colab choose the interface colors based on lighting conditions. You can also configure display and access settings on this tab.

>> **Editor:** Determines how text appears onscreen and how the interface works. For example, you can set the key bindings to work like those in *Vim* (a text editor included on Unix and Linux systems, generally as the vi utility, `https://www.vim.org/`) if desired. You can also select font size, spaces for each level of indentation, and a plethora of other settings.

>> **Colab Pro:** Provides an advertisement for Colab Pro (`https://colab.research.google.com/signup`), which gives you some significant benefits like faster GPUs, longer runtimes, and more memory — all of which let you get more work done in a shorter time.

TECHNICAL STUFF

>> **GitHub (optional):** Shows that your GitHub account is connected to Colab when this tab appears. The various options let you remove GitHub access and determine whether you can see private repositories when opening files. Figure 2-2 doesn't show this particular tab because you won't normally see it until you grant GitHub access using the instructions found at `https://medium.com/analytics-vidhya/how-to-use-google-colab-with-github-via-google-drive-68efb23a42d`. You can find some additional insights at `https://stackoverflow.com/questions/67553747/how-do-i-link-a-github-repository-to-a-google-colab-notebook`.

>> **Miscellaneous:** Contains fun settings. You can choose from three visual effects: adding thunder and lightning using the Power Level setting; letting a Corgi run across the top of the display; and allowing a kitten to run across the top of the display. You can choose any mix of these visual effects.

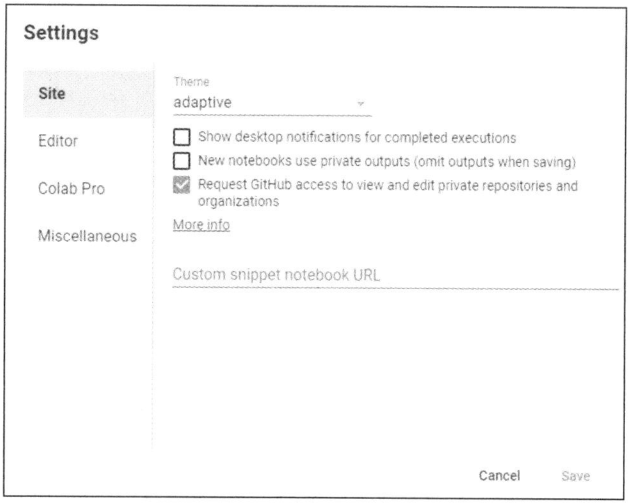

Settings

Site	Theme adaptive
Editor	☐ Show desktop notifications for completed executions
	☐ New notebooks use private outputs (omit outputs when saving)
Colab Pro	☑ Request GitHub access to view and edit private repositories and organizations
	More info
Miscellaneous	Custom snippet notebook URL

Cancel   Save

FIGURE 2-2:
The Settings dialog box helps you configure the Colab IDE.

Customizing keyboard shortcuts

If you don't like the default keyboard shortcuts, you can customize them to match your needs. To do so, choose Tools⇨ Keyboard Shortcuts, and you see the Keyboard Preferences dialog box, shown in Figure 2-3. If you see Set Shortcut, it means that the command doesn't currently have a shortcut, so you can add one if desired. Here's how you work with shortcuts:

>> To add or change a shortcut, place the cursor in the box next to the command and press the shortcut key you want to use for that command.

>> To remove a shortcut, press Delete.

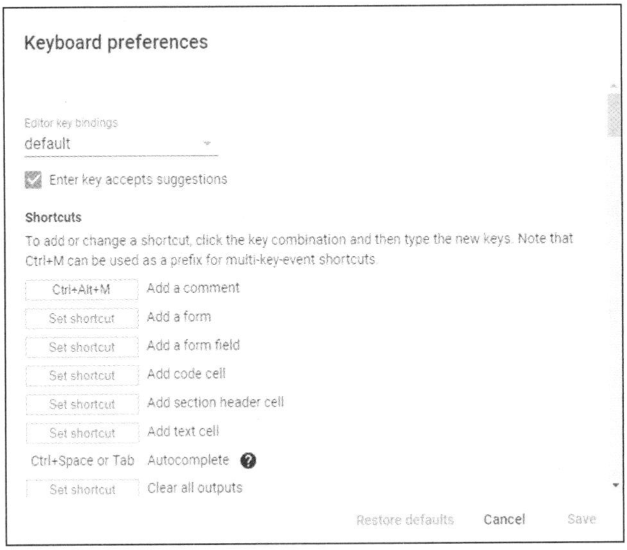

FIGURE 2-3:
Customize
shortcut keys for
speed of access
to commands.

Comparing files

Sometimes you need to compare two files to see how they differ. When you select Tools⇨ Diff Notebooks, Colab opens a new browser tab and shows you two notebooks side by side, as shown in Figure 2-4. These are files selected by random from your Google Drive. To select the files you actually want to work with, click the down arrow next to the file path in each pane. The differences appear onscreen.

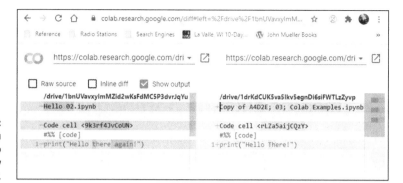

FIGURE 2-4:
Colab lets you compare two files to see how they differ.

Working with Notebooks

The notebook forms the basis for interactions with Colab. In fact, Colab is built on notebooks, as previously mentioned. When you place the mouse on certain parts of the Welcome page at `https://colab.research.google.com/notebooks/welcome.ipynb`, you see opportunities for interacting with the page by adding either code or text entries (which you can use for notes as needed). These entries are active, so you can interact with them. You can also move cells around and copy the resulting material to your Google Drive. Of course, although interacting with the Welcome page is both unexpected and fun, the real purpose of this chapter is to demonstrate how to interact with Colab notebooks. The following sections describe how to perform basic notebook-related tasks with Colab.

Creating a new notebook

To create a new notebook, choose File ⇨ New Notebook. You see a new Python 3 notebook, like the one shown in Figure 2-5.

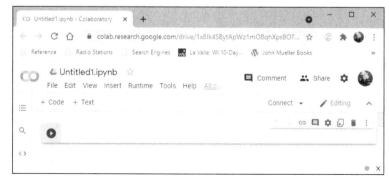

FIGURE 2-5:
Create a new Python 3 Notebook.

The notebook shown in Figure 2-5 lets you change the filename by clicking it. To run the code in a particular cell, you click the right-pointing arrow on the left side of that cell. After you run the code, you must choose the next cell directly.

Opening existing notebooks

You can open existing notebooks found in local storage, on Google Drive, or on GitHub. You can also open any of the Colab examples or upload files from sources that you can access, such as a network drive on your system. In all cases, you begin by choosing File ⇨ Open Notebook. You see the dialog box shown in Figure 2-6.

Examples	Recent	Google Drive	GitHub		Upload
Filter notebooks					
Title		Last opened ▲	First opened ▼		🗑
🔺 Untitled1.ipynb		4:12 PM	4:12 PM	🖿	☑
◌◌ Welcome To Colaboratory		4:10 PM	Aug 27, 2018		☑
🔺 A4D2E; 03; Colab Examples.ipynb		3:44 PM	3:41 PM	🖿	☑
◌◌ Welcome To Colaboratory		3:43 PM	May 2		☑
🔺 A4D2E; 03; Colab Examples.ipynb		3:22 PM	Nov 30, 2020	🖿	☑
					Cancel

FIGURE 2-6: Use this dialog box to open existing notebooks.

The default view shows all the files you opened recently, regardless of location. The files appear in alphabetical order. You can filter the number of items displayed by typing a string into the Filter Notebooks field. Across the top are other options for opening notebooks.

TIP

Even if you're not logged in, you can still access the Colab example projects. These projects help you understand Colab but won't allow you to do anything with your own projects. Even so, you can still experiment with Colab without logging into Google first. The following sections tell you more details about these options.

Using Google Drive for existing notebooks

Google Drive is the default location for many operations in Colab, and you can always choose it as a destination. When working with Google Drive, you see a list of files similar to those shown in Figure 2-6. To open a particular file, you click its link in the dialog box. The file opens in the current tab of your browser.

Using GitHub for existing notebooks

When working with GitHub, you initially need to provide the location of the source code online by modifying the Repository field, as shown in Figure 2-7. If the project contains more than one branch (path of code changes), you must also select an option in the Branch field. The location must point to a public project or a private project owned by you; you can't use Colab to access other people's private projects.

FIGURE 2-7:
When using GitHub, you must provide the location of the source code.

After you make the connection to GitHub, you see two lists: repositories, which are containers for code related to a particular project; and branches, a particular implementation of the code. Selecting a repository and branch displays a list of notebook files that you can load into Colab. Simply click the required link, and it loads as if you were using a *Google Drive* (https://drive.google.com/), which is another type of online storage.

Using local storage for existing notebooks

If you want to use the downloadable source for this book, or any local source for that matter, you select the Upload tab of the dialog box. In the center is a single button, Choose File. Clicking this button opens the File Open dialog box for your browser. You locate the file you want to upload, just as you normally would for opening any file.

REMEMBER

Selecting a file and clicking Open uploads the file to Google Drive. If you make changes to the file, those changes appear on Google Drive, not on your local drive. Depending on your browser, you usually see a new window open with the code loaded. However, you may also simply see a success message, in which case you must now open the file using the same technique as you would when using Google Drive. In some cases, your browser asks whether you want to leave the current page. You should tell the browser to do so.

TIP

The File⇨Upload Notebook command also uploads a file to Google Drive. In fact, uploading a notebook works like uploading any other kind of file, and you see the same dialog box. If you want to upload other kinds of files, using the File⇨Upload Notebook command is likely faster.

Saving notebooks using GitHub

Colab provides a significant number of options for saving your notebook. However, none of these options works with your local drive. After you upload content from your local drive to Google Drive or GitHub, Colab manages the content in the cloud and not on your local drive. To save updates to your local drive, you must download the file to your local drive by choosing one of the options on the File⇨Download menu (either an .ipynb or a .py file format). The following sections review the cloud-based options for saving notebooks.

Using Drive to save notebooks

The default location for storing your data is Google Drive. When you choose File⇨Save, the content you create goes to the root directory of your Google Drive. If you want to save the content to a different folder, you need to select that folder in Google Drive.

REMEMBER

Colab tracks the versions of your project as you perform saves. However, as these revisions age, Colab removes them. To save a version that won't age, you use the File⇨Save and Pin Revision command. To see the revisions for your project, choose File⇨Revision History.

You can also save a copy of your project by choosing File⇨Save a Copy In Drive. The copy receives the word *Copy* as part of its name. Of course, you can rename it later. Colab stores the copy in the current Google Drive folder.

Using GitHub to save notebooks

GitHub provides an alternative to Google Drive for saving content. It offers an organized method of sharing code for the purpose of discussion, review, and distribution. You can find GitHub at `https://github.com/`. The source code for this book appears at `https://github.com/JohnPaulMueller/BPP4D3E`, so you can access it easily from Colab.

REMEMBER

You may use only public repositories and private repositories that you own when working with GitHub from Colab, even though GitHub also supports private repositories. To save a file to GitHub, choose File ➪ Save a Copy in GitHub. If you aren't already signed into GitHub, Colab displays a window that requests your sign-in information. After you sign in, you see a dialog box similar to the one shown in Figure 2-8.

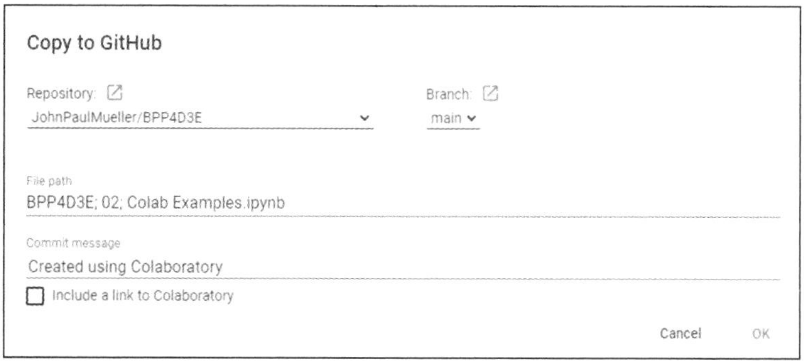

Copy to GitHub

Repository: ☑   Branch: ☑
JohnPaulMueller/BPP4D3E   ∨   main ∨

File path
BPP4D3E; 02; Colab Examples.ipynb

Commit message
Created using Colaboratory

☐ Include a link to Colaboratory

                                            Cancel   OK

FIGURE 2-8:
Using GitHub
means storing
your data in a
repository.

If your account doesn't currently have a repository, you must either create a new repository or choose an existing repository in which to store your data. After you save the file, it appears in the GitHub repository of your choice. The repository can include a link to open the data in Colab by default when you check the Include a Link to Colaboratory option.

Getting the gist of things

You use GitHub gists as a means of sharing single files or other resources with other people. Some people use them for full projects as well, but the idea is that you have a concept you want to share — something that isn't quite fully formed and doesn't necessarily represent a usable application. You can read more about gists at `https://docs.github.com/en/get-started/writing-on-github/editing-and-sharing-content-with-gists/creating-gists`.

WARNING

Gists come in two forms, public and secret. A secret gist isn't private; anyone who has the URL can see it. The only difference between a public and a secret gist is that someone can't use Discover (`https://gist.github.com/discover`) to locate the gist. If you really need to keep your code private, you need to use a GitHub private repository instead of a gist.

When you choose File ⇨ Save a Copy as a GitHub gist, Colab opens a new copy of the file for you and places it on GitHub gist as a secret gist. The saved file automatically includes an Open in Colab button (badge) so that you can open the file in Colab as needed. The problem is that you really don't know much about the gist (not even where Colab put it), so here are some helpful pointers:

>> **Locate:** To locate your gist, open Discover (`https://gist.github.com/discover`), type the name of the file in the Search field, and press Enter. You see a list of matching files, one of which is going to be the one you saved. It's also possible to locate your gists by accessing them on your gist page, such as `https://gist.github.com/JohnPaulMueller`.

>> **Delete:** You may not want to keep the file around because it contains secrets, or perhaps you're just embarrassed about it. Open the file and click the Delete button that appears at the top of the browser page. GitHub displays a dialog box asking whether you're positive that you want to delete the file. Click OK to complete the action.

>> **Publicize:** After your masterpiece is complete, you may want to share it with the world. To perform this task, open the file and click Edit at the top of the page. GitHub will display the editable form of the file for you. Click Make Public at the top of the page.

WARNING

Making your gist public is a one-way trip. After the gist is public, you can't make it private again, so your only option is to delete the gist if you want to keep it out of the public view.

>> **Share:** You have multiple options for sharing your gist: Embed, Share, Clone via HTTPS, and Clone via SSH. To share a gist, choose the option you want to use from the drop-down box (Embed is the default) and then click the Copy button to the right of the option selection. You can now paste the link to your gist anywhere you need to.

>> **Download:** If you need a local copy of your gist, click the Download ZIP button. GitHub will download a `.zip` file to your local drive that contains the gist.

Working with Drive

When you upload a file or obtain it from another source, such as GitHub, you can choose to save a copy of it to Drive by choosing File ⇨ Save a Copy in Drive. When you choose this option, Colab opens another copy of the file in a window that says Copy Of and then the original name of the file. When you open Google Drive, you see a new folder named Colab Notebooks with the copy of the file in it. You can double-click this entry to open the notebook in Colab later.

Performing Common Tasks

Most tasks in Colab and Notebook work the same. Each has both code cells and noncode cells, and you can create code cells in both Colab and Notebook by using the options on the Insert menu. Likewise, both environments have noncode cells that come in three forms:

» Text

» Section header

» Form field, which comes in these types:

- Drop-down

- Input

- Slider

- Markdown

Noncode cells in Colab work somewhat differently from the Markdown cells found in Notebook, but the idea is the same. Two interesting additions in Colab that aren't found in Notepad are the scratch code cell, which allows you to experiment with code in real time, and code snippets, which are canned code for performing specific tasks (you just insert them where needed).

You can also edit and move cells. One important difference between the two environments is that you can't change a cell type in Colab but you can in Notebook. A cell that you create as a section header can't suddenly transform into a code cell. The following sections offer a brief overview of the various features.

Creating code cells

The first cell that Colab creates for you is a code cell. Colab and Notebook share the same features with regard to code, so code you write in Colab also works in Notepad (and vice versa). However, off to the side of the cell, you see a menu of extras that you can use with Colab (see Figure 2-9); these aren't present in Notebook.

FIGURE 2-9:
Colab code cells
contain a few
extras not found
in Notebook.

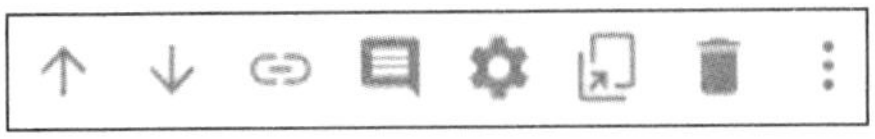

You use the icons shown in Figure 2-9 to augment your Colab code experience. Here's what these features do (in order of appearance, left to right, in the figure):

>> **Move cell up:** Moves the cell up one position in the cell ordering.

>> **Move cell down:** Moves the cell down one position in the cell ordering.

>> **Link to cell:** Displays a dialog box containing a link you can use to access a specific cell within the notebook. You can embed this link anywhere on a web page or within a notebook to allow someone to access that specific cell. The person still sees the entire notebook but doesn't have to search for the cell you want to discuss.

>> **(Optional) Add a comment (assuming that you have the right to make a comment):** Creates a comment balloon to the right of the cell. This is not the same as a code comment, which exists inline with the code, but this kind of comment affects the entire cell. You can edit, delete, or resolve comments. A resolved comment is one that received attention and is no longer applicable.

>> **Open editor settings:** Opens the same dialog box shown in Figure 2-2 and discussed in the "Working with Google Colab features" section, earlier in this chapter. This option appears when you are editing a cell.

>> **Mirror cell in tab:** Mirrors the currently selected cell in a Cell pane that appears on the right side of the window. You can scroll wherever you want within the code in the left pane and keep this code accessible. The right-pointing arrow lets you execute the cell at any time after making changes in left-pane code. A pair of double-pointing arrows lets you move the focus back to the selected code in the left pane with a single click. You can also move the cell code to a scratch cell, where you can play with it without modifying your original code. You can have more than one Cell pane. You simply select the one you want and move between them as needed, which lets you move easily from place to place in your code. Close a Cell pane by clicking the X next to the word *Cell*.

>> **Delete Cell:** Removes the cell from the notebook.

>> **Vertical ellipses:** Contains a number of additional features in a menu (not all of which may appear because they depend on the file you have opened, the tasks you have performed, and your rights to work with the file content):

  • **Select Cell:** Highlights the entire content of the current cell, including the output, which is a convenient way to copy the material for use elsewhere.

- **Copy Cell:** Copies the content of the currently selected cell to the Clipboard.

- **Cut Cell:** Deletes the content of the currently selected cell and places it on the Clipboard.

- **Clear Output:** Removes the output from the cell. You must run the code again to regenerate the output.

- **View Output Fullscreen:** Displays the output (not the entire cell or any other part of the notebook) in full-screen mode on the host device. This option is useful when displaying a significant amount of content, or when a detailed view of graphics helps explain a topic. Press Esc to exit full-screen mode.

- **Add a Form:** Inserts a form into the cell to the right of the code. You use forms to provide a graphical input for parameters. Forms don't appear in Notebook, but because of how you create them, they won't prevent you from running the code in Notebook. You can read more about forms at `https://colab.research.google.com/notebooks/forms.ipynb`.

Code cells also tell you about the code and its execution. The little icon next to the output displays information about the execution when you hover your mouse over it. Clicking the icon clears the output. You must run the code again to regenerate the output.

Creating text cells

Text cells work much like Markdown cells in Notebook. However, Figure 2-10 shows that you receive additional help in formatting the text using a graphical interface. The markdown is the same, but you have the option of allowing the GUI to help you create the markdown. For example, in this case, to create the hash sign (#) for a heading, you click the double *T* icon that appears first in the list. Clicking the double *T* icon again would increase the header level. To the right, you see how the text will appear in the notebook.

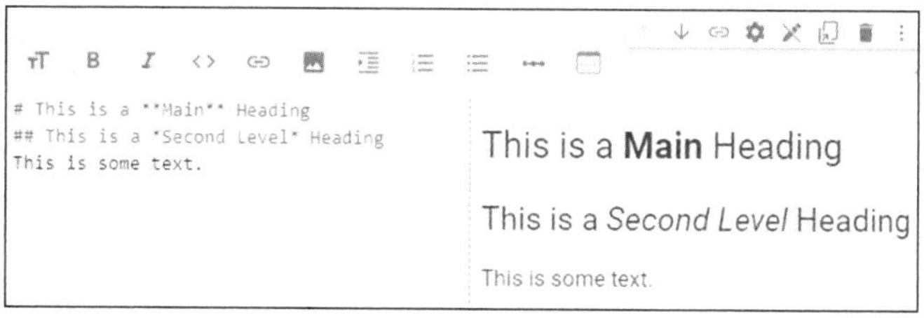

FIGURE 2-10:
Use the GUI to make formatting your text easier.

Notice the menu to the right of the text cell. This menu contains many of the same options that a code cell does. For example, you can create a list of links to help people access specific parts of your notebook through an index. In contrast to Notebook, you can't execute text cells to resolve the markup they contain.

TIP

You can find details of Colab markdown at `https://colab.research.google.com/notebooks/markdown_guide.ipynb`. The tutorial at `https://www.datacamp.com/community/tutorials/markdown-in-jupyter-notebook` is helpful in discovering how to use both Colab and Notebook markdown.

Creating special cells

The special cells that Colab provides are variations of the text cell. These special cells, which you access using the Insert menu option, make creating the required cells faster. However, you shouldn't use these special cells if you need to maintain compatibility between Colab and Notebook. The following sections describe each of these special cell types.

Working with headings

When you choose Insert ⇨ Section Header Cell, you see a new cell created below the currently selected cell that has the appropriate header level-1 entry in it. You can increase the heading level by clicking the double *T* icon. The GUI looks the same as the one in Figure 2-10, shown previously, so you have all the standard formatting features for your text.

Working with a table of contents

An interesting addition to Colab is the automatic generation of a table of contents for your notebook. To use this feature, click the Table of Contents icon on the left side of the window. The table of contents contains one entry for each heading you provide in your notebook. The entries are automatically organized according to level, so you see the hierarchy of your code. Clicking an entry automatically takes you to that location in your code.

Editing cells

Both Colab and Notebook have Edit menus that contain the options you expect, such as the ability to cut, copy, and paste cells. The two products also have some interesting differences. For example, Notebook allows you to split and merge cells. Colab contains an option to show or hide the code as a toggle. These differences give each product a slightly different flavor but don't really change your ability to use each one to create and modify Python code.

Moving cells

The same technique you use for moving cells in Notebook also works with Colab. The only difference is that Colab relies exclusively on toolbar buttons (refer to in Figure 2-9); Notebook also has cell movement options on the Edit menu. To move a cell, select it and then click the Move Cell Up or Move Cell Down buttons as needed.

Using Hardware Acceleration

Even though you won't need it for the examples in this book, Colab does offer hardware acceleration in the form of a Graphics Processing Unit (GPU) or Tensor Processing Unit (TPU). Both of these special processors offer the ability to process multiple sets of data in parallel at high speed. When working with big data in a machine learning or deep learning environment, a GPU or TPU can make a huge difference in the time required to accomplish a task. The main difference between a GPU and a TPU is that a GPU appears as part of most high-end display adapters today and can double for rendering complex graphics, while a TPU is a custom processor designed by Google specifically for machine learning and deep learning tasks. (There are other differences, but they aren't important for this book.)

GPU and TPU support are disabled by default in Colab. To enable GPU or TPU support, choose Runtime ⇨ Change Runtime Type. A Notebook Settings dialog box appears. In this dialog box is the Hardware Accelerator drop-down list, from which you can choose None (the default), GPU, or TPU.

Executing the Code

For your code to be useful, you need to run it at some point. Previous sections have mentioned the right-pointing arrow that appears in the current cell. Clicking it runs just the current cell. Of course, you have other options than clicking the right-pointing arrow, and all these options appear on the Runtime menu (the Cell menu in Notebook). The following list summarizes these options:

» **Running the current cell:** Instead of clicking the right-pointing arrow, you can also choose Runtime ⇨ Run the Focused Cell to execute the code in the current cell.

» **Running other cells:** Colab provides options on the Runtime menu for executing the code in the next cell, the previous cell, or a selection of cells.

Simply choose the option that matches the cell or set of cells you want to execute.

>> **Running all the cells:** In some cases, you want to execute all the code in a notebook. In this case, choose Runtime ⇨ Run All. Execution starts at the top of the notebook, in the first cell containing code, and continues to the last cell that contains code in the notebook. You can stop execution at any time by choosing Runtime ⇨ Interrupt Execution.

TIP

Choosing Runtime ⇨ Manage Sessions displays a dialog box containing a list of all the sessions that are currently executing for your account on Colab. You can use this dialog box to determine when the code in that notebook last executed and how much memory the notebook consumes. Click the trash can icon (also shown as a TERMINATE link) to end execution for a particular notebook.

Getting Help

The most obvious place to obtain help with Colab is from the Colab Help menu. The menu doesn't have a general help link, but you can find it at `https://colab.research.google.com/notebooks/welcome.ipynb` (which requires you to log into the Colab site). This menu does contain all the usual entries (some of which may not appear on your browser):

>> **Frequently Asked Questions (FAQs):** Takes you to a page with questions that other people have asked.

>> **View Release Notes:** Takes you to a page that contains the release notes for the current Colab version, along with all of the versions before it.

>> **Search Code Snippets:** Opens a pane showing common tasks, such as working with a camera, in which you can search for example code that may meet your needs with a little modification. Clicking the Insert button inserts the code at the current cursor location in the cell that has focus. Each of the entries also shows an example of the code.

>> **Report a Bug:** Takes you to a page where you can report Colab errors.

>> **Ask a Question on Stack Overflow:** Displays a new browser tab, where you can ask questions from other users. You see a login screen if you haven't already logged in to Stack Overflow.

>> **Send Feedback:** Displays a dialog box with links for locations where you can obtain additional information. If you really do want to send feedback, you click the Continue Anyway link at the bottom of the dialog box.

Chapter **3**

Interacting with Python

U ltimately, any application you create interacts with the computer and the data it contains. The focus is on data because without data, there isn't a good reason to have an application. Any application you use (even one as simple as Solitaire) manipulates data in some way. In fact, the acronym CRUD sums up what most applications do:

» Create

» Read

» Update

» Delete

If you remember CRUD, you'll be able to summarize what most applications do with the data your computer contains (and some applications really are quite cruddy). However, before your application accesses the computer, you have to interact with a programming language that creates a list of tasks to perform in a language the computer understands. That's the purpose of this chapter. You begin interacting with Python. Python takes the list of steps you want to perform on the computer's data and changes those steps into bits the computer understands. The chapter helps you understand how to obtain help about data manipulation methods, work with functions and objects that interact with data, and use the Python inspect module to perform detective work on your data.

You don't have to type the source code for this chapter manually. In fact, using the downloadable source is a lot easier. You can find the source for this chapter in the `BPP4D3E; 03; Working with Commands.ipynb` file of the downloadable source. See the Introduction for details on how to find these source files.

Typing a Command

When you tame your lion (or cat or dog), you teach it commands such as sit, stay, and don't eat me. Each command instructs the animal to perform a task or do something else interesting. Likewise, using commands in Python makes it possible to perform application tasks, test ideas that you have for writing your application, and discover more about Python. Using the commands let you gain hands-on experience with how Python actually works.

UNDERSTANDING THE IMPORTANCE OF THE README FILE

Many applications include a README file (not necessarily named README). The README file usually provides updated information that didn't make it into the documentation before the application was put into a production status. Unfortunately, most people ignore the README file and some don't even know it exists. As a result, people who should know something interesting about their shiny new product never find out.

The version of Python you use has a Release Notes file (just because the developers didn't want to call it a README file) that contains essential information about Python. If you download and install a copy of Python on your local machine, this Release Notes file is named NEWS.txt and it appears in the main Python folder. If you use Colab and don't download anything, you can find the same information online. For example, the Python 3.10.3 Release Notes appear at https://docs.python.org/release/ 3.10.3/whatsnew/changelog.html. You can find Release Notes links for other version of Python at https://www.python.org/downloads/. When you open this file, you find all sorts of really interesting information, most of which centers on upgrades to Python that you really need to know about.

Opening and reading the Release Notes file (named NEWS.txt or changelog.html because people were apparently ignoring the other file) will help you become a Python genius. People will be amazed that you really do know something interesting about Python and will ask you all sorts of questions (deferring to your wisdom). Of course, you could always just sit there, thinking that the README is just too much effort to read.

Telling the computer what to do

Python, like every other programming language in existence, relies on commands. A *command* is simply a step in a procedure. In Chapter 1, you see how "Get the bread and butter from the refrigerator" is a step in a procedure for making toast. When working with Python, a command, such as `print()`, is simply the same thing: a step in a procedure.

To tell the computer what to do, you issue one or more commands that Python understands. Python translates these commands into instructions that the computer understands, and then you see the result. A command such as `print()` can display the results onscreen so that you get an instant result. However, Python supports all sorts of commands, many of which don't display any results onscreen but still do something important.

As the book progresses, you use commands to perform all sorts of tasks. Each of these tasks will help you accomplish a goal, just as the steps in a procedure do. When it seems as if all the Python commands become far too complex, simply remember to look at them as steps in a procedure. Even human procedures become complex at times, but if you take them one step at a time, you begin to see how they work. Python commands are the same way. Don't get overwhelmed by them; instead, look at them one at a time and focus on just that step in your procedure.

Telling the computer you're done

At some point, the procedure you create ends. When you make toast, the procedure ends when you finish buttering the toast. Computer procedures work precisely the same way. They have a starting and an ending point. When typing commands, the ending point for a particular step is the Enter key. You press Enter to tell the computer that you're done typing the command.

TIP

Pressing Enter doesn't actually run the command; you need to click Run Cell in Colab or click Run in Jupyter Notebook. As an alternative, you can also type a single command in a code cell and then press Ctrl+Enter in either IDE to run it.

As the book progresses, you find that Python provides a number of ways to signify that a step, group of steps, or even an entire application is complete. No matter how the task is accomplished, computer programs always have a distinct starting and stopping point.

Seeing the result

You now know that a command is a step in a procedure and that each command has a distinct starting and ending point. In addition, groups of commands and entire applications also have a distinct starting and ending point. So, take a look at how this works. The following procedure helps you see the result of using a command:

1. **Start a copy of either Google Colab or Jupyter Notebook and then create a new Python 3 Notebook as described in the "Creating a new notebook" section of Chapter 2.**

   You see a code cell where you can type a command.

2. **Type** print("This is a line of text.") **in the code cell.**

   Notice that nothing happens. Yes, you typed a command, but you haven't signified that the command is complete.

3. **Press Ctrl+Enter.**

   The command is complete, so you see a result like the one shown in Figure 3-1.

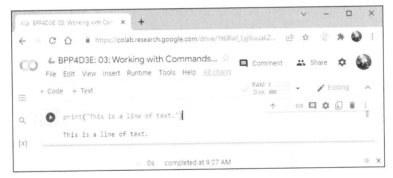

FIGURE 3-1:
Issuing commands tells Python what to tell the computer to do.

This exercise shows you how things work within Python. Each command that you type performs some task, but only after you tell Python that the command is complete in some way. The `print()` command displays data onscreen. In this case, you supplied text to display. Notice that the output shown in Figure 3-1 comes immediately after the command because this is an interactive environment — one in which you see the result of any given command immediately after Python performs it. Later, as you start creating applications, you notice that sometimes a result doesn't appear immediately because the application environment delays it. Even so, the command is executed by Python immediately after the application tells Python that the command is complete.

PYTHON'S CODING STYLES

Most programming languages are dedicated to using just one coding style, which reduces flexibility for the programmer. However, Python is different. You can use a number of coding styles to achieve differing effects with Python. The four commonly used Python coding styles are

- **Functional:** Every statement is a kind of math equation. This style lends itself well to use in parallel processing activities.

- **Imperative:** Computations occur as changes to program state. This style is most used for manipulating data structures.

- **Object-oriented:** This is the style commonly used with other languages to simplify the coding environment by using objects to model the real world. Python doesn't fully implement this coding style because it doesn't support features like data hiding, but you can still use this approach to a significant degree. You see this style used later in the book.

- **Procedural:** All the code you've written so far (and much of the initial code in this book) is procedural, meaning that tasks proceed a step at a time. This style is most used for iteration, sequencing, selection, and modularization. It's the simplest form of coding you can use.

Even though this book doesn't cover all these coding styles (and others that Python supports), it's useful to know that you aren't trapped using a particular coding style. Because Python supports multiple coding styles and you can mix and match those styles in a single application, you have the advantage of being able to use Python in the manner that works best for a particular need. You can read more about the coding styles at https://newrelic.com/blog/nerd-life/python-programming-styles.

Getting Python's Help

Python is a computer language, not a human language. As a result, you won't speak it fluently at first. If you think about it for a moment, it makes sense that you won't speak Python fluently (and as with most human languages, you won't know every command even after you do become fluent). Having to discover Python commands a little at a time is the same thing that happens when you learn to speak another human language. If you normally speak English and try to say something in German, you find that you must have some sort of guide to help you along. Otherwise, anything you say is gibberish and people will look at you quite oddly. Even if you manage to say something that makes sense, it may not be what you want. You might go to a restaurant and order hot hubcaps for dinner when what you really wanted was a steak.

Likewise, when you try to speak Python, you need a guide to help you. Fortunately, Python is quite accommodating and provides immediate help to keep you from ordering something you really don't want. The help provided inside Python works at two levels:

>> **Help mode,** in which you can browse the available commands

>> **Direct help,** in which you ask about a specific command

There isn't a correct way to use help — just the method that works best for you at a particular time. The following sections describe how to obtain help.

Entering into help mode

One of the ways in which Jupyter Notebook excels over Google Colab is that Jupyter Notebook provides a good language reference as part of the Help menu. In fact, you can also find references for NumPy, SciPy, MatPlotLib, SymPy, and pandas. However, it's also important to realize that you have access to other forms of help that are supported by both Jupyter Notebook and Colab in the form of the four commands shown in the following list:

>> `copyright()`

>> `credits()`

>> `license()`

>> `help()`

All four commands provide you with help, of a sort, about Python. For example, the `copyright()` command tells you about who holds the right to copy, license, or otherwise distribute Python. The `credits()` command tells you who put Python together. The `license()` command describes the usage agreement between you and the copyright holder. Unlike `copyright()` and `credits()`, `license()` requires that you either press Enter to obtain more licensing information or type **q** and press Enter to exit the licensing screen, as shown in Figure 3-2, when working with Colab. (Jupyter Notebook simply prints the following: See `https://www.python.org/psf/license/`.) Notice that the Run Cell icon to the left of the cell continues to remain active as long as there is more licensing information to see.

The command you most want to know about is simply `help()`. To enter help mode, type **help()** and click Run Cell. Notice that you must include the parentheses after the command. Every Python command has parentheses associated with it. After you enter this command, Python goes into help mode and you see a display similar to the one shown in Figure 3-3.

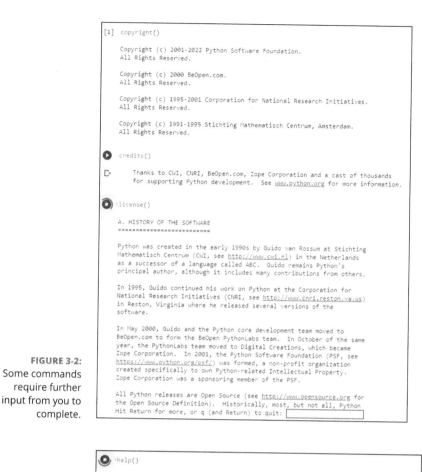

```
[1]  copyright()

     Copyright (c) 2001-2022 Python Software Foundation.
     All Rights Reserved.

     Copyright (c) 2000 BeOpen.com.
     All Rights Reserved.

     Copyright (c) 1995-2001 Corporation for National Research Initiatives.
     All Rights Reserved.

     Copyright (c) 1991-1995 Stichting Mathematisch Centrum, Amsterdam.
     All Rights Reserved.

     credits()

         Thanks to CWI, CNRI, BeOpen.com, Zope Corporation and a cast of thousands
         for supporting Python development.  See www.python.org for more information.

     license()

     A. HISTORY OF THE SOFTWARE
     ==========================

     Python was created in the early 1990s by Guido van Rossum at Stichting
     Mathematisch Centrum (CWI, see http://www.cwi.nl) in the Netherlands
     as a successor of a language called ABC.  Guido remains Python's
     principal author, although it includes many contributions from others.

     In 1995, Guido continued his work on Python at the Corporation for
     National Research Initiatives (CNRI, see http://www.cnri.reston.va.us)
     in Reston, Virginia where he released several versions of the
     software.

     In May 2000, Guido and the Python core development team moved to
     BeOpen.com to form the BeOpen PythonLabs team.  In October of the same
     year, the PythonLabs team moved to Digital Creations, which became
     Zope Corporation.  In 2001, the Python Software Foundation (PSF, see
     https://www.python.org/psf/) was formed, a non-profit organization
     created specifically to own Python-related Intellectual Property.
     Zope Corporation was a sponsoring member of the PSF.

     All Python releases are Open Source (see http://www.opensource.org for
     the Open Source Definition).  Historically, most, but not all, Python
     Hit Return for more, or q (and Return) to quit: [              ]
```

FIGURE 3-2: Some commands require further input from you to complete.

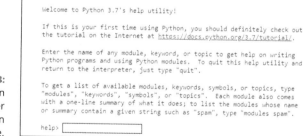

```
     help()

     Welcome to Python 3.7's help utility!

     If this is your first time using Python, you should definitely check out
     the tutorial on the Internet at https://docs.python.org/3.7/tutorial/.

     Enter the name of any module, keyword, or topic to get help on writing
     Python programs and using Python modules.  To quit this help utility and
     return to the interpreter, just type "quit".

     To get a list of available modules, keywords, symbols, or topics, type
     "modules", "keywords", "symbols", or "topics".  Each module also comes
     with a one-line summary of what it does; to list the modules whose name
     or summary contain a given string such as "spam", type "modules spam".

     help> [              ]
```

FIGURE 3-3: You ask Python about other commands in help mode.

REMEMBER

You can always tell that you're in help mode by the help> prompt that you see in the cell and that the Run Cell icon remains active. As long as you see the help> prompt, you know that you're in help mode.

Asking for help

To obtain help, you need to know what question to ask. The initial help message that you see when you go into help mode (refer to Figure 3-3) provides some helpful tips about the kinds of questions you can ask. If you want to explore Python, the four basic topics are

>> `modules`

>> `keywords`

>> `symbols`

>> `topics`

The first two topics won't tell you much for now. You won't need the `modules` topic until Chapter 11. The `keywords` topic will begin proving useful in Chapter 5. However, the `symbols` and `topics` keywords are already useful because they help you understand where to begin your Python adventure. When you type **symbols** and press Enter, you see a list of symbols used in Python. To see what topics are available, type **topics** and press Enter. You see a list of topics similar to those shown in Figure 3-4.

```
help> topics

Here is a list of available topics.  Enter any topic name to get more help.

ASSERTION            DELETION             LOOPING              SHIFTING
ASSIGNMENT           DICTIONARIES         MAPPINGMETHODS       SLICINGS
ATTRIBUTEMETHODS     DICTIONARYLITERALS   MAPPINGS             SPECIALATTRIBUTES
ATTRIBUTES           DYNAMICFEATURES      METHODS              SPECIALIDENTIFIERS
AUGMENTEDASSIGNMENT  ELLIPSIS             MODULES              SPECIALMETHODS
BASICMETHODS         EXCEPTIONS           NAMESPACES           STRINGMETHODS
BINARY               EXECUTION            NONE                 STRINGS
BITWISE              EXPRESSIONS          NUMBERMETHODS        SUBSCRIPTS
BOOLEAN              FLOAT                NUMBERS              TRACEBACKS
CALLABLEMETHODS      FORMATTING           OBJECTS              TRUTHVALUE
CALLS                FRAMEOBJECTS         OPERATORS            TUPLELITERALS
CLASSES              FRAMES               PACKAGES             TUPLES
CODEOBJECTS          FUNCTIONS            POWER                TYPEOBJECTS
COMPARISON           IDENTIFIERS          PRECEDENCE           TYPES
COMPLEX              IMPORTING            PRIVATENAMES         UNARY
CONDITIONAL          INTEGER              RETURNING            UNICODE
CONTEXTMANAGERS      LISTLITERALS         SCOPING
CONVERSIONS          LISTS                SEQUENCEMETHODS
DEBUGGING            LITERALS             SEQUENCES

help>
```

FIGURE 3-4: The `topics` help topic provides you with a starting point for your Python adventure.

REMEMBER

Chapter 7 begins the discussion of `symbols` when you explore the use of operators in Python. When you see a topic that you like, such as `FUNCTIONS`, simply type that topic and press Enter. To see how this works, type **FUNCTIONS** and press Enter (you must type the word in uppercase — don't worry, Python won't think you're shouting). You see help information similar to that shown in Figure 3-5.

```
help> FUNCTIONS
Functions
*********

Function objects are created by function definitions.  The only
operation on a function object is to call it: "func(argument-list)".

There are really two flavors of function objects: built-in functions
and user-defined functions.  Both support the same operation (to call
the function), but the implementation is different, hence the
different object types.

See Function definitions for more information.

Related help topics: def, TYPES

help> [                    ]
```

FIGURE 3-5:
You must use
uppercase when
requesting topic
information.

As you work through examples in the book, you use commands that look interesting, and you might want more information about them. For example, in the "Seeing the result" section of this chapter, you use the `print()` command. To see more information about the `print()` command, type **print** and press Enter (notice that you don't include the parentheses this time because you're requesting help about `print()`, not actually using the command). Figure 3-6 shows typical help information for the `print()` command.

```
help> print
Help on built-in function print in module builtins:

print(...)
    print(value, ..., sep=' ', end='\n', file=sys.stdout, flush=False)

    Prints the values to a stream, or to sys.stdout by default.
    Optional keyword arguments:
    file:  a file-like object (stream); defaults to the current sys.stdout.
    sep:   string inserted between values, default a space.
    end:   string appended after the last value, default a newline.
    flush: whether to forcibly flush the stream.

help> [                    ]
```

FIGURE 3-6:
Request
command help
information by
typing the
command using
whatever case it
actually uses.

TIP

Unfortunately, reading the help information probably doesn't help much yet because you need to know more about Python. However, you can ask for more information. For example, you might wonder what sys.stdout means — and the help topic certainly doesn't tell you anything about it. Type **sys.stdout** and press Enter. You see the help information shown in Figure 3-7.

You may still not find the information as helpful as you need, but at least you know a little more. In this case, help has a lot to say and it can't all fit on one screen (Figure 3-7 is a truncated view). To see more of the information, you'll need to scroll up or down in the cell.

```
help> sys.stdout
Help on OutStream in sys object:

sys.stdout = class OutStream(io.TextIOBase)
 |  sys.stdout(session, pub_thread, name, pipe=None, echo=None)
 |
 |  A file like object that publishes the stream to a 0MQ PUB socket.
 |
 |  Output is handed off to an IO Thread
 |
 |  Method resolution order:
 |      OutStream
 |      io.TextIOBase
 |      _io._TextIOBase
 |      io.IOBase
 |      _io._IOBase
 |      builtins.object
 |
 |  Methods defined here:
 |
 |  __init__(self, session, pub_thread, name, pipe=None, echo=None)
 |      Initialize self.  See help(type(self)) for accurate signature.
 |
 |  close(self)
 |      Flush and close the IO object.
 |
 |      This method has no effect if the file is already closed.
```

FIGURE 3-7:
You can ask for help on the help you receive.

Leaving help mode

At some point, you need to leave help mode to perform useful work. All you have to do is press Enter without typing anything. When you press Enter, you see a message about leaving help, and then the Run Cell icon changes to the standard Python prompt, as shown in Figure 3-8.

FIGURE 3-8:
Exit help mode by pressing Enter without typing anything.

```
help>

You are now leaving help and returning to the Python interpreter.
If you want to ask for help on a particular object directly from the
interpreter, you can type "help(object)".  Executing "help('string')"
has the same effect as typing a particular string at the help> prompt.
```

Obtaining help directly

Entering help mode isn't necessary unless you want to browse, which is always a good idea, or unless you don't actually know what you need to find. If you have a good idea of what you need, all you need to do is ask for help directly (a really nice thing for Python to do). So, instead of fiddling with help mode, you simply type the word *help*, followed by a left parenthesis and single quote, whatever you want to find, another single quote, and the right parenthesis. For example, if you want to know more about the print() command, you type **help('print')** and click Run Cell. Figure 3-9 shows typical output when you access help this way.

You can browse directly within a cell, too. For example, when you type **help('topics')** and press Enter, you see a list of topics like the one that appears in Figure 3-10. You can compare this list with the one shown in Figure 3-4. The two lists are identical, even though you typed one while in help mode and the other while at the Python prompt.

```
help('print')

Help on built-in function print in module builtins:

print(...)
    print(value, ..., sep=' ', end='\n', file=sys.stdout, flush=False)

    Prints the values to a stream, or to sys.stdout by default.
    Optional keyword arguments:
    file:  a file-like object (stream); defaults to the current sys.stdout.
    sep:   string inserted between values, default a space.
    end:   string appended after the last value, default a newline.
    flush: whether to forcibly flush the stream.
```

FIGURE 3-9:
Python lets you obtain help whenever you need it without leaving the Python prompt.

```
help('topics')

Here is a list of available topics.  Enter any topic name to get more help.

ASSERTION            DELETION             LOOPING              SHIFTING
ASSIGNMENT           DICTIONARIES         MAPPINGMETHODS       SLICINGS
ATTRIBUTEMETHODS     DICTIONARYLITERALS   MAPPINGS             SPECIALATTRIBUTES
ATTRIBUTES           DYNAMICFEATURES      METHODS              SPECIALIDENTIFIERS
AUGMENTEDASSIGNMENT  ELLIPSIS             MODULES              SPECIALMETHODS
BASICMETHODS         EXCEPTIONS           NAMESPACES           STRINGMETHODS
BINARY               EXECUTION            NONE                 STRINGS
BITWISE              EXPRESSIONS          NUMBERMETHODS        SUBSCRIPTS
BOOLEAN              FLOAT                NUMBERS              TRACEBACKS
CALLABLEMETHODS      FORMATTING           OBJECTS              TRUTHVALUE
CALLS                FRAMEOBJECTS         OPERATORS            TUPLELITERALS
CLASSES              FRAMES               PACKAGES             TUPLES
CODEOBJECTS          FUNCTIONS            POWER                TYPEOBJECTS
COMPARISON           IDENTIFIERS          PRECEDENCE           TYPES
COMPLEX              IMPORTING            PRIVATENAMES         UNARY
CONDITIONAL          INTEGER              RETURNING            UNICODE
CONTEXTMANAGERS      LISTLITERALS         SCOPING
CONVERSIONS          LISTS                SEQUENCEMETHODS
DEBUGGING            LITERALS             SEQUENCES
```

FIGURE 3-10:
You can browse at the Python prompt if you really want to.

TIP

You might wonder why Python has a help mode at all if you can get the same results directly as a cell command. The answer is convenience. It's easier to browse in the help mode. In addition, even though you don't do a lot of extra typing as a separate cell command, you do perform less typing while in help mode. Help mode also provides additional helps, such as by listing topics that you can type, as shown previously in Figure 3-4. So you have all kinds of good reasons to enter help mode when you plan to ask Python a lot of help questions.

REMEMBER

No matter where you ask for help, you need to observe the correct capitalization of help topics. For example, if you want general information about functions, you must type **help('FUNCTIONS')** and not help('Functions') or help('functions'). When you use the wrong capitalization, Python will tell you that it doesn't know what you mean or that it couldn't find the help topic. It won't know to tell you that you used the wrong capitalization. Someday computers will know what you meant to type, rather than what you did type, but that hasn't happened yet.

Finding Out More about Functions and Objects

The help feature in Python offers an overview of the various functions and objects found in an application. However, you often need to know more than what help provides. In this case, you can use a type of alternative approach to help as described in the following sections.

Yelling "Hello There" doesn't help: Use dir() instead

There is a need to determine the details of what an application requires without expending a lot of effort. Of course, you could try simply asking, starting with "Hello There!" as a form of greeting, but extensive testing shows that speaking to your computer won't work. The dir() function gives you a means of discovering new things about functions and objects in Python. It also provides more information in some respects to using help() and is more flexible to boot. Using the dir() function by itself displays a listing of functions, classes, and objects that are currently available and are similar to this list (your list could vary depending on what you have loaded into Python):

```
['In', 'Out', '_', '__', '___', '__builtin__',
 '__builtins__', '__doc__', '__loader__', '__name__',
 '__package__', '__spec__', '_dh', '_i', '_i1', '_ih',
 '_ii', '_iii', '_oh', '_sh', 'exit', 'get_ipython',
 'quit']
```

Note that this list is reformatted into horizontal form to save space in the book. You'll actually see it in a vertical format that can be a little hard to read.

As you import packages, classes, and functions and execute code, the list will change to reflect the new additions. For example, when you execute the following code:

```
myNum = 2056
dir(myNum)
```

you see a list of the functions you can use with myNum, as shown here:

```
['__abs__', '__add__', '__and__', '__bool__',
 '__ceil__', '__class__', '__delattr__', '__dir__',
```

```
'__divmod__', '__doc__', '__eq__', '__float__',
'__floor__', '__floordiv__', '__format__', '__ge__',
'__getattribute__', '__getnewargs__', '__gt__',
'__hash__', '__index__', '__init__',
'__init_subclass__', '__int__', '__invert__', '__le__',
'__lshift__', '__lt__', '__mod__', '__mul__', '__ne__',
'__neg__', '__new__', '__or__', '__pos__', '__pow__',
'__radd__', '__rand__', '__rdivmod__', '__reduce__',
'__reduce_ex__', '__repr__', '__rfloordiv__',
'__rlshift__', '__rmod__', '__rmul__', '__ror__',
'__round__', '__rpow__', '__rrshift__', '__rshift__',
'__rsub__', '__rtruediv__', '__rxor__', '__setattr__',
'__sizeof__', '__str__', '__sub__', '__subclasshook__',
'__truediv__', '__trunc__', '__xor__',
'as_integer_ratio', 'bit_length', 'conjugate',
'denominator', 'from_bytes', 'imag', 'numerator',
'real', 'to_bytes']
```

That's quite a list of things you can do with myNum! What this list tells you is the details about myNum, an object that you created. So, you could type **myNum.bit_length()** and press Enter to see that the bit length for this particular variable is 12. Using dir() can help jog your memory or make you aware of new features you might not have known about.

What are those double underscores all about?

Python lacks the concept of private variables, classes, functions, and so on. Some developers feel that this makes the object-oriented programming (OOP) features in Python incomplete (see https://www.geeksforgeeks.org/data-hiding-in-python/ for a conversation about the topic). The creator of Python, Guido van Rossum, put it this way, "We are all adults. Feel free to shoot yourself in the foot if you must." So, Python lacks true data hiding and the benefits and problems that data hiding provides. What it has instead is double underlines (__), which indicates that the member is private and you shouldn't use it, but many developers do anyway.

TECHNICAL STUFF

Some Python implementations enforce the double underline as private, even though this functionality isn't part of the specification. For example, myNum.__eq__(2056) returns True if myNum actually does contain the value 2056, but the __eq__() function is listed as private so what you should use in your code instead is myNum == 2056.

Drilling, drilling, drilling down into classes

In any OOP implementation, classes inherit from other classes, so you end up with an object hierarchy. Drilling down into this hierarchy can tell you a lot about how to interact with Python objects in ways that you might not have considered in the past. For example, when working with myNum, you can use the myNum.to_bytes(4, byteorder = 'big') call to display myNum as a series of bytes: b'\x00\x00\x08\x08'. The output is another object. Consequently, you can use dir(myNum.to_bytes(4, byteorder = 'big')) call to find out more about how you can use this new object:

```
['__add__', '__class__', '__contains__', '__delattr__',
 '__dir__', '__doc__', '__eq__', '__format__', '__ge__',
 '__getattribute__', '__getitem__', '__getnewargs__',
 '__gt__', '__hash__', '__init__', '__init_subclass__',
 '__iter__', '__le__', '__len__', '__lt__', '__mod__',
 '__mul__', '__ne__', '__new__', '__reduce__',
 '__reduce_ex__', '__repr__', '__rmod__', '__rmul__',
 '__setattr__', '__sizeof__', '__str__',
 '__subclasshook__', 'capitalize', 'center', 'count',
 'decode', 'endswith', 'expandtabs', 'find', 'fromhex',
 'hex', 'index', 'isalnum', 'isalpha', 'isascii',
 'isdigit', 'islower', 'isspace', 'istitle', 'isupper',
 'join', 'ljust', 'lower', 'lstrip', 'maketrans',
 'partition', 'replace', 'rfind', 'rindex', 'rjust',
 'rpartition', 'rsplit', 'rstrip', 'split',
 'splitlines', 'startswith', 'strip', 'swapcase',
 'title', 'translate', 'upper', 'zfill']
```

TECHNICAL STUFF

Oddly enough, you can replace some of the bytes in the value with different bytes using myNum.to_bytes(4, byteorder = 'big').replace(b'\x00', b'\x01'), which provides an output of: b'\x01\x01\x08\x08'. However, you might not have known you could do this without drilling down into the original myNum object using dir().

If you really want to get fancy, you can start combining bits of knowledge you obtain while drilling down into objects. For example, myNum.from_bytes(myNum.to_bytes(4, byteorder = 'big').replace(b'\x00', b'\x01'), 'big') produces a new myNum value of 16844808. That's a really large number, but it also shows that you can work with Python to produce a wide assortment of interesting effects just by playing with dir().

Playing the Part of Inspector

The `inspect` module (see `https://docs.python.org/3/library/inspect.html`) allows you to get even more in depth than the `dir()` function by playing the role of a detective. You can query any object, class, or variable about its details in a detailed manner. The following sections give you the briefest overview of what you can do because this module can become really involved. As with all tools, you need to spend time with `inspect` before you become proficient at using it.

Gaining access to inspect

The `inspect` module isn't included with the standard Python setup, so you must import it into the environment so that you can use it by adding the following line of code:

```
import inspect
```

REMEMBER

This code imports the entire `inspect` module. If you want to use a limited number of features, you can also use other Python methods of importation, such as

```
from inspect import isfunction
```

Instead of importing everything, this approach imports just the `isfunction()` method.

Using inspect

There are a lot of different ways to use `inspect`. For example, you can use it to ask direct questions such as `inspect.ismodule(inspect)`, which returns `True` because `inspect` is a module. It's also possible to use `inspect` on any object, including those you create. The query `inspect.getmembers(myNum)` returns a considerable amount of information, as shown here (in part; the actual list is much longer):

```
[('__abs__', <method-wrapper '__abs__' of int object at
    0x7f71e52ea4b0>),
 ('__add__', <method-wrapper '__add__' of int object at
    0x7f71e52ea4b0>),
 ('__and__', <method-wrapper '__and__' of int object at
    0x7f71e52ea4b0>),
 ('__bool__', <method-wrapper '__bool__' of int object
    at 0x7f71e52ea4b0>),
 ('__ceil__', <function int.__ceil__>),
 ('__class__', int),
```

```
('__delattr__',
    <method-wrapper '__delattr__' of int object at
    0x7f71e52ea4b0>),
('__dir__', <function int.__dir__>),
('__divmod__', <method-wrapper '__divmod__' of int
    object at 0x7f71e52ea4b0>),

...


('bit_length', <function int.bit_length>),
('conjugate', <function int.conjugate>),
('denominator', 1),
('from_bytes', <function int.from_bytes>),
('imag', 0),
('numerator', 2056),
('real', 2056),
('to_bytes', <function int.to_bytes>)]
```

TIP

Most of the added information tells you what a particular member is, such as a method or a function. In some cases, you also get the member value. For example, the denominator() function output is 1.

It may take some time for you to go through all the inspect features, but it's worth the effort. For example, you can quickly check whether a function is built in. A call to inspect.isbuiltin(dir) returns True because the dir() function is part of the default Python functionality.

Is reflection really like looking in a mirror?

The process used by the inspect module to obtain detailed information about your code is called *reflection*, but it has nothing to do with looking in a mirror. Instead, reflection looks back through the compiled code in an effort to reconstruct the original element information. Another term, *introspection*, means essentially the same thing when it comes to viewing code, and some people would say that the inspect module performs introspection.

TECHNICAL STUFF

In addition to viewing element information, reflection can also allow you to modify the underlying objects, but this is an extremely advanced technique that most developers don't really need. For the purposes of this book, looking back through code to find out more about it is called *reflection*, just to keep things simple (and to keep the terminology on par with what other languages use). You can discover more about the differences between introspection and reflection at https://betterprogramming.pub/python-reflection-and-introspection-97b348be54d8 and see some advanced used of reflection at https://www.geeksforgeeks.org/reflection-in-python/.

Chapter **4**

Writing Your First Application

Many people view application development as some sort of magic practiced by wizards called geeks who wave their keyboard to produce software both great and small. However, the truth is a lot more mundane.

Application development follows a number of processes. It's more than a strict procedure, but is most definitely not magic of any sort. As Arthur C. Clark once noted, "Any sufficiently advanced technology is indistinguishable from magic." This chapter is all about removing the magic from the picture and introducing you to the technology. By the time you're finished with this chapter, you, too, will be able to develop a simple application (and you won't use magic to do it).

As with any other task, people use tools to write applications. In the case of Python, you don't have to use a tool, but using a tool makes the task so much easier that you really will want to use one. In this chapter, you use a commonly available Integrated Development Environment (IDE) named Google Colab (discussed in Chapter 2). An *IDE* is a special kind of application that makes writing, testing, and debugging code significantly easier. You can also use Jupyter Notebook for desktop development, which appears as part of the Anaconda tool collection (https://www.anaconda.com/products/distribution) or you can get Jupyter Notebook as a separate download at https://jupyter.org/install.

TIP

A vast number of other tools are available for you to use when writing Python applications. This book doesn't tell you much about them because *Conda* (a command-line tool provided with Jupyter Notebook) performs every task needed and it's readily available free of charge. However, as your skills increase, you might find the features in other tools such as Komodo Edit (`https://www.activestate.com/products/komodo-ide/downloads/edit/`) more to your liking. You can find a great list of these tools at `https://wiki.python.org/moin/IntegratedDevelopmentEnvironments`.

REMEMBER

You don't have to type the source code for this chapter manually. In fact, using the downloadable source is a lot easier. You can find the source for this chapter in the `BPP4D3E; 04; Comments.ipynb`, `BPP4D3E; 04; Indentation.ipynb`, and `BPP4D3E; 04; Sample.ipynb` files of the downloadable source. See the Introduction for details on how to find these source files.

Understanding Why IDEs Are Important

A good question to ask is, why do you need an IDE to work with Python? It does come with a command-line tool that you can open by typing **python** and pressing Enter at a command line or terminal window for desktop setups. (You can make things easier by ensuring that the folder in which Python is installed appears as part of your system's PATH environment variable or by installing Anaconda, which comes with its own Anaconda prompt.) For that matter, Python actually comes with a limited IDE called Integrated Development and Learning Environment (IDLE) that appears in the `Lib\idlelib` folder of your Python installation (again, for desktop setups, but please, no more email about just how dead the desktop really is; I get it). Many people probably question the need for anything more during the learning process and possibly to develop full-fledged applications.

REMEMBER

Unfortunately, the tools that come with Python are interesting and even helpful in getting started, but they won't help you create useful applications with any ease. In addition, accessing these tools means creating a desktop setup that may not provide the flexibility you require because now you can't program on your tablet (or smart phone, if you're really adept). If you choose to work with Python long term, you really need a better tool for the reasons described in the following sections.

Creating better code

A good IDE contains a certain amount of intelligence. For example, the IDE can suggest alternatives when you type the incorrect keyword, or it can tell you that a certain line of code simply won't work as written. The more intelligence that an

IDE contains, the less hard you have to work to write better code. Writing better code is essential because no one wants to spend hours looking for errors, called *bugs*.

TIP

IDEs vary greatly in the level and kind of intelligence they provide, which is why so many IDEs exist. You may find the level of help obtained from one IDE to be insufficient to your needs, but another IDE hovers over you like a mother hen. Every developer has different needs and, therefore, different IDE requirements. The point is to obtain an IDE that helps you write clean, efficient code quickly and easily.

Debugging functionality

Finding bugs (errors) in your code is a process called *debugging*. Even the most expert developer in the world spends time debugging. Writing perfect code on the first pass is nearly impossible, especially when squinting to see the text on your smart phone. When you do, it's cause for celebration because it won't happen often. Consequently, the debugging capabilities of your IDE are critical. Unfortunately, the debugging capabilities of the native Python tools are almost nonexistent. If you spend any time at all debugging, you quickly find the native tools annoying because of what they don't tell you about your code.

TIP

The best IDEs double as training tools. Given enough features, an IDE can help you explore code written by true experts. Tracing through applications using a debugger is a time-honored method of learning new skills and honing the skills you already possess. A seemingly small advance in knowledge can often become a huge savings in time later. When looking for an IDE, don't just look at debugging features as a means to remove errors — see them also as a means to learn new things about Python.

Defining why notebooks are useful

Most IDEs look like fancy text editors, and that's precisely what they are. Yes, you get all sorts of intelligent features, hints, tips, code coloring, and so on, but at the end of the day, they're all text editors. There's nothing wrong with text editors, and this chapter isn't telling you anything of the sort. However, given that Python developers often focus on scientific applications that require something better than pure text presentation, using notebooks instead can be helpful.

REMEMBER

A *notebook* differs from a text editor in that it focuses on a technique advanced by Stanford computer scientist Donald Knuth called literate programming. You use *literate programming* to create a kind of presentation of code, notes, math equations, and graphics. In short, you wind up with a scientist's notebook full of everything needed to understand the code completely. You commonly see literate programming techniques used in high-priced packages such as Mathematica and MATLAB (see *MATLAB For Dummies,* 2nd Edition, by John Paul Mueller and Jim Sizemore [Wiley] for details). Notebook development excels at

>> Demonstration

>> Collaboration

>> Research

>> Teaching objectives

>> Presentation

This book uses Colab and Jupyter Notebook because these IDEs provide you with a great Python coding experience, as well as help you discover the enormous potential of literate programming techniques. If you spend a lot of time performing scientific tasks, Colab and products like it are essential. In addition, both Colab and Jupyter Notebook are free, so you get the benefits of the literate programming style without the cost of other packages.

REMEMBER

When working through this book, you see Colab used to reference Google Colab specifically, Jupyter Notebook used to reference Jupyter Notebook specifically, and Notebook (by itself) to refer to both Colab and Jupyter Notebook generically. There are differences between the two products that you need to know about, and the book points them out for you.

Creating the Application

You've actually created your first Python application by using the steps in the "Seeing the result" section of Chapter 3. The print() method may not seem like much, but you use it quite often. However, the literate programming approach provided by Colab requires a little more knowledge than you currently have. The following sections don't tell you everything about this approach, but they do help you gain an understanding of what literate programming can provide in the way of functionality. However, before you begin, make sure you have the BPP4D3E; 04; Sample.ipynb file open for use because you need it to explore Notebook.

Developing the code

Real applications do something more than print a message using the print() method. Starting with Part 2 of the book, you develop the skills required to do something really interesting. For now though, it's time to do something a little better than just printing a message, even if you don't quite understand everything that the code does. (You definitely will later in the book.) Create a new notebook (see the "Creating a new notebook" section of Chapter 2 if you need some help in this regard) and type the following code into a code cell:

```
def addSomething(value1, value2):
    return value1 + value2


print(addSomething(1, 2))
```

When you click the Run Cell icon (or click the Run button in Jupyter Notebook), you see the result of 3 magically appear. Of course, the delight in seeing code that you typed run is momentary. A second impression might be that this is an interesting group of gibberish letters that really don't mean much to most humans. So it's a good time to break this code down a little and add comments to it so that you can remember what it does. Add the following comments (in bold), as shown here:

```
# Define a function to encapsulate task code that accepts
# two pieces of information in boxes called variables
# named value1 and value2.
def addSomething(value1, value2):

    # Add the two values together and return the result
    # to the caller.
    return value1 + value2


# Call the addSomething() function with two numbers to
# add and then use print() to display the result.
print(addSomething(1, 2))
```

Comments always begin with a hashtag (#) so that the Python interpreter doesn't mistake them for code. It's amazing what a difference a few comments can make. Of course, you still might not understand the code completely, but you have a better idea of how it works, which is why you always comment your code.

Adding documentation cells

Cells come in a number of different forms. This book doesn't use them all. However, knowing how to use the documentation cells can come in handy. Select the first cell (the one with the code you just created in it). Click the +Text button in Colab or choose Insert ➪ Insert Cell Above in Jupyter Notebook. You see a new cell added to the notebook. (When working with Jupyter Notebook, you need to select Markdown from the drop-down list that currently contains Code in it.) Type **#** **Creating the Application** because this is the parent heading for this section. The #

symbol is called *markup*, which is a method of telling Notebook how to format text (the "Working with text cells" section of the chapter talks about using markup in more detail). Select the next cell in Colab or click Run in Jupyter Notebook. You see the text change into a heading. Click the Move Cell Up button in Colab as needed to place the heading correctly, as shown in Figure 4-1.

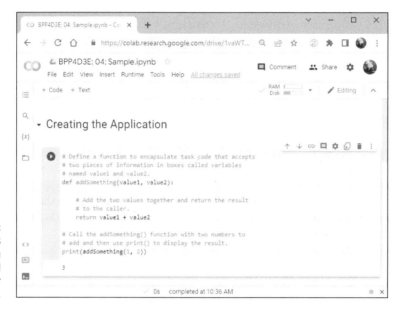

FIGURE 4-1:
Adding headings helps you separate and document your code.

About now, you may be thinking that these special cells act just like HTML pages, and you'd be right. Use the same process you did for adding the first heading to add a second heading by typing **## Developing the code**. As you can see in Figure 4-2, the number of hashes (#) you add to the text affects the heading level, but the hashes don't show up in the actual heading.

TIP

Notice that you have also documented precisely where the code appears in the book. The other source code examples in the book follow this same strategy so that you can easily match the source code to the section that describes it.

Other cell content

This chapter (and book) doesn't demonstrate all the kinds of cell content that you can see by using Colab and Jupyter Notebook. However, you can add things like graphics to your notebooks, too. When the time comes, you can output (print) your notebook as a report and use it in presentations of all sorts. The literate programming technique is different from what you may have used in the past, but it has definite advantages, as you see in upcoming chapters.

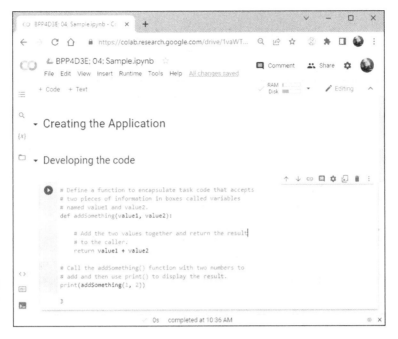

FIGURE 4-2: Using heading levels provides emphasis for cell content.

Playing around with scratch cells

There are times when you want to experiment without making code a part of your main application. You may also need to access a shell while working with Colab. For example, the Linux `ls` command (`https://linuxize.com/post/how-to-list-files-in-linux-using-the-ls-command/`) displays a list of files and directories found in the location where you're executing the Colab code. In this case, you can create a scratch cell, like the one shown in Figure 4-3, by choosing Insert ⇨ Scratch Code Cell. This feature is available only in Colab and not in Jupyter Notebook.

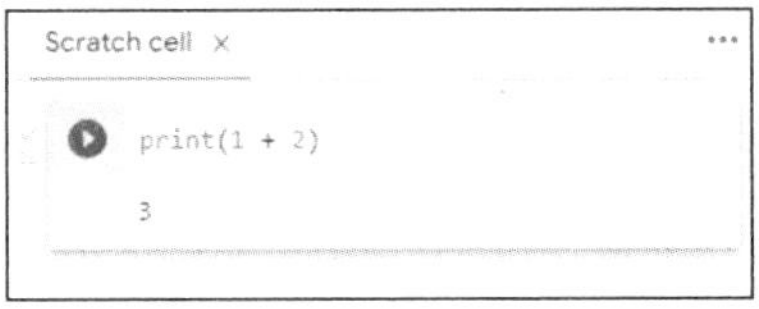

FIGURE 4-3: A scratch cell provides a place to experiment and run shell commands.

Clicking the ellipsis in the upper-right corner displays tasks you can perform with the scratch cell. Here are some of the most important options:

» **Copy Cell:** Copies the cell contents to the Clipboard where you can paste the information to another application.

» **Clear Output:** Clears the cell output before you run the scratch code again.

» **View Output Fullscreen:** Displays the cell data full screen so that you can see all of it at one time outside the Colab panes. Press Esc to exit the full-screen mode.

» **Move Tab to Next Pane:** Places the scratch cell in the next available pane. Normally, a scratch cell opens in its own pane, which may take up too much screen real estate in some cases.

» **Move Tab to Previous Pane:** Places the scratch cell in the previous pane, which may be the pane originally used to hold it.

» **Close Tab:** Closes the selected scratch cell tab without affecting any other tabs.

» **Close All Tabs:** Closes all the scratch cell tabs without affecting any other Colab cells. Note that you may also see options for closing all the tabs to the left of the current tab and all the tabs to the right of the current tab.

» **Change Page Layout:** Determines the appearance of Colab with regard to scratch cells. The default is to use two columns, but you can also use a single column view where the scratch cell tabs appear across the top with a separate tab labeled Notebook that holds your code. It's also possible to place the scratch cells below the last line in the current Notebook pane.

TIP

You can have more than one scratch cell at a time. Every time you choose Insert ⇨ Scratch Code Cell, Colab creates another scratch cell tab for you. You can close the tabs in any order desired.

Interacting with form fields

Form fields let the user enter values that a program can then use as input. Just as Jupyter Notebook doesn't provide scratch cells, it also doesn't provide access to form fields. So even though adding form fields to your Colab notebook won't prevent the code from also running in Jupyter Notebook, you also won't see the functionality that form fields provide in Jupyter Notebook.

WARNING

Using form fields adds the potential for incompatibility to your notebooks. Unless you have a good reason to add GUI elements to your notebook, it's usually best to skip the form fields and use standard Python data-entry methods instead, like the input() function shown here:

```
name = input("Type your name: ")
print(f"Your name is: {name}")
```

Choosing a form field type

If you do decide to use form fields in your program, you choose Insert ⇨ Add A Form Field. You see the Add New Form Field dialog box, shown in Figure 4-4. The Form Field Type field contains a list of GUI elements you can add, which include `input`, `dropdown`, `slider`, and `markdown`.

Add new form field

Form field type
input

Variable type
string

Variable name
variable_name

Cancel   Save

FIGURE 4-4:
The Add New
Form Field dialog
box allows you to
add GUI inputs to
your notebook.

The form field type that you choose determines how the Add New Form Field dialog box appears. For example, if you choose `dropdown`, you need to add a list of drop-down options. A `slider` requires that you add minimum and maximum values, and the size of the steps between values.

TIP

The markdown option is interesting because it allows you to add what amounts to a text cell within a code cell. You type **Colab markdown** (`https://colab.research.google.com/notebooks/markdown_guide.ipynb`) in the Markdown field. This means that you really can mix code and markdown together to create a better looking notebook.

Defining the variable type and name

To use a form field, all you need to do is fill in the blanks. Follow these steps for this example:

1. **Choose input in the Form Field Type field.**

   You see the dialog box shown in Figure 4-4.

2. **Choose string in the Variable Type field.**

3. **Type** YourName **in the Variable Name field; then click Save.**

   You see the combination of code and GUI presentation shown in Figure 4-5.

TIP

Displaying both code and GUI presentation may seem counterproductive because you want a nice display for your notebook. To get rid of the code, choose the ellipsis in the cell toolbar and then select Form ⇨ Hide Code from the menu.

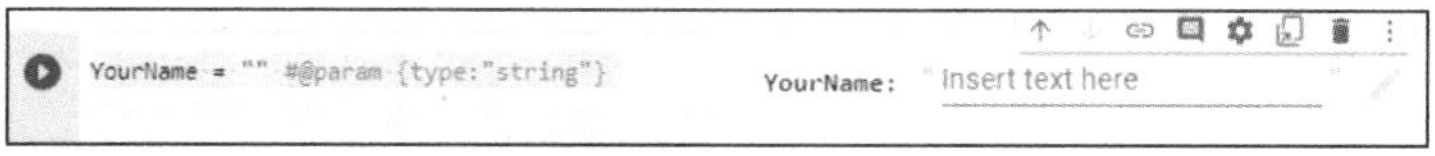

FIGURE 4-5:
Adding a form field to your notebook displays a combination of code and GUI presentation.

YourName = "" #@param {type:"string"}   YourName: Insert text here

Using the form field

One of the interesting aspects of form fields is that they exist as part of a code cell, so you can add code directly below the form field entry to interact with the form field. Type **print(f"Your name is: {YourName}")** directly below the YourName = "" #@param {type:"string"} entry in the cell. Type your name in the form field, and you see that the code changes as well. Now, click Run Cell and you see that the code interacts with the form field as, shown in Figure 4-6.

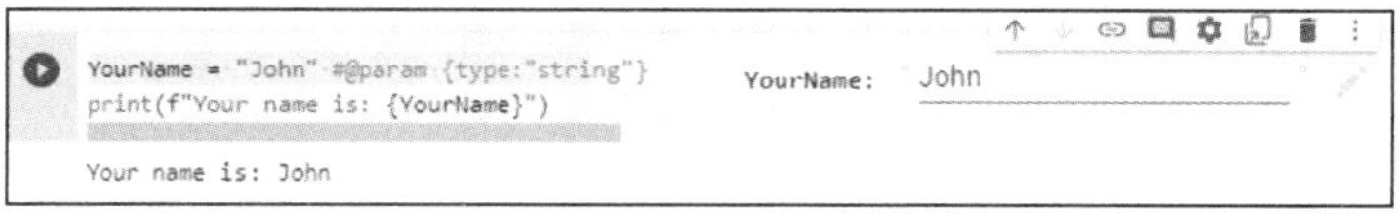

FIGURE 4-6:
Design code to interact with the form fields you create.

YourName = "John" #@param {type:"string"}   YourName: John
print(f"Your name is: {YourName}")

Your name is: John

REMEMBER

By linking a number of form fields together in the same cell, you can create the appearance of a form used in any other application. The user fills out the form and clicks Run Cell to see the result. When you hide the code area, the GUI presentation looks seamless, and because it resides in a notebook, you have access to the presentation features that a notebook can provide as well.

Running the Application

In general, an application consists of the current notebook and any linked resources. It's not an application in the traditional sense because you can run it just one cell at a time, but it does help to view the application as being the entire notebook.

Seeing the result

To this point, you have seen applications run one cell at a time. To see the entire result without having to click Run Cell in each and every cell like an annoying little habit that drives sane people a little batty, you can use the following options:

- **Runtime ⇨ Run All:** Runs all the cells without clearing the output first.

- **Runtime ⇨ Run Before:** Runs all the cells above the cell that currently has focus.

- **Selected cells:** Select multiple cells using Shift+Up Arrow or Shift+Down Arrow; then choose Runtime ⇨ Run Selection to run just the selected cells.

- **Runtime ⇨ Run After:** Runs all the cells below the cell that currently has focus.

- **Runtime ⇨ Restart and Run All:** Runs all the cells after restarting the runtime and clearing the output.

The Jupyter Notebook options are similar, but different enough to warrant separate coverage.

TIP

- **Selected cells:** Select multiple cells using Shift+Down Arrow or Shift+Up Arrow; then choose Cell ⇨ Run Cells to run just the selected cells. You can also choose Cell ⇨ Run Cells and Select Below to run the selected cells and choose the next cell as the focused cell. If there is no next cell, Jupyter Notebook creates one for you. Choosing Cell ⇨ Run Cells and Insert Below runs the selected cells and then inserts a new cell as the focused cell even if there is an existing cell to use.

  When using this method, ensure that you have the cell selected and not the text within the cell. Jupyter Notebook highlights the selected cells for you in a light color.

- **Cell ⇨ Run All:** Runs all the cells without clearing the output first.

- **Cell ⇨ Run All Above:** Runs all the cells above the cell that currently has focus.

- **Cell ⇨ Run All Below:** Runs all the cells below the cell that currently has focus.

- **Kernel ⇨ Restart & Clear Output:** Clears the output from the previous runs without running the code. This is an important feature if you want to run just some of the cells without having previous results interfere with the current test.

- **Kernel ⇨ Restart & Run All:** Runs all the cells after restarting the runtime and clearing the output.

Viewing the executed code history

It's helpful to see the history of code that you've run while creating an application. Doing so can help you locate errors in logic or even execution order. Sometimes, viewing the code history simply reminds you to restart the runtime or kernel because things have gotten messy with variables dangling about (staying when you don't need them any longer) and causing problems. To see the code history in Colab, choose View ⇨ Executed Code History. Figure 4-7 shows a typical execution history for the example found in the previous sections.

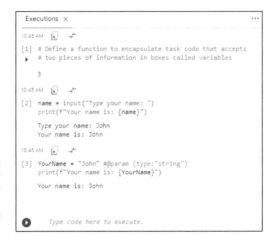

FIGURE 4-7:
Viewing the executed code history can tell you a lot about your code.

The top of each entry contains the time that you executed the code. Next to the time stamp is an icon you can click to copy the code to a scratch cell for further analysis. The last icon in the time stamp row scrolls the display to the code in question and selects it so that you don't have to manually look for it.

TIP

At the bottom of the window is a cell where you can try ideas as you browse the executed code. It acts like a scratch cell, and you use it like any other cell.

Understanding the Use of Indentation

As you work through the examples in this book, you see that certain lines are indented. In fact, the examples also provide a fair amount of white space (such as extra lines between lines of code). The indentation is also functional. Python uses indentation to define code regions such as code associated with functions and loops. So, adding indentation is an important part of your Python program.

The various uses of indentation will become more familiar as you work your way through the examples in the book. However, you should know at the outset why indentation is used and how it gets put in place. So it's time for another example. The following steps help you create a new example that uses indentation to make the relationship between application elements a lot more apparent and easier to figure out later.

1. **Open a new notebook by selecting New Notebook in the Colab notebook opening dialog box, New ⇨ Python3 in Jupyter Notebook, or by choosing File ⇨ New Notebook (optionally choosing the correct notebook type) if you already have a notebook open.**

   Colab or Jupyter Notebook creates a new notebook for you.

2. **Type** print("This is a really long line of text that will" +.

   You see the text displayed normally onscreen, just as you expect. The plus sign (+) tells Python that there is additional text to display. (Don't add the period at the end of the sentence.) Adding text from multiple lines together into a single long piece of text is called *concatenation*. You learn more about using this feature later in the book, so you don't need to worry about it now.

3. **Press Enter.**

   The insertion point doesn't go back to the beginning of the line, as you might expect. Instead, it ends up directly under the first double quote, as shown in Figure 4-8. This feature is called automatic indention and it's one of the features that differentiates a regular text editor from one designed to write code.

FIGURE 4-8:
The Edit window automatically indents some types of text.

```
print("This is a really long line of text that will " +
    |
```

4. **Type** "appear on multiple lines in the source code file.") **and press Enter.**

   Notice that the insertion point goes back to the beginning of the line. When Notebook senses that you have reached the end of the code, it automatically outdents the text to its original position.

5. **Click Run.**

   You see the output shown in Figure 4-9. Even though the text appears on multiple lines in the source code file, it appears on just one line in the output.

FIGURE 4-9:
Use concatena-
tion to make
multiple lines of
text appear on a
single line in the
output.

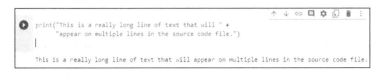

Adding Comments

People create notes for themselves all the time. When you need to buy groceries, you look through your cabinets, determine what you need, and write it down on a list or dictate it into your phone. When you get to the store, you review your list to remember what you need. Using notes comes in handy for all sorts of needs, such as tracking the course of a conversation between business partners or remember-ing the essential points of a lecture. Humans need notes to jog their memories. Comments in source code are just another form of note. You add them to the code so that you can remember what task the code performs later. The following sec-tions describe comments in more detail.

Understanding comments

Computers need some special way to determine that the text you're writing is a comment, not code to execute. Python provides two methods of defining text as a comment and not as code. The first method is the single-line comment. It uses the number sign (#), like this:

```
# This is a comment.
print("Hello from Python!") #This is also a comment.
```

HEADINGS VERSUS COMMENTS

You may find headings and comments a bit confusing at first. Headings appear in sepa-rate cells; comments appear with the source code. They serve different purposes. Headings serve to tell you about an entire code grouping, and individual comments tell you about individual code steps or even lines of code. Even though you use both of them for documentation, each serves a unique purpose. Comments are generally more detailed than headings.

REMEMBER

A single-line comment can appear on a line by itself or it can appear after executable code. It appears on only one line. You typically use a single-line comment for short descriptive text, such as an explanation of a particular bit of code. Notebook shows comments in a distinctive color (usually blue or green) and in italics.

Creating multiline comments

Python doesn't actually support a multiline comment directly, but you can create one using a triple-quoted string (called a *docstring*). A multiline comment both starts and ends with three double quotes (""") or three single quotes (''') like this:

```
"""
    Application: Comments.py
    Written by: John
    Purpose: Shows how to use comments.
"""
```

REMEMBER

Unlike single-line comments, multiline docstrings used as comments normally appear in red and in roman type. The interpreter does read them, but you can still use them for comments. These lines aren't executed. Python won't display an error message when they appear in your code. However, Notebook treats them differently, as shown in Figure 4-10.

FIGURE 4-10:
Multiline comments do work, but they also provide output.

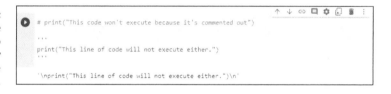

Note that the actual Python comments, those preceded by a hash (#) in cell 1, don't generate any output. The triple-quote docstrings, however, do generate output. If you plan to output your notebook as a report, you need to avoid using triple-quoted docstrings. (Some IDEs, such as IDLE, ignore the triple-quoted strings completely.)

TECHNICAL STUFF

You can also assign a docstring to a variable, which isn't possible with a comment. The code and output shown in Figure 4-11 shows what a docstring looks like as output when assigned to a variable. Notice that the docstring isn't printed in this case because it appears as a variable assignment. The docstring formatting does remain in place, though, unlike the concatenation example shown in the "Understanding the Use of Indentation" section, earlier in this chapter.

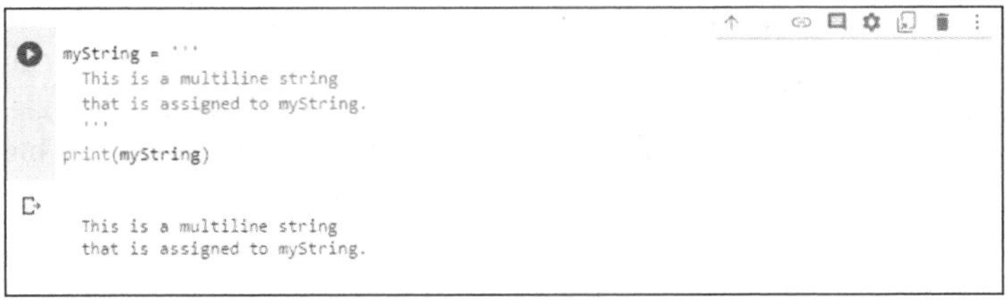

FIGURE 4-11:
Use docstrings
for strings that
require multiple
lines.

You typically use multiline docstrings for longer explanations of who created an application, why it was created, and what tasks it performs. Of course, there aren't any hard rules on precisely how you use comments. The main goal is to tell the computer precisely what is and isn't a comment so that it doesn't become confused.

Using comments to leave yourself reminders

A lot of people don't really understand comments — they don't quite know what to do with notes in code. Keep in mind that you might write a piece of code today and then not look at it for years. You need notes to jog your memory so that you remember what task the code performs and why you wrote it. In fact, here are some common reasons to use comments in your code:

» Reminding yourself about what the code does and why you wrote it

» Recording who wrote the code when involved in a multiperson project (usually along with other information, such as how to contact the person)

» Telling others how to maintain your code

» Making your code accessible to other developers

» Listing ideas for future updates

» Providing a list of documentation sources you used to write the code

» Maintaining a list of improvements you've made

You can use comments in a lot of other ways, too, but these are the most common ways. Look at the way comments are used in the examples in the book, especially as you get to later chapters where the code becomes more complex. As your code becomes more complex, you need to add more comments and make the comments pertinent to what you need to remember about it.

Using comments to keep code from executing

Developers also sometimes use the commenting feature to keep lines of code from executing (referred to as *commenting out*). You might need to do this in order to determine whether a line of code is causing your application to fail. As with any other comment, you can use either single line commenting or multiline commenting. However, when using multiline commenting, you do see the code that isn't executing as part of the output (and it can actually be helpful to see where the code affects the output). Figure 4-12 shows an example of code commenting techniques.

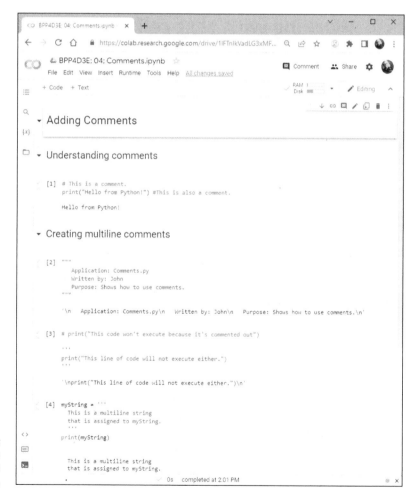

FIGURE 4-12: Use comments to keep code from executing.

Making Your Notebook Informative, Descriptive, and Pretty

After putting a lot of time and effort into creating headings and code for your notebook, you don't want to falter at the end and not add the fit and finish items that will truly make your notebook stand out from any competition. Fortunately, you don't need a degree in media to make notebooks interesting and even pretty. Adding pizzazz does require a little time, but the payoff is worth it when you make a presentation. The following sections offer some ideas on how to dress your notebook up.

Working with text cells

So far, you have worked with text cells that contain headings. You've also been exposed to some of the other markup options you can employ in a heading, such as adding italics. Boring! When you open a text cell in Colab, you see a toolbar containing all sorts of interesting options, like those found in Figure 4-13.

FIGURE 4-13: The text cell toolbar contains a variety of interesting options.

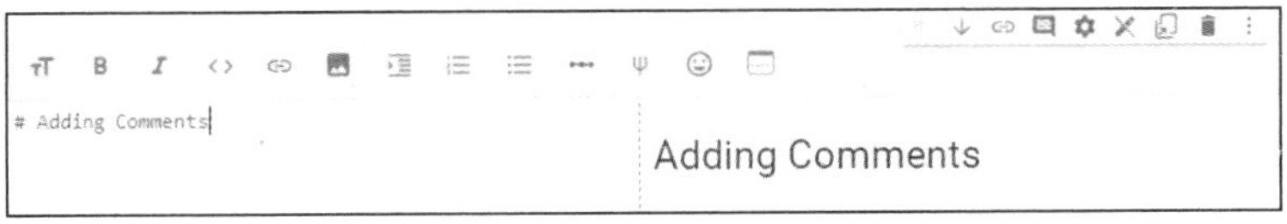

Here is what those buttons do:

>> **Toggle Heading:** Cycles through the various heading levels so that you can see how the text appears in various sizes.

>> **Bold:** Makes the selected text appear in bold type.

>> **Italics:** Makes the selected text appear in italics type.

>> **Format as Code:** Sets the selected text to appear as code rather than regular text. You can use this option for things like calling syntax or examples of usage.

>> **Insert Link:** Adds a URL to the text cell so that the user can click it and see other online resources. This is also a handy way to create reference notes for yourself as you write the code so that you can simply go back to the website that contains the really good coding idea.

>> **Insert Image:** Places an image at the current cursor position, making it possible to add graphical documentation to your notebook in addition to text. This is also a dandy way to personalize your notebook so that you can see a loved one as you type.

>> **Indent:** Adds an indent to the current text. You can also use this feature to create multiple-level bulleted and numbered lists.

>> **Add Numbered List:** Creates a new numeric list at the current cursor position.

TIP

You can add bulleted sublists to a numeric list and vice versa simply by using the indent feature. For example, Figure 4-14 shows what a nested list looks like. Notice the use of the > symbol to increase the indent level. Also notice that the bullet type changes to make the indent level.

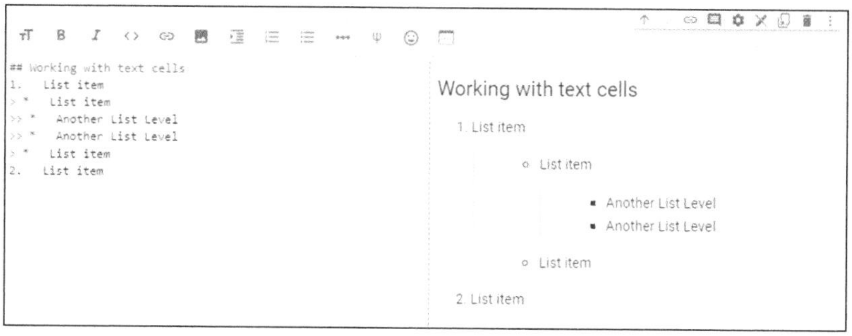

FIGURE 4-14: Use indents to create nested lists for your documentation.

>> **Add Bulleted List:** Creates a new bulleted list at the current cursor position.

>> **Add Horizontal Rule:** Places a line across the text cell to separate one group of material from another.

>> **LaTeX:** Allows use of LaTeX markup (https://www.latex-project.org/) in the text cell.

>> **Insert Emoji:** Places the selected emoji at the current cursor location. When you click this option, what you see is a list of standard emojis. Note that emoji support comes with Colab, but you may have to install it on Jupyter Notebook as described at https://sawanrai777.medium.com/have-fun-with-emojis-in-jupyter-notebook-f74db7f45210. Note that you can copy and paste emojis from websites and other locations into your code, but place them within a string to ensure correct interpretation by the IDE.

Adding section headers

A section heading is simply a text cell with a heading already defined in it. You can promote or demote the section heading level using fewer or more # characters in front of the heading. The only difference is that Colab does some of the work for you. Add a new section header to your notebook by choosing Insert ⇨ Section Header Cell.

Interacting with the table of contents

The table of contents is a feature that is supported by Colab and not Jupyter Notebook. To see the Table of Contents, choose View ⇨ Table of Contents or click the Table of Contents button on the left toolbar. Figure 4-15 shows typical output.

FIGURE 4-15:
The Table of Contents feature provides an outline of your notebook.

To use the Table of Contents, simply click the heading that contains the material you want to see. The currently selected heading appears in bold so that you know where you're currently at in the notebook.

REMEMBER Figure 4-15 points out the need to use separate text cells for each heading level in your notebook, rather than combine all the headers for a particular area into one text cell (even though it would look acceptable that way in the document). If you don't place each heading level in its own text cell, the feature won't work as intended and you'll get really frustrated trying to make it behave itself.

Renaming a notebook

The notebooks you create should have descriptive names. Otherwise, they become too difficult to find after you've accumulated enough of them. It's sort of like having a closet at home that's stocked floor to ceiling with unmarked boxes (or worse yet, boxes that have the wrong content marked on them). The only way to find something is to take the boxes out one at a time and open them to see what's inside. To rename a notebook, just click the filename at the top of the notebook such as BPP4D3E; 04; Comments.ipynb and type a new name for it.

Closing and Halting a Notepad

There is no need (or option) to close and halt notebooks when working with Colab. However, when working with Jupyter Notebook, you have a local server (called a *kernel*), and you need to interact with that server to ensure that all the changes you make to a notebook are recorded. With this idea in mind, the following list contains the menu options you use to interact with the server to ensure that your changes are saved and that the server itself is halted when you want to end a session.

- » **File ⇨ Save and Checkpoint:** Saves any changes you made to disk and creates a checkpoint so that you can restore a previous version of your file. However, Jupyter Notebook saves only one previous version, so your undo options are somewhat limited.

- » **File ⇨ Revert to Checkpoint:** Presents a list of checkpoint files for this notebook. There is usually just one such file, and selecting it will restore the file from the previous checkpoint.

- » **File ⇨ Close and Halt:** Closes the file and halts the server for this notebook. The overall server functionality is unaffected. To completely shut the server down, you must click Quit in the main Jupyter Notebook screen (the one where you select which file to open).

- » **Kernel ⇨ Reconnect:** Allows recovery after a software glitch if the server breaks the connection with the current notebook. You can tell that the connection is broken because you see a No Kernel message at the right side of the menu bar.

- » **Kernel ⇨ Shutdown:** Shuts the kernel down without closing the file. You see a No Kernel message at the right side of the menu bar when the shutdown is complete.

- » **Kernel ⇨ Change Kernel:** Selects an alternative kernel to use when running the current notebook. You might install multiple versions of Python, for example, and need to test the code with each one. (The "Seeing the result" section of the chapter talks about various restart options you can use to ensure you have a clean environment to use between tests.)

Chapter **5**

Performing Magic

M ost everyone likes magic. You see it in films, books, magazines, online, video games, and a seemingly endless assortment of other sources. Watching a magician perform tricks is nothing short of amazing. Unlike other programming languages, Python comes with its own built-in set of *magic* commands. A magic command is a special kind of function that does something to the programming environment, rather than work as code. These magical words can make you look just like a magician on a stage; others will wonder how you created a certain effect, and the secret of your magic commands will remain yours alone. The first part of this chapter discusses the ins and outs of magic commands in a little more detail.

Of course, you'll want to start performing magic commands immediately, so the second part of the chapter gets you started with a few beginner tricks designed to tantalize without being too hard to use. Some magic commands can become involved, just like those on the stage (but your code won't ever disappear and no one will get locked up in a tank of water).

The third part of this chapter provides an overview of the magic commands keywords that you need to know. Each entry comes with a short description so that you know which magic commands will fulfill needs you have with your notebooks. Spending time working with the magic commands is the only way to learn them well.

REMEMBER

You don't have to type the source code for this chapter manually. In fact, using the downloadable source is a lot easier. You can find the source for this chapter in the `BPP4D3E; 05; Magics.ipynb` file of the downloadable source. See the Introduction for details on how to find these source files.

Understanding the Concept of a Magic Command

A magic command really isn't magic. The magic is in the output. For example, instead of displaying graphic output in a separate window, you can choose to display it within the cell, as if by magic (because the cells appear to hold only text). Or you can use magic to check the performance of your application, and do so without all the usual added code that such performance checks require.

A *magic command* begins with either a percent sign (%) or double percent sign (%%). Those with a % sign work within the environment, and those with a %% sign work at the cell level. For example, if you want to obtain a list of magic commands, type **%lsmagic** and then run the command in Colab or Notebook to see them, as shown in Figure 5-1. (You may see the output all on one line, in which case you can apply the fix described in the "Adding magic to the magic commands" sidebar.)

```
%lsmagic

Available line magics:
%alias  %alias_magic  %autocall  %automagic  %autosave  %bookmark  %cat  %cd  %clear  %colors  %config  %connect_info
%cp  %debug  %dhist  %dirs  %doctest_mode  %ed  %edit  %env  %gui  %hist  %history  %killbgscripts  %ldir  %less  %lf
%lk  %ll  %load  %load_ext  %loadpy  %logoff  %logon  %logstart  %logstate  %logstop  %ls  %lsmagic  %lx  %macro  %magic
%man  %matplotlib  %mkdir  %more  %mv  %notebook  %page  %pastebin  %pdb  %pdef  %pdoc  %pfile  %pinfo  %pinfo2  %pip
%popd  %pprint  %precision  %profile  %prun  %psearch  %psource  %pushd  %pwd  %pycat  %pylab  %qtconsole  %quickref
%recall  %rehashx  %reload_ext  %rep  %rerun  %reset  %reset_selective  %rm  %rmdir  %run  %save  %sc  %set_env  %shell
%store  %sx  %system  %tb  %tensorflow_version  %time  %timeit  %unalias  %unload_ext  %who  %who_ls  %whos  %xdel
%xmode

Available cell magics:
%%!  %%HTML  %%SVG  %%bash  %%bigquery  %%capture  %%debug  %%file  %%html  %%javascript  %%js  %%latex  %%perl  %%prun
%%pypy  %%python  %%python2  %%python3  %%ruby  %%script  %%sh  %%shell  %%svg  %%sx  %%system  %%time  %%timeit
%%writefile

Automagic is ON, % prefix IS NOT needed for line magics.
```

FIGURE 5-1:
The `%lsmagic` command displays a list of magic commands for you.

ADDING MAGIC TO THE MAGIC COMMANDS

Depending on the IDE and browser you use (Colab tends to have this problem; Notebook doesn't), you may notice that certain commands display a very long line of text without any text wrap, which means you must scroll back and forth to see the entire line. Of course, this can prove frustrating, especially if you're already having a bad day. Rather than throw your shoe at the monitor, however, you can add the following piece of code to the beginning of your notebook and run it in a separate cell from your other code:

```
from IPython.display import HTML, display

def set_css():
  display(HTML('''
  <style>
    pre {
        white-space: pre-wrap;
    }
  </style>
  '''))
get_ipython().events.register('pre_run_cell', set_css)
```

TECHNICAL STUFF

It's not essential to understand this code to make use of it, although understanding it would be nice. This code tells the IDE to provide text wrapping using a specific Cascading Style Sheets (CSS) style, `pre {white-space: pre-wrap;}`, as documented at `https://developer.mozilla.org/en-US/docs/Web/CSS/white-space`. You access this style by using the `IPython.display.HTML` class documented at `https://ipython.readthedocs.io/en/stable/api/generated/IPython.display.html`. You can see other `IPython.display.HTML` examples at `https://www.programcreek.com/python/example/83957/IPython.display.HTML`.

The call to `get_ipython()` obtains a copy of the interactive shell object that you then use to register a new event handler named `pre_run_cell` (see `https://ipython.readthedocs.io/en/stable/api/generated/IPython.core.getipython.html` and `https://ipython.readthedocs.io/en/stable/config/callbacks.html` for details). Every time you run a cell, the event handler adds the bit of CSS code defined by the `set_css()` function to ensure that text lines will wrap for you. You can see other `get_ipython()` call examples at `https://www.programcreek.com/python/example/50972/IPython.get_ipython`. The point is that the code fixes the text wrapping problem for you.

Each of these magic commands is part of the IPython module that is automatically loaded when you load Python, no matter where or how you load it. So when you work at the command line (something you won't do in this book), you can still use many of the magic commands. Of course, you have to have Python installed on your machine to test it by typing **ipython** and pressing Enter at a command prompt or in a terminal window. (Note that this is the interactive Python (ipython) command, not the standard Python (python) command.) Some magic commands don't have a use at the command line, such as %autosave, because the environment is different. The point is that Python provides magic commands no matter where you work with it.

What Kind of Magic Do You Want to Perform?

Magic functions are all about the programming environment rather than the application code. When you issue a magic command, what you're doing is accessing the underlying interactive shell in a manner that doesn't require you to write code similar to that found in the "Adding Magic to the Magic Commands" sidebar in the chapter. All this code is already encapsulated for you in the form of the magic functions. There are two kinds of magic commands: line and cell, as described in the sections that follow.

Working with line magic commands

Line magic commands affect a single line in your code. When you start reviewing them in the "An overview of line magic commands" section of the chapter, you see that this limitation makes sense. For example, if you perform a directory listing using the %ls function, you don't want to have it keep affecting every other cell in the application. All you really want to see are the items (files and other directories) in the current directory.

Any line magic functions that affect settings do continue to modify the environment. For example, the settings you use with the %matplotlib function remain in effect until you change them again. However, like any other line magic commands, the %matplotlib affects only the current line where the setting is made. That the setting remains permanent is a matter of application state, rather than having the %matplotlib function remain active.

REMEMBER

It's important to note that the magic functions work directly with the interactive shell and aren't actually part of your application. For example, you can't write `myDir = %ls` and expect that `myDir` will contain a directory listing after you execute the command. What will happen instead is that you see a directory listing and `myDir` remains empty (a call to `print(myDir)` will produce an output of `None`).

Working with cell magic commands

Cell magic commands affect an entire cell in your code and some affect all cells after the cell in which the magic command appears. For example, the `%%debug` function affects only the current cell, but it does so in a manner that affects the application as a whole because it activates the built-in debugger. You can use this debugger to locate errors in your code much faster and with better accuracy than using the `print()` function, which is how most developers debug their Python code. The article at `https://towardsdatascience.com/4-little-known-magic-commands-that-boost-your-productivity-af1ba4268c57` tells you more about the built-in debugger (a feature that few people even know about).

Depending on how you use `%%prun` and `%%time` functions, they can affect the application as a whole because you're using them to monitor performance. In fact, `%%prun` actually shows all the external calls involved in running your code (the listing can become quite long). So it's important to view cell magic commands as running in the current cell, but possibly affecting other cells as well.

Learning the Magic Commands

Like any good magician, you need to learn the magic words before you can perform magic commands. The following sections provide you with the information needed to make creating magic in your notebooks a reality.

Getting magic command details

As previously mentioned, you can use the `%lsmagic` command to obtain a simple listing of available magic commands. Tables 5-1 and 5-2 list the most common magic commands and their purpose. To obtain a full detail listing, type **%quickref** and click Run Cell in Colab or Notebook to display output like that shown in Figure 5-2. You can also find a full listing of the magic commands at `https://damontallen.github.io/IPython-quick-ref-sheets/`.

WATCHING FOR ENVIRONMENTAL DIFFERENCES

Most of the magic commands you read about in this chapter will work in most environments. However, some magic commands don't work with Colab, and others don't work with Jupyter Notebook. Unfortunately, the support you see for magic commands changes all the time, so your best option is to try a magic command in the environment in which you want to use it and see if it works. For example, %cp --help works fine in Colab, but doesn't work in Jupyter Notebook (at least, not now). You may also get different results from some commands based on environment because the environment helps to determine the information you receive. A directory listing for Colab will definitely differ from a directory listing in Jupyter Notebook. You also see differences based on platform — output from a Windows platform will differ from the output on a Linux platform.

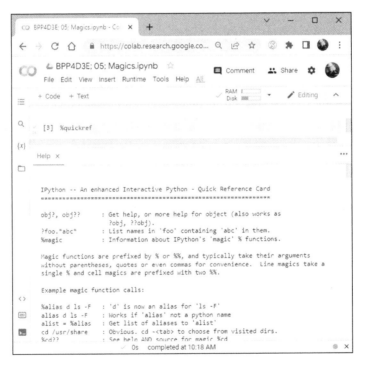

FIGURE 5-2:
The %quickref function displays more detailed magic command information for you.

TIP

In some cases, %quickref shows :: for an output, rather than a description, to indicate that this particular magic command doesn't have a specific output. For example, when working with %debug or %%debug, the output depends on the code that you debug. In other cases, %quickref does provide help text, but it doesn't really tell you how to work with the magic command, such as with %%prun, where you must supply the code to run as part of the cell, as shown in Figure 5-3. In this case, the output from the code appears as part of the cell as usual, but the performance information appears in a help screen.

FIGURE 5-3:
The %quickref
function may
not tell you
everything you
need to know.

It's possible to obtain even more detailed information about a particular magic command by adding --help to the function. For example, %cp --help tells you about the arguments used with the %cp function. However, this feature doesn't work with all magic commands.

An overview of line magic commands

Table 5-1 shows a listing of common line magic commands and their purpose. The table also tells you when you can use the line magic command by itself. For example, when you use the %alias magic command alone, you obtain a listing of the currently defined aliases for system commands as a list of tuples, such as ('ldir', 'ls -F -o --color %l | grep /$'), where ldir is the alias for ls -F -o --color %l | grep /$. Typing ldir is much shorter, of course, but it accomplishes so much. Note that Table 5-1 doesn't include a few of the most advanced magic commands, such as %gui, or those that seem incompatible or somewhat useless, such a %dirs. In addition, you won't find deprecated (that is, no longer supported) magic commands such as %profile and %sc.

TABLE 5-1 **Common IPython Line Magic Commands**

Magic Command	Type Alone Provides Status?	Description
%alias	Yes	Assigns or displays an alias for a system command.
%alias_magic	No	Assigns an alias for a magic command. You must supply the new name you want to use and the name of the magic command that it represents. It's also possible to specify –c for cell magic commands and –l for line magic commands.
%autocall	Yes	Enables you to call functions without including the parentheses. The settings are Off, Smart (default), and Full. The Smart setting applies the parentheses only if you include an argument with the call.
%automagic	Yes	Enables you to call the line magic commands without including the percent (%) sign. The settings are False (default) and True.
%autosave	Yes	Displays or modifies the intervals between automatic Notebook saves. The default setting is every 120 seconds.
%bookmark	No	Makes it possible to create a bookmark in your code so that you don't have to remember where you're at between sessions. You must supply the bookmark name. Use the %cd –b function to go to a bookmark in your code.
%cd	Yes	Changes directory to a new storage location. You can also use this command to move through the directory history or to change directories to a bookmark. When used by itself, you see the current directory on disk.
%clear	No	Clears the terminal window (may not be available in all environments).
%cls	No	Clears the screen (may not be available in all environments).
%colors	No	Specifies the colors used to display text associated with prompts, the information system, and exception handlers. You can choose between NoColor (black and white), Linux (default), and LightBG.
%config	Yes	Enables you to configure IPython.
%connect_info	Yes	Displays the connection information for the notebook's interactive environment.

Magic Command	Type Alone Provides Status?	Description
%conda	No	Runs the specified conda command, assuming that you have conda installed on your system (may not be available in all environments).
%cp	No	Copies a file from a source to a destination (may not be available in all environments).
%debug and %%debug.	No	Places the interactive environment into debug mode.
%dhist	Yes	Displays a list of directories visited during the current session.
%dirs, %popd, %pushd, %pwd	Yes	Pushes the current directory on the directory stack (%pushd), pops a saved directory from the directory stack (%popd), shows the list of directories on the directory stack (%dirs), and shows the current working directory (%pwd).
%doctest_mode	No	Toggles the interactive environment between doctest mode and standard environment behavior. In doctest mode, the environment behaves more like the plain Python environment in reporting errors and outputting information, which makes it easier to copy and paste the information into doctests (see https://docs.python.org/3/library/doctest.html and https://www.digitalocean.com/community/tutorials/how-to-write-doctests-in-python for additional details).
%env and %set_env	Yes	Displays (%env) and sets (%set_env) the environment variables for the current machine. When the name of an environment variable is provided, the output shows just the information for that environment variable.
%file	No	Outputs the name of the file that contains the source code for the object. (May not be available in all environments.)
%hist and %history	Yes	Displays a list of magic commands issued during the current session.
%install_ext	No	Installs the specified extension. (May not be available in all environments.)
%ldir	Yes	Provides a directory listing of the current directory (no files). It's also possible to add the path to a directory that you want to search.

(continued)

TABLE 5-1 *(continued)*

Magic Command	Type Alone Provides Status?	Description
`%load` and `loadpy`	No	Loads application code from another source, such as an online example.
`%load_ext`	No	Loads a Python extension using its module name.
`%logoff`, `%logon`, `%logstart`, `%log-state`, and `%logstop`	Yes	Starts, stops, queries, and pauses Python logging of application activity. The `%logstart` and `%logstop` functions start and stop the log. Use `%logoff` and `%logon` to pause and continue the log. The `%logstate` function shows the current logging status.
`%lsmagic`	Yes	Displays a list of the currently available magic commands.
`%magic`	Yes	Displays a help screen showing information about the magic commands.
`%matplotlib`	Yes	Sets the back-end processor used for plots. Using the inline value displays the plot within the cell for an IPython Notebook file. The possible values are: `'gtk'`, `'gtk3'`, `'inline'`, `'nbagg'`, `'osx'`, `'qt'`, `'qt4'`, `'qt5'`, `'tk'`, and `'wx'`.
`%mkdir`	No	Creates a new directory in the location specified.
`%notebook`	No	Exports the current environment history to the specified notebook file that you can import and review.
`%paste`	No	Pastes the content of the Clipboard into the IPython environment (may not be available in all environments).
`%pdef`	No	Shows how to call the object (assuming that the object is callable).
`%pdoc`	No	Displays the `docstring` for an object.
`%pinfo`	No	Displays detailed information about the object (often more than provided by help alone).
`%pinfo2`	No	Displays extra detailed information about the object (when available).
`%pip`	No	Runs the specified pip command assuming that you have pip (package installer for Python) installed on your system (may not be available in all environments).
`%pprint`	No	Toggles pretty printing (how output appears) of content on and off.

Magic Command	Type Alone Provides Status?	Description
%precision	No	Sets the precision for pretty printing of floating-point values.
%prun	Yes	Profiles the specified function that appears on the same line as the magic command, rather than the code found in a cell as the %%prun function does. When run by itself, you see the calls used to run %prun, making it easier to separate the %prun calls from those made by your code.
%psearch	No	Performs a pattern search for desired objects in the environment. For example, using %psearch d* would search for all objects beginning with the letter d.
%pylab	Yes	Provides additional support for plotting using MatPlotLib as described at https://www.tutorialspoint.com/matplotlib/matplotlib_pylab_module.htm.
%quickref	Yes	Displays a reference sheet for all the available magic commands on a particular system (see the "Getting magic command details" section of the chapter for details).
%reload_ext	No	Reloads a previously installed extension.
%reset and %reset_selective	No	Resets the namespace, removing all the variables when used alone. It's also possible to specify which variables to reset. Clearing the variables allows execution of code in a clean environment but means that you must recreate any lost variables.
%rm and %rmdir	No	Removes a directory from the specified location. Note that the directory must be empty before you can remove it.
%run	No	Loads the specified Python module and runs it.
%source	No	Displays the source code for the object, assuming that the source is available (may not be available in all environments).
%store	No	Provides the means to store variables long term in Python. The article at https://www.blopig.com/blog/2020/05/storing-variables-in-jupyter-notebooks-using-store-magic/ provides details on how to use this magic command effectively.
%time and %timeit	No	Calculates the best performance time for an instruction.
%unalias	No	Removes a previously created alias from the list.

(continued)

TABLE 5-1 *(continued)*

Magic Command	Type Alone Provides Status?	Description
%unload_ext	No	Unloads the specified extension.
%who, %who_ls, and %whos	Yes	Provides a listing of currently defined variables. The %who and %who_ls functions provide overviews. The %whos function provides the most detailed output.
%xdel	No	Deletes a variable, even when the variable has several aliases. The variable is also removed from the output history.
%xmode	No	Toggles between exception handling verbosity levels: Minimal, Plain, Context, and Verbose. By setting the verbosity level correctly, you can usually reduce the time needed to find errors in your application.

An overview of cell magic commands

Cell magic commands tend to provide greater functionality in many ways than line magic commands do. You can perform tasks that might seem impossible, but they actually do work (making them quite magical indeed). For example, you may want to create an HTML presentation as part of your notebook, which would seem impossible because notebooks don't execute HTML very well, or do they? Using the following code lets you execute HTML within your notebook to get just the right presentation:

```
%%HTML

<p>This is a list.</p>
<ul>
   <li>Morning</li>
   <li>Noon</li>
   <li>Night</li>
</ul>
```

When you execute the cell, you get precisely the output you intend. Table 5-2 tells you more about the magical nature of cell magic commands. Unlike line magic commands, cell magic commands don't provide status information.

TABLE 5-2   Common IPython Cell Magic Commands

Magic Comand	Description
`%%!`, `%%bash`, `%sx`, `%%sx`, `%system`, and `%%system`	Performs a list of system-specific commands. The commands must match the underlying operating system. When working with Colab, this means using Linux commands, such as `ls`. When working with Notebook, it may mean using Windows commands, such as `dir`. Even though `ls` and `dir` are equivalent, you can't mix and match them, which makes this particular kind of magic command brittle (prone to breaking). The `%%bash` function is available only on Linux systems and provides the additional functionality detailed at `https://tldp.org/LDP/Bash-Beginners-Guide/html/Bash-Beginners-Guide.html` for bash users.
`%%capture`	Records the `stdout`, `stderr`, and IPython's rich `display()` calls for later use. The resulting object acts as a macro that you can play back as needed. The article at `https://notebook.community/lifeinoppo/littlefishlet-scode/RES/REF/python_sourcecode/ipython-master/examples/IPython%20Kernel/Capturing%20Output` provides an example of how to use this feature.
`%%file` and `%%writefile`	Writes the contents of a cell to the specified file.
`%%HTML` and `%%html`	Runs the specified HTML script immediately following the magic command in the same cell.
`%%javascript` and `%%js`	Runs the specified JavaScript script immediately following the magic command in the same cell.
`%%latex`	Renders the cell as a block of LaTeX (`https://www.latex-project.org/`). The level of LaTeX support depends on the environment you're using. For example, Jupyter Notebook supports only the level described at `https://docs.mathjax.org/en/v2.5-latest/tex.html`. The tutorial at `https://www.overleaf.com/learn/latex/Learn_LaTeX_in_30_minutes` tells you more about how to work with LaTeX. You can also use LaTeX directly in markup cells as described in the "Working with text cells" section of Chapter 4.
`%%prun`	Performance tests the code found in the remainder of the cell and provides detailed statistics about it. This magic command is different from the `%prun` function, so don't confuse the two.
`%%SVG` and `%%svg`	Renders the cell as a Scalable Vector Graphics (SVG) literal, so you can create images as part of your notebook. The tutorial at `https://www.w3schools.com/graphics/svg_intro.asp` tells you more about working with SVG.
`%%time` and `%%timeit`	Calculates the best performance time for all the instructions in a cell, apart from the one placed on the same cell line as the cell magic (which could therefore be an initialization instruction).

2

Talking the Talk

IN THIS PART . . .

Working with various kinds of data

Changing how Python views data

Choosing paths in applications

Performing tasks more than once

Dealing with exceptional situations

Chapter **6**

Storing and Modifying Information

hapter 3 introduces you to CRUD, that is, Create, Read, Update, and Delete — not that Chapter 3 contains cruddy material. This acronym provides an easy method to remember precisely what tasks all computer programs perform with information you want to manage. Of course, geeks use a special term for information — data, but either information or data works fine for this book.

To make information useful, you have to have some means of storing it permanently. Otherwise, every time you turned the computer off, all your information would be gone and the computer would provide limited value. In addition, Python must provide some rules for modifying information. The alternative is to have applications running amok, changing information in any and every conceivable manner. This chapter is about controlling information — defining how information is stored permanently and manipulated by applications you create.

REMEMBER

You don't have to type the source code for this chapter manually. In fact, using the downloadable source is a lot easier. You can find the source for this chapter in the `BPP4D3E; 06; Storing And Modifying Information.ipynb` file of the downloadable source. See the Introduction for details on how to find these source files.

Storing Information

An application requires fast access to information or else it will take a long time to complete tasks. As a result, applications store information in memory. However, memory is temporary. When you turn off the machine, the information must be stored in some permanent form, such as on your hard drive, a Universal Serial Bus (USB) flash drive, a Secure Digital (SD) card, or on the Internet using a cloud-based solution. In addition, you must also consider the form of the information, such as whether it's a number or text. The following sections discuss the issue of storing information as part of an application in more detail.

Seeing variables as storage boxes

When working with applications, you store information in variables. A *variable* is a kind of storage box. Whenever you want to work with the information, you access it using the variable. If you have new information you want to store, you put it in a variable. Changing information means accessing the variable first and then storing the new value in the variable. Just as you store things in boxes in the real world, so you store things in variables when working with applications.

REMEMBER

Computers are actually pretty tidy. Each variable stores just one piece of information. Using this technique makes it easy to find the particular piece of information you need — unlike in your closet, where things from ancient Egypt could be hidden. Even though the examples you work with in previous chapters don't use variables, most applications rely heavily on variables to make working with information easier.

Using the right box to store the data

People tend to store things in the wrong sort of box. For example, you might find a pair of shoes in a garment bag and a supply of pens in a shoebox. However, Python likes to be neat. As a result, you find numbers stored in one sort of variable and text stored in an entirely different kind of variable. Yes, you use variables in both cases, but the variable is designed to store a particular kind of information. Using specialized variables makes it possible to work with the information inside in particular ways. You don't need to worry about the details just yet — just keep in mind that each kind of information is stored in a special kind of variable.

TECHNICAL STUFF

Python uses specialized variables to store information to make things easy for the programmer and to ensure that the information remains safe. However, computers don't actually know about information types. All that the computer knows about are 0s and 1s, which is the absence or presence of a voltage. At a higher level, computers do work with numbers, but that's the extent of what computers do.

Numbers, letters, dates, times, and any other kind of information you can think about all come down to 0s and 1s in the computer system. For example, the letter *A* is actually stored as 01000001 or the number 65. The computer has no concept of the letter *A* or of a date such as 8/31/2022.

Defining the Essential Python Data Types

Every programming language defines variables that hold specific kinds of information, and Python is no exception. The specific kind of variable is called a *data type*. Knowing the data type of a variable is important because it tells you what kind of information you find inside. In addition, when you want to store information in a variable, you need a variable of the correct data type to do it. Python doesn't allow you to store text in a variable designed to hold numeric information. Doing so would damage the text and cause problems with the application. You can generally classify Python data types as numeric, string, and Boolean, although there really isn't any limit on just how you can view them. The following sections describe each of the standard Python data types within these classifications.

Putting information into variables

To place a value into any variable, you make an assignment using the assignment operator (=). Chapter 7 discusses the whole range of basic Python operators in more detail, but you need to know how to use this particular operator to some extent now. For example, to place the number 5 into a variable named myVar, you type **myVar = 5**. Even though Python doesn't provide any additional information to you, you can always type the variable name and click Run Cell to see the value it contains, or use a print() function as shown in Figure 6-1.

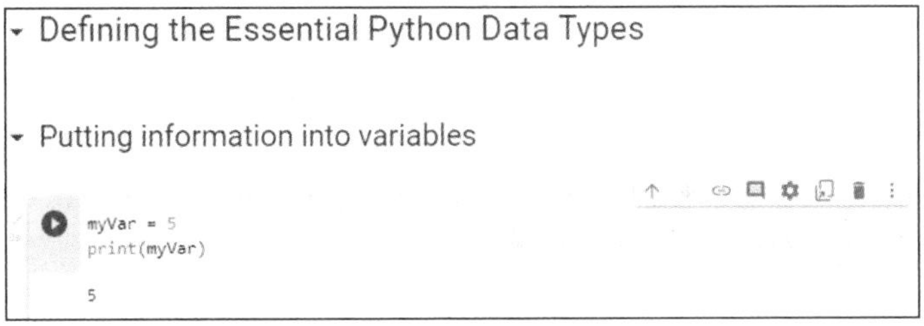

FIGURE 6-1:
Use the assignment operator to place information into a variable.

- Defining the Essential Python Data Types

- Putting information into variables

```
myVar = 5
print(myVar)

5
```

Understanding the numeric types

Humans tend to think about numbers in general terms. We view 1 and 1.0 as being the same number — one of them simply has a decimal point. However, as far as we're concerned, the two numbers are equal and we could easily use them interchangeably. Python views them as being different kinds of numbers because each form requires a different kind of processing. The following sections describe the integer, floating-point, and complex number classes of data types that Python supports.

Integers

Any whole number is an *integer*. For example, the value 1 is a whole number, so it's an integer. On the other hand, 1.0 isn't a whole number; it has a decimal part to it, so it's not an integer. Integers are represented by the `int` data type.

TECHNICAL STUFF

Unlike many programming languages, Python doesn't have an `int` capacity limit — you can make an `int` any size you need it. In case you want to understand how this unlimited size feature works, the site at `https://jakevdp.github.io/PythonDataScienceHandbook/02.01-understanding-data-types.html` provides additional details, but you really don't need to know how things work under the hood to work with Python. This unlimited size feature can cause problems with working with third-party libraries, such as NumPy (`https://numpy.org/doc/stable/user/basics.types.html`), where there are different integer data types with specific sizes, so you need to be aware of this issue when writing an application using third-party libraries.

When working with the `int` type, you have access to a number of interesting features. Many of them appear later in the book, but one feature is the ability to use different numeric bases:

>> **Base 2:** Uses only 0 and 1 as numbers.

>> **Base 8:** Uses the numbers 0 through 7.

>> **Base 10:** Uses the usual numeric system.

>> **Base 16:** Is also called *hex* (or *hexadecimal*) and uses the numbers 0 through 9 and the letters A through F to create 16 different possible values.

To tell Python when to use bases other than base 10, you add a 0 and a special letter to the number. For example, `0b100` is the value one-zero-zero in base 2. Here are the letters you normally use:

>> **b:** Base 2

>> **o:** Base 8

>> **x:** Base 16

You can also convert numeric values to other bases by using the bin(), oct(), and hex() functions. So, putting everything together, you can see how to convert between bases using the functions shown in Figure 6-2. Try the function shown in the figure yourself so that you can see how the various bases work. Using a different base actually makes things easier in many situations, and you'll encounter some of those situations later in the book. For now, all you really need to know is that integers support different numeric bases.

```
▼ Understanding the numeric types

▼ Integers

                                                      ↑ ↓ ⊘ ▢ ✿ ▣ ▮ ⋮

⏺   Test = 0b100
    print("100 Binary: ", Test)

    Test = 0o100
    print("100 Octal: ", Test)

    Test = 100
    print ("100 Decimal: ", Test)

    Test = 0x100
    print("100 Hexadecimal:", Test)

    print(bin(Test))
    print(oct(Test))
    print(hex(Test))

[→  100 Binary:  4
    100 Octal:  64
    100 Decimal:  100
    100 Hexadecimal: 256
    0b100000000
    0o400
    0x100
```

FIGURE 6-2:
Integers have many interesting features, including the capability to use different numeric bases.

Floating-point values

Any number that includes a decimal portion is a floating-point value. For example, 1.0 has a decimal part, so it's a floating-point value. Many people get confused about whole numbers and floating-point numbers, but the difference is easy to remember. If you see a decimal in the number, then it's a floating-point value. Python stores floating-point values in the float data type.

REMEMBER

Floating-point values have an advantage over integer values in that you can store values with a fractional portion in them. Unlike integers, floating-point variables do have a storage capacity because of the way in which they're stored using IEEE 754 format (see https://www.geeksforgeeks.org/ieee-standard-754-floating-point-numbers/ for details). In their case, the maximum value that a variable can contain is $\pm 1.7976931348623157 \times 10^{308}$ and the minimum value that a variable can contain is $\pm 2.2250738585072014 \times 10^{-308}$ on most platforms.

UNDERSTANDING THE NEED FOR MULTIPLE NUMBER TYPES

A lot of new developers (and even some older ones) have a hard time understanding why there is a need for more than one numeric type. After all, humans can use just one kind of number. To understand the need for multiple number types, you have to understand a little about how a computer works with numbers.

An integer is stored in the computer as simply a series of bits that the computer reads directly. A value of 0100 in binary equates to a value of 4 in decimal. On the other hand, numbers that have decimal points are stored in an entirely different manner. Think back to all those classes you slept through on exponents in school — they actually come in handy sometimes. A floating-point number is stored as a sign bit (plus or minus), *mantissa* (the fractional part of the number), and *exponent* (the power of 2). (Some texts use the term *significand* in place of mantissa — the terms are interchangeable.) To obtain the floating-point value, you use the equation:

```
Value = Sign Bit, Mantissa * 2^Exponent
```

At one time, computers all used different floating-point representations, but they all use the IEEE-754 standard (https://standards.ieee.org/ieee/754/6210/) now. You can read about this standard at https://www.geeksforgeeks.org/ieee-standard-754-floating-point-numbers/. A full explanation of precisely how floating-point numbers work is outside the scope of this book, but you can read a fairly understandable description at https://www.cprogramming.com/tutorial/floating_point/understanding_floating_point_representation.html. Nothing helps you understand a concept like playing with the values. You can find a really interesting floating-point number converter at https://www.h-schmidt.net/FloatConverter/IEEE754.html, where you can click the individual bits (to turn them off or on) and see the floating-point number that results.

As you might imagine, floating-point numbers tend to consume more space in memory because of their complexity. In addition, they use an entirely different area of the processor — one that works more slowly than the part used for integer math. Finally, integers are precise, as contrasted to floating-point numbers, which can't precisely represent some numbers, so you get an approximation instead. The bottom line is that decimals are unavoidable in the real world, so you need floating-point numbers. Computer systems have many trade-offs, and this one is unavoidable.

When working with floating-point values, you can assign the information to the variable in a number of ways. The two most common methods are to provide the number directly and to use scientific notation. When using scientific notation, an *e* separates the number from its exponent. Figure 6-3 shows both methods of making an assignment. Notice that using a negative exponent results in a fractional value.

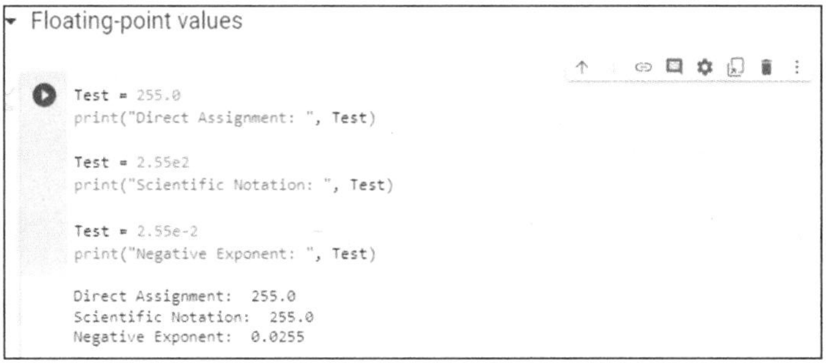

FIGURE 6-3:
Floating-point values provide multiple assignment techniques.

Complex numbers

You may or may not remember complex numbers from school. A *complex number* consists of a real number and an imaginary number that are paired together. Just in case you've completely forgotten about complex numbers, you can read about them at `https://www.mathsisfun.com/numbers/complex-numbers.html`. Real-world uses for complex numbers include:

» Electrical engineering

» Fluid dynamics

» Quantum mechanics

» Computer graphics

» Dynamic systems

Complex numbers have other uses, too, but this list should give you some ideas. In general, if you aren't involved in any of these disciplines, you probably won't ever encounter complex numbers. However, Python is one of the few languages that provides a built-in data type to support them. As you progress through the book, you find other ways in which Python lends itself especially well to science and engineering.

The imaginary part of a complex number always appears with a *j* after it in Python. So, if you want to create a complex number with 3 as the real part and 4 as the imaginary part, you make an assignment like this:

```
myComplex = 3 + 4j
```

If you want to see the real part of the variable, you simply type **print(myComplex. real)**. Likewise, if you want to see the imaginary part of the variable, you type **print(myComplex.imag)**.

Understanding Boolean values

It may seem amazing, but computers always give you a straight answer! A computer will never provide "maybe" as output. Every answer you get is either True or False. In fact, there is an entire branch of mathematics called Boolean algebra (`https://www.tutorialspoint.com/computer_logical_organization/boolean_algebra.htm`) that was originally defined by George Boole (`https://plato.stanford.edu/entries/boole/`), a super-geek of his time, that computers rely upon to make decisions. Contrary to common belief, Boolean algebra has existed since 1854 — long before the time of computers.

When using Boolean values in Python, you rely on the bool type. A variable of this type can contain only two values: True or False. You can assign a value by using the True or False keywords, or you can create an expression that defines a logical idea that equates to true or false. For example, you could say, myBool = 1 > 2, which would equate to False because 1 is most definitely not greater than 2. You see the bool type used extensively in the book, so don't worry about understanding this concept right now.

DETERMINING A VARIABLE'S TYPE

Sometimes you might want to know the variable type. Perhaps the type isn't obvious from the code or you've received the information from a source whose code isn't accessible. Whenever you want to see the type of a variable, use the type() method. For example, if you start by placing a value of 5 in myInt by typing **myInt = 5** and clicking Run Cell, you can find the type of myInt by typing **type(myInt)** and pressing Enter. The output will be <class 'int'>, which means that myInt contains an int value.

Understanding strings

Of all the data types, strings are the most easily understood by humans and not understood at all by computers. If you have read the previous chapters in this book, you have already seen strings used quite often. For example, all the example code in Chapter 4 relies on strings. A *string* is simply any grouping of characters you place within double or single quotes. For example, myString = "Python is a great language." assigns a string of characters to myString.

The computer doesn't see letters at all. Every letter you use is represented by a number in memory. For example, the letter *A* is actually the number 65. To see this for yourself, type **print(ord("A"))** and click Run Cell. You see 65 as output. You can convert any single letter to its numeric equivalent by using the ord() function.

Because the computer doesn't really understand strings, but strings are so useful in writing applications, you sometimes need to convert a string to a number. You can use the int() and float() functions to perform this conversion. For example, if you type **myInt = int("123")** and click Run Cell, you create an int named myInt that contains the value 123. Figure 6-4 shows how you can perform this task and validate the content and type of myInt.

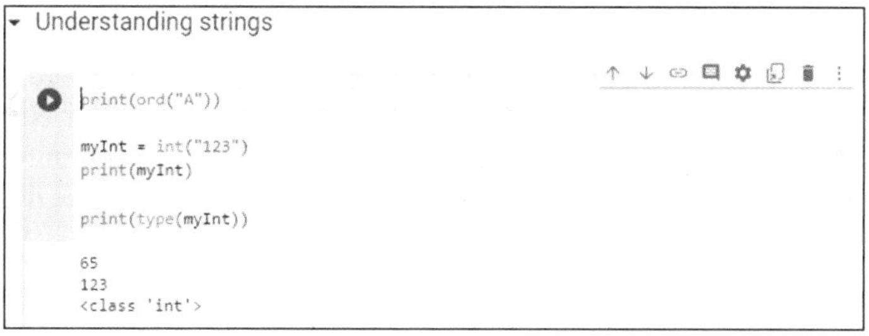

FIGURE 6-4: Converting a string to a number is easy by using the int() and float() functions.

You can convert numbers to a string as well by using the str() function. For example, if you type **myStr = str(1234.56)** and click Run Cell, you create a string containing the value "1234.56" and assign it to myStr. Figure 6-5 shows this type of conversion and the test you can perform on it. The point is that you can go back and forth between strings and numbers with great ease. Later chapters demonstrate how these conversions make a lot of seemingly impossible tasks quite doable.

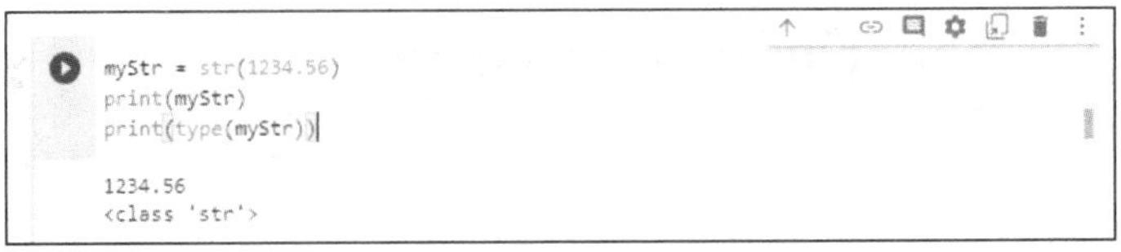

FIGURE 6-5:
You can convert
numbers to
strings as well.

```
myStr = str(1234.56)
print(myStr)
print(type(myStr))

1234.56
<class 'str'>
```

Working with Dates and Times

Dates and times are items that most people work with quite a bit. Society bases almost everything on the date and time that a task needs to be or was completed. We make appointments and plan events for specific dates and times. Most of our day revolves around the clock. Because of the time-oriented nature of humans, it's a good idea to look at how Python deals with interacting with dates and time (especially storing these values for later use). As with everything else, computers understand only numbers — the date and time don't really exist.

REMEMBER

To work with dates and times, you need to perform a special task in Python. When writing computer books, chicken-and-egg scenarios always arise, and this is one of them. To use dates and times, you must issue a special `import datetime` function. Technically, this act is called *importing a package,* and you learn more about it in Chapter 11. Don't worry how the function works right now — just use it whenever you want to do something with date and time.

Computers do have clocks inside them, but the clocks are for the humans using the computer. Yes, some software also depends on the clock, but again, the emphasis is on human needs rather than anything the computer might require. To get the current time, you can simply type **print(datetime.datetime.now())** and click Run Cell. You see the full date and time information as found on your computer's clock (see Figure 6-6).

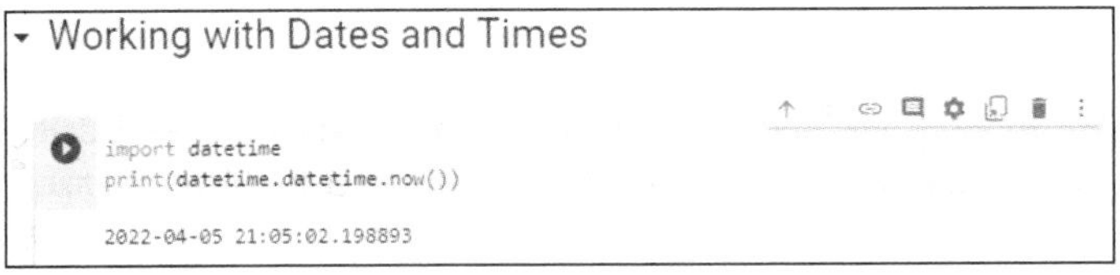

FIGURE 6-6:
Get the current
date and time by
using the now( )
function.

▼ Working with Dates and Times

```
import datetime
print(datetime.datetime.now())

2022-04-05 21:05:02.198893
```

You may have noticed that the date and time are a little hard to read in the existing format. Say that you want to get just the current date, in a readable format. It's time to combine a few things you discovered in previous sections to accomplish that task. Type **print(str(datetime.datetime.now().date()))** and click Run Cell. Figure 6-7 shows that you now have something a little more usable.

```
print(str(datetime.datetime.now().date()))

2022-04-05
```

Interestingly enough, Python also has a time() function (https://docs.python. org/3/library/time.html), which you can use to obtain the current time. You can obtain separate values for each of the components that make up date and time by using the day, month, year, hour, minute, second, and microsecond values. Later chapters help you understand how to use these various date and time features to keep application users informed about the current date and time on their system.

Chapter **7**

Managing Information

W hether you use the term *information* or *data* to refer to the content that applications manage, the fact is that you must provide some means of working with it or your application really doesn't have a purpose. Throughout the rest of the book, you see *information* and *data* used interchangeably because they really are the same thing, and in real-world situations, you'll encounter them both, so getting used to both is a good idea. No matter which term you use, you need some means of assigning data to variables, modifying the content of those variables to achieve specific goals, and comparing the result you receive with desired results.

Also essential is to start working through methods of keeping your code understandable. Yes, you could write your application as a really long procedure, but trying to understand such a procedure is incredibly hard, and you'd find yourself repeating some steps because they must be done more than once. Functions are one way for you to package code so that you can more easily understand and reuse as needed.

Applications also need to interact with the user. Yes, some perfectly usable applications exist that don't really interact with the user, but they're rare. To provide a useful service, most applications interact with the user to discover how the user wants to manage data.

REMEMBER

You don't have to type the source code for this chapter manually. In fact, using the downloadable source is a lot easier. You can find the source for this chapter in the BPP4D3E; 07; Managing Information.ipynb file of the downloadable source. See the Introduction for details on how to find these source files.

Controlling How Python Views Data

As discussed in Chapter 6, all data on your computer is stored as 0s and 1s. The computer doesn't understand the concept of letters, Boolean values, dates, times, or any other kind of information except numbers. In addition, a computer's capability to work with numbers is both inflexible and relatively simplistic. When you work with a string in Python, you depend on Python to translate the concept of a string into a form the computer can understand. The storage containers that your application creates and uses in the form of *variables* tell Python how to treat the 0s and 1s that the computer has stored. The Python view of data isn't the same as your view of data or the computer's view of data — Python acts as an intermediary to make your applications functional.

REMEMBER

To manage data within an application, the application must control the way in which Python views the data. The use of operators, packaging methods such as functions, and the introduction of user input all help applications control data. All these techniques rely, in part, on making comparisons. Determining what to do next means understanding what state the data is in now as compared to some other state.

Making comparisons

Python uses *operators* to make comparisons. In fact, operators play a major role in manipulating data as well. The upcoming "Working with Operators" section discusses how operators work and how you can use them in applications to control data in various ways. Later chapters use operators extensively as you discover techniques for creating applications that can make decisions, perform tasks repetitively, and interact with the user in interesting ways.

In some cases, you use some fancy methods to perform *comparisons* (the strict measuring of one value or one result against another) in an application. For example, you can compare the output of two functions (as described in the "Comparing function output" section, later in this chapter). With Python, you can perform comparisons at a number of levels so that you can manage data without a problem in your application. Using these techniques hides detail so that you can focus on the point of the comparison and define how to react to that comparison. Your choice of techniques to perform comparisons affects the manner in which Python views the data and determines the sorts of things you can do to manage the data after the comparison is made. Applications require comparisons to interact with data correctly.

Understanding how computers make comparisons

Computers don't understand packaging, such as functions, or any of the other structures that you create with Python. All this packaging is for your benefit, not the computer's. However, computers do directly support the concept of operators at the processor level. Most Python operators have a direct corollary with a command that the computer understands directly. For example, when you ask whether one number is greater than another number, the computer can actually perform this computation directly, using its hardware.

REMEMBER

Some comparisons aren't direct. Computers work only with numbers. So, when you ask Python to compare two strings, what Python actually does is compare the numeric value of each character in the string. For example, the letter *A* is actually the number 65 in the computer. A lowercase letter *a* has a different numeric value — 97. Consequently, the computer sees ABC as different from abc because the numeric values of their individual letters are different.

Working with Operators

Operators are the basis for both control and management of data within applications. You use operators to define how one piece of data is compared to another and to modify the information within a single variable. In fact, operators are essential to performing any sort of math-related task and to assigning data to variables in the first place.

REMEMBER

When using an operator, you must supply either a variable or an expression. You already know that a variable is a kind of storage box used to hold data. An *expression* is an equation or formula that provides a description of a mathematical concept. In most cases, the result of evaluating an expression is a Boolean (true or false) value. The following sections describe operators in detail because you use them everywhere throughout the rest of the book.

Defining the operators

An *operator* accepts one or more inputs in the form of variables or expressions, performs a task (such as comparison or addition), and then provides an output consistent with that task. Operators are classified partially by their effect and partially by the number of elements they require. For example, a unary operator works with a single variable or expression; a binary operator requires two; a ternary operator requires three. Python doesn't support anything above three because that would really be ridiculous (and possibly confusing).

The elements provided as input to an operator are called *operands.* The operand on the left side of the operator is called the left operand, while the operand on the right side of the operator is called the right operand (ternary operators are special, as you find out in the "Understanding Python's one ternary operator" sidebar, so don't worry about it for now). The following list shows the categories of operators that you use within Python:

>> Unary

>> Arithmetic

>> Relational

>> Logical

>> Bitwise

>> Assignment

>> Membership

>> Identity

Each of these categories performs a specific task. For example, the arithmetic operators perform math-based tasks, while relational operators perform comparisons. The following sections describe the operators based on the category in which they appear.

UNDERSTANDING PYTHON'S ONE TERNARY OPERATOR

A ternary operator requires three elements. Python supports just one such operator, and you use it to determine the truth value of an expression. This ternary operator takes the following form (it apparently has no actual name, but you can call it the if. . .else operator if desired):

```
TrueValue if Expression else FalseValue
```

When the Expression is true, the operator outputs TrueValue. When the expression is false, it outputs FalseValue. As an example, if you type

```
"Hello" if True else "Goodbye"
```

the operator outputs a response of 'Hello'. However, if you type

```
"Hello" if False else "Goodbye"
```

the operator outputs a response of 'Goodbye'. This is a handy operator for times when you need to make a quick decision and don't want to write a lot of code to do it.

One of the advantages of using Python is that it normally has more than one way to do things. Python has an alternative form of this ternary operator — an even shorter short-cut. It takes the following form:

```
(FalseValue, TrueValue)[Expression]
```

As before, when Expression is true, the operator outputs TrueValue; otherwise, it outputs FalseValue. Notice that the TrueValue and FalseValue elements are reversed in this case. An example of this version is

```
("Hello", "Goodbye")[True]
```

In this case, the output of the operator is 'Goodbye' because that's the value in the TrueValue position. Of the two forms, the first is a little clearer, while the second is shorter.

Unary

The unary operators shown in Table 7-1 require a single variable or expression as input. You often use these operators as part of a decision-making process.

TABLE 7-1   ## Python Unary Operators

Operator	Description	Example
~	Inverts the bits in a number so that all the 0 bits become 1 bits and vice versa.	~4 results in a value of –5
–	Negates the original value so that positive becomes negative and vice versa.	–(–4) results in 4 and –4 results in –4
+	Is provided purely for the sake of completeness. This operator returns the same value that you provide as input.	+4 results in a value of 4

Arithmetic

The complex math tasks that Python performs are often based on much simpler math tasks, such as addition, as shown in Table 7-2. You can always create your own libraries of math functions using these simple operators as well.

TABLE 7-2   **Python Arithmetic Operators**

Operator	Description	Example
+	Adds two values together	5 + 2 = 7
–	Subtracts the right operand from the left operand	5 – 2 = 3
*	Multiplies the right operand by the left operand	5 * 2 = 10
/	Divides the left operand by the right operand	5 / 2 = 2.5
%	Divides the left operand by the right operand and returns the remainder	5 % 2 = 1
**	Calculates the exponential value of the left operand raised to the power of the right operand	5 ** 2 = 25
//	Performs integer division, in which the left operand is divided by the right operand and only the whole number is returned (also called floor division)	5 // 2 = 2

Relational

The relational operators compare one value to another and tell you when the relationship you've provided is true as shown in Table 7-3. For example, 1 is less than 2, but 1 is never greater than 2.

Logical

The logical operators shown in Table 7-4 combine the true or false value of variables or expressions so that you can determine their resultant truth value. You use the logical operators to create Boolean expressions that help determine whether to perform tasks.

Bitwise

The bitwise operators shown in Table 7-5 interact with the individual bits in a number. For example, the number 6 is actually 0b0110 in binary. A bitwise operator would interact with each bit within the number in a specific way. When working with a logical bitwise operator, a value of 0 counts as false and a value of 1 counts as true.

TABLE 7-3   **Python Relational Operators**

Operator	Description	Example
==	Determines whether two values are equal. Notice that the relational operator uses two equals signs. A mistake many developers make is using just one equals sign, which results in one value being assigned to another.	1 == 2 is False
!=	Determines whether two values are not equal. Some older versions of Python allowed you to use the <> operator in place of the != operator. Using the <> operator results in an error in current versions of Python.	1 != 2 is True
>	Verifies that the left operand value is greater than the right operand value.	1 > 2 is False
<	Verifies that the left operand value is less than the right operand value.	1 < 2 is True
>=	Verifies that the left operand value is greater than or equal to the right operand value.	1 >= 2 is False
<=	Verifies that the left operand value is less than or equal to the right operand value.	1 <= 2 is True

TABLE 7-4   **Python Logical Operators**

Operator	Description	Example
and	Determines whether both operands are true.	True and True is True
		True and False is False
		False and True is False
		False and False is False
or	Determines when one of two operands is true.	True or True is True
		True or False is True
		False or True is True
		False or False is False
not	Negates the truth value of a single operand. A true value becomes false and a false value becomes true.	not True is False
		not False is True

TABLE 7-5

Python Bitwise Operators

Operator	Description	Example
& (And)	Determines whether both individual bits within two operands are true and sets the resulting bit to true when they are.	0b1100 & 0b0110 = 0b0100
| (Or)	Determines whether either of the individual bits within two operands is true and sets the resulting bit to true when one of them is.	0b1100 | 0b0110 = 0b1110
^ (Exclusive or)	Determines whether just one of the individual bits within two operands is true and sets the resulting bit to true when one is. When both bits are true or both bits are false, the result is false.	0b1100 ^ 0b0110 = 0b1010
~ (One's complement)	Calculates the one's complement value of a number.	~0b1100 = –0b1101 ~0b0110 = –0b0111
<< (Left shift)	Shifts the bits in the left operand left by the value of the right operand. All new bits are set to 0 and all bits that flow off the end are lost.	0b00110011 << 2 = 0b11001100
>> (Right shift)	Shifts the bits in the left operand right by the value of the right operand. All new bits are set to 0 and all bits that flow off the end are lost.	0b00110011 >> 2 = 0b00001100

Assignment

The assignment operators shown in Table 7-6 place data within a variable, MyVar, which has a starting value of 5. The simple assignment operator appears in previous chapters of the book, but Python offers a number of other interesting assignment operators that you can use. These other (compound) assignment operators can perform mathematical tasks during the assignment process, which makes it possible to combine assignment with a math operation.

Membership

The membership operators shown in Table 7-7 detect the appearance of a value within a list or sequence and then output the truth value of that appearance. Think of the membership operators as you would a search routine for a database. You enter a value that you think should appear in the database, and the search routine finds it for you or reports that the value doesn't exist in the database.

Identity

The identity operators shown in Table 7-8 determine whether a value or expression is of a certain class or type. You use identity operators to ensure that you're actually working with the sort of information that you think you are.

TABLE 7-6   # Python Assignment Operators

Operator	Description	Example
=	Assigns the value found in the right operand to the left operand.	MyVar = 5 results in MyVar containing 5
+=	Adds the value found in the right operand to the value found in the left operand and places the result in the left operand.	MyVar += 2 results in MyVar containing 7
−=	Subtracts the value found in the right operand from the value found in the left operand and places the result in the left operand.	MyVar −= 2 results in MyVar containing 3
*=	Multiplies the value found in the right operand by the value found in the left operand and places the result in the left operand.	MyVar *= 2 results in MyVar containing 10
/=	Divides the value found in the left operand by the value found in the right operand and places the result in the left operand.	MyVar /= 2 results in MyVar containing 2.5
%=	Divides the value found in the left operand by the value found in the right operand and places the remainder in the left operand.	MyVar %= 2 results in MyVar containing 1
**=	Determines the exponential value found in the left operand when raised to the power of the value found in the right operand and places the result in the left operand.	MyVar **= 2 results in MyVar containing 25
//=	Divides the value found in the left operand by the value found in the right operand and places the integer (whole number) result in the left operand.	MyVar //= 2 results in MyVar containing 2

TABLE 7-7   # Python Membership Operators

Operator	Description	Example
in	Determines whether the value in the left operand appears in the sequence found in the right operand.	"Hello" in "Hello Goodbye" is True
not in	Determines whether the value in the left operand is missing from the sequence found in the right operand.	"Hello" not in "Hello Goodbye" is False

TABLE 7-8   # Python Identity Operators

Operator	Description	Example
is	Evaluates to true when the type of the value or expression in the right operand points to the same type in the left operand.	type(2) is int is True
is not	Evaluates to true when the type of the value or expression in the right operand points to a different type than the value or expression in the left operand.	type(2) is not int is False

Understanding operator precedence

When you create simple statements that contain just one operator, the order of determining the output of that operator is also simple. However, when you start working with multiple operators, it becomes necessary to determine which operator to evaluate first. For example, you should know whether 1 + 2 * 3 evaluates to 7 (where the multiplication is done first) or 9 (where the addition is done first). An order of operator precedence tells you that the answer is 7 unless you use parentheses to override the default order. In this case, (1 + 2) * 3 would evaluate to 9 because the parentheses have a higher order of precedence than multiplication does. Table 7-9 defines the order of operator precedence for Python.

TABLE 7-9   **Python Operator Precedence**

Operator(s)	Description
( )	You use parentheses to group expressions and to override the default precedence so that you can force an operation of lower precedence (such as addition) to take precedence over an operation of higher precedence (such as multiplication).
**	Exponentiation raises the value of the left operand to the power of the right operand.
~ + −	Unary operators interact with a single variable or expression.
* / % //	Multiply, divide, modulo, and floor division.
+ −	Addition and subtraction.
>> <<	Right and left bitwise shift.
&	Bitwise AND.
^ |	Bitwise exclusive OR and standard OR.
<= < > >=	Comparison operators.
== !=	Equality operators.
= %= /= //= −= += *= **=	Assignment operators.
is is not	Identity operators.
in not in	Membership operators.
not or and	Logical operators.

Creating and Using Functions

To manage information properly, you need to organize the tools used to perform the required tasks. Each line of code that you create performs a specific task, and you combine these lines of code to achieve a desired result. Sometimes you need to repeat the instructions with different data, and in some cases your code becomes so long that keeping track of what each part does is hard. Functions serve as organization tools that keep your code neat and tidy. In addition, functions make it easy to reuse the instructions you've created as needed with different data. This section of the chapter tells you all about functions.

Viewing functions as code packages

You go to your closet, open the door, and everything spills out. In fact, it's an avalanche, and you're lucky that you've survived. That bowling ball in the top shelf could have done some severe damage! However, you're armed with storage boxes and soon you have everything in the closet in neatly organized boxes. After you're done, you can find anything you want in the closet without fear of injury. Functions are just like that: They take messy code and place it in packages that make it easy to see what you have and understand how it works.

Understanding code reusability

You go to your closet, take out new pants and shirt and put them on. At the end of the day, you take everything off and throw it in the trash. Hmmm . . . That really isn't what most people do. Most people take the clothes off, wash them, and then put them back into the closet for reuse. Functions are reusable, too. No one wants to keep repeating the same task; it becomes monotonous and boring. When you create a function, you define a package of code that you can use over and over to perform the same task. All you need to do is tell the computer to perform a specific task by telling it which function to use.

REMEMBER

When you work with functions, the code that needs services from the function is named the *caller*, and it calls upon the function to perform tasks for it. Much of the information you see about functions refers to the caller. The caller must supply information to the function, and the function returns information to the caller.

At one time, computer programs didn't include the concept of code reusability. As a result, developers had to keep reinventing the same code. It didn't take long for someone to come up with the idea of functions, though, and the concept has evolved over the years until functions have become quite flexible. You can make functions do anything you want. Code reusability is a necessary part of applications to

>> Reduce development time

>> Reduce programmer error

>> Increase application reliability

>> Allow entire groups to benefit from the work of one programmer

>> Make code easier to understand

>> Improve application efficiency

Defining a function

Creating a function doesn't require much work. The following steps show you the process of creating a function that you can later access:

1. **Create a new notebook in Notebook.**

   The book uses the filename BPP4D3E; 07; Managing Information.ipynb, which is where you find all the source code for this chapter. See the Introduction for information on using the downloadable source.

2. **Type** def Hello(): **and press Enter.**

   This step tells Python to define a function named Hello. The parentheses are important because they define any requirements for using the function. (There aren't any requirements in this case.) The colon at the end tells Python that you're done defining the way in which people will access the function. Notice that the insertion pointer is now indented, as shown in Figure 7-1. This indentation is a reminder that you must give the function a task to perform.

FIGURE 7-1:
Define the name
of your function.

3. **Type** print("This is my first Python function!") **and press Enter.**

   You should notice something special. The insertion pointer is still indented because Notebook is waiting for you to provide the next step in the function.

4. **Click Run Cell.**

   The function is now complete.

Even though this is a really simple function, it demonstrates the pattern you use when creating any Python function. You define a name, provide any requirements for using the function (none in this case), and provide a series of steps for the function to perform. A function ends when the insertion point is at the left side or you move to the next cell.

Accessing functions

After you define a function, you probably want to use it to perform useful work. Of course, this means knowing how to access the function. In the previous section, you create a new function named Hello(). To access this function, you type **Hello()** and click Run Cell. Figure 7-2 shows the output you see when you execute this function.

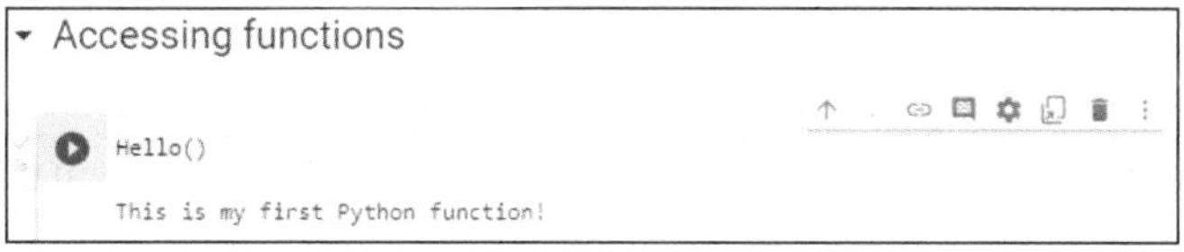

FIGURE 7-2: Whenever you type the function's name, you get the output the function provides.

Every function you create provides a similar pattern of usage. You type the function name, an open parenthesis, any required input, and a closed parenthesis; then you click Run Cell. In this case, you have no input, so all you type is **Hello()**.

Sending information to functions

The Hello() example in the previous section is nice because you don't have to keep typing that long string every time you want to say Hello(). However, it's also quite limited because you can use it to say only one thing. Functions should allow you to do more than just one thing. Otherwise, you end up writing a lot of functions that vary by the data they use rather than the functionality they provide. Using arguments helps you create functions that are flexible and can use a wealth of data.

Understanding arguments

The term *argument* doesn't mean that you're going to have a fight with the function; it means that you supply information to the function to use in processing a request. Perhaps a better word for it would be input, but the term *input* has been used for so many other purposes that developers decided to use something a bit different: argument. An argument makes it possible for you to send data to the function so that the function can use it when performing a task, making your function more flexible.

The Hello() function is currently inflexible because it prints just one string. Adding an argument to the function can make it a lot more flexible because you can send strings to the function to say anything you want. To see how arguments work, create a new function in the notebook. This version of Hello(), Hello2(), requires an argument:

```
def Hello2(Greeting):
    print(Greeting)
```

Notice that the parentheses are no longer empty. They contain a word, Greeting, which is the argument for Hello2(). The Greeting argument is a variable that you can pass to print() to see it onscreen.

REMEMBER

Make sure you click Run Cell after you create Hello2() or you will get a NameError message when you try to use the function in the next section.

Sending required arguments

You have a new function, Hello2(). This function requires that you provide an argument to use it. At least, that's what you've heard so far. Type **Hello2()** and click Run Cell. You see an error message, as shown in Figure 7-3, telling you that Hello2() requires an argument.

```
▾ Sending required arguments

                                              ↑  ⊖ ▢ ✿ ▯ ▮ ⋮

○ ● Hello2()

    ----------------------------------------------------------------
    TypeError                          Traceback (most recent call last)
    <ipython-input-5-62b0700617ba> in <module>()
    ----> 1 Hello2()

    TypeError: Hello2() missing 1 required positional argument: 'Greeting'

    SEARCH STACK OVERFLOW
```

FIGURE 7-3:
You must supply an argument or you get an error message.

Not only does Python tell you that the argument is missing, it tells you the name of the argument as well. Creating a function the way you have done so far means that you must supply an argument. Type **Hello2("This is an interesting function.")** and click Run Cell. (Note that if you're using Jupyter Notebook, you automatically advance to the next cell after clicking Run Cell.) This time, you see the expected output. However, you still don't know whether Hello2() is flexible enough to print multiple messages. Press Enter (as needed) to start another line, type **Hello2("Another message...")**, and click Run Cell. You see the expected output again, so Hello2() is indeed an improvement over Hello().

You might easily assume that Greeting will accept only a string from the tests you have performed so far. Create a new cell (if necessary). Type **Hello2(1234)**, click Run Cell, and you see 1234 as the output. Likewise, type **Hello2(5 + 5)** in a new cell, and click Run Cell. This time you see the result of the expression, which is 10.

Sending arguments by name

As your functions become more complex and the methods to use them do as well, you may want to provide a little more control over precisely how you call the function and provide arguments to it. Up until now, you have *positional arguments,* which means that you have supplied values in the order in which they appear in the argument list for the function definition. However, Python also has a method for sending arguments by name. In this case, you supply the name of the argument followed by an equals sign (=) and the argument value. To see how this works, type the following function in the notebook and run it:

```
def AddIt(Value1, Value2):
    print(Value1, " + ", Value2, " = ", (Value1 + Value2))
```

Notice that the print() function argument includes a list of items to print and that those items are separated by commas. In addition, the arguments are of different types. Python makes it easy to mix and match arguments in this manner.

Time to test AddIt(). Of course, you want to try the function using positional arguments first, so type **AddIt(2, 3)** in a new cell and click Run Cell. You see the expected output of 2 + 3 = 5. Now type **AddIt(Value2 = 3, Value1 = 2)** and click Run Cell. Again, you receive the output 2 + 3 = 5 even though the positions of the arguments have been reversed.

Giving function arguments a default value

Whether you make the call using positional arguments or named arguments, the functions to this point have required that you supply a value. Sometimes a function can use default values when a common value is available. Default values make the function easier to use and less likely to cause errors when a developer doesn't provide an input. To create a default value, you simply follow the argument name with an equals sign and the default value. To see how this works, type the following function in a new cell of the notebook and click Run Cell:

```
def Hello3(Greeting = "No Value Supplied"):
    print(Greeting)
```

This is yet another version of the original `Hello()` and updated `Hello2()` functions, but `Hello3()` automatically compensates for individuals who don't supply a value. When someone tries to call `Hello3()` without an argument, it doesn't raise an error. Type **Hello3()** and click Run Cell to see for yourself. Type **Hello3("This is a string.")** and click Run Cell to see a normal response. Lest you think the function is now unable to use other kinds of data, type **Hello3(5)** and click Run Cell; then **Hello3(2 + 7)** and click Run Cell. Figure 7-4 shows the output from all these tests.

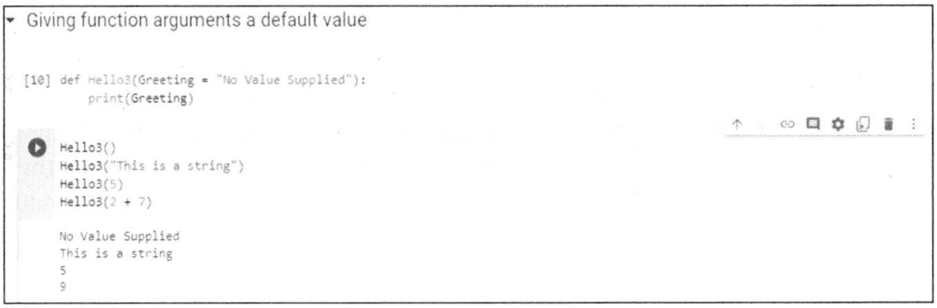

FIGURE 7-4:
Supply default arguments when possible to make your functions easier to use.

Creating functions with a variable number of arguments

In most cases, you know precisely how many arguments to provide with your function. It pays to work toward this goal whenever you can because functions with a fixed number of arguments are easier to troubleshoot later. However, sometimes you simply can't determine how many arguments the function will receive at the outset. For example, when you create a Python application that works at the command line, the user might provide no arguments, the maximum number of arguments (assuming there is more than one), or any number of arguments in between.

Fortunately, Python provides a technique for sending a variable number of arguments to a function. You simply create an argument that has an asterisk in front of it, such as *VarArgs. The usual technique is to provide a second argument that contains the number of arguments passed as an input. However, you can eliminate the second argument and simply use the `len()` function to obtain the number of arguments passed to the function. Here is an example of a function that can print a variable number of elements. (Don't worry too much if you don't understand it completely now — you haven't seen some of these techniques used before.)

```
def Hello4(ArgCount, *VarArgs):
    print("You passed ", ArgCount, " arguments.")
    for Arg in VarArgs:
        print(Arg)
```

This example uses something called a `for` loop (described in Chapter 9). For now, all you really need to know is that it takes the arguments out of `VarArgs` one at a time, places the individual argument into `Arg`, and then prints `Arg` using `print()`. After you type the code, click Run Cell.

In a new cell, type **Hello4(1, "A Test String.")** and click Run Cell. You should see the number of arguments and the test string as output — nothing too exciting there. In the next new cell type **Hello4(3, "One", "Two", "Three")** and click Run Cell. As shown in Figure 7-5, the function handles a variable number of arguments without problem.

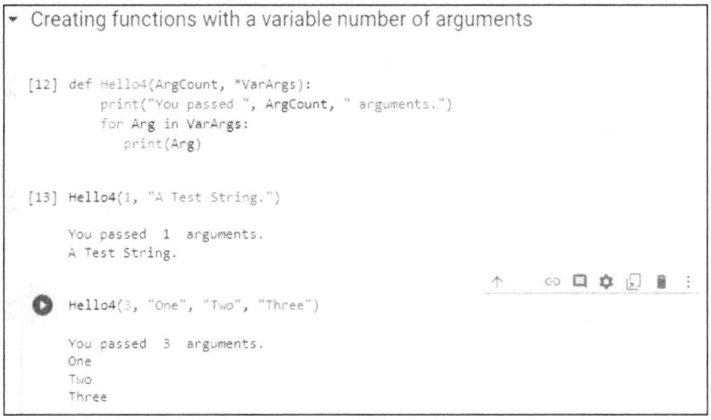

FIGURE 7-5: Variable argument functions can make your applications more flexible.

Returning information from functions

Functions can display data directly or they can return the data to the caller so that the caller can do something more with it. In some cases, a function displays data directly as well as returns data to the caller, but more commonly, a function either displays the data directly or returns it to the caller. Just how a function works depends on the task the function is supposed to perform; a function that performs a math-related task is more likely to return the data to the caller than other functions.

To return data to a caller, a function needs to include the keyword return, fol-lowed by the data to return. You have no limit on what you can return to a caller. Here are some types of data that you commonly see returned by a function to a caller:

>> **Values:** Any value is acceptable. You can return numbers, such as 1 or 2.5; strings, such as "Hello There!"; or Boolean values, such as True or False.

>> **Variables:** The content of any variable works just as well as a direct value. The caller receives whatever data is stored in the variable.

>> **Expressions:** Many developers use expressions as a shortcut. For example, you can simply return A + B rather than perform the calculation, place the result in a variable, and then return the variable to the caller. Using the expression is faster and accomplishes the same task.

>> **Results from other functions:** You can actually return data from another function as part of the return of your function.

It's time to see how return values work. Type the following code into the notebook and click Run Cell:

```
def DoAdd(Value1, Value2):
    return Value1 + Value2
```

This function accepts two values as input and then returns the sum of those two values. Yes, you could probably perform this task without using a function, but this is how many functions start. To test this function, type **print("The sum of 3 + 4 is ", DoAdd(3, 4))** in a new cell and click Run Cell. You see The sum of 3 + 4 is 7.

Comparing function output

You use functions with return values in a number of ways. For example, the previ-ous section of this chapter shows how you can use functions to provide input for another function. You use functions to perform all sorts of tasks. One of the ways to use functions is for comparison purposes. You can actually create expressions from them that define a logical output.

To see how this might work, use the DoAdd() function from the previous section. Type **print("3 + 4 equals 2 + 5 is ", (DoAdd(3, 4) == DoAdd(2, 5)))** and click Run Cell. You see the truth value of the statement that 3 + 4 equals 2 + 5, as shown in Figure 7-6.

FIGURE 7-6:
Use your
functions to
perform a wide
variety of tasks.

Getting User Input

Very few applications exist in their own world — that is, apart from the user. In fact, most applications interact with users in a major way because computers are designed to serve user needs. To interact with a user, an application must provide some means of obtaining user input. The most commonly used technique for obtaining input is also relatively easy to implement; you use the `input()` function.

REMEMBER

The `input()` function always outputs a string. Even if a user types a number, the output from the `input()` function is a string. This means that if you are expecting a number, you need to convert it after receiving the input. The `input()` function also lets you provide a string prompt. This prompt is displayed to tell the user what to provide in the way of information. The following example shows how to use the `input()` function in a simple way:

```
Name = input("Tell me your name: ")
print("Hello ", Name)
```

In this case, the `input()` function asks the user for a name. After the user types a name and presses Enter, the example outputs a customized greeting to the user. Try running this example. Figure 7-7 shows typical results when you input John as the username.

FIGURE 7-7:
Provide a
username and
see a greeting as
output.

> ▾ Getting User Input
>
> ```
> Name = input("Tell me your name: ")
> print("Hello ", Name)
> ```
> Tell me your name: John
> Hello John

You can use `input()` for other kinds of data; all you need is the correct conversion function. The code in the following example provides one technique for performing such a conversion:

```
ANumber = float(input("Type a number: "))
print("You typed: ", ANumber)
```

When you run this example, the application asks for a numeric input. The call to float() converts the input to a number. After the conversion, print() outputs the result. When you run the example using a value such as 5.5, you obtain the desired result.

Understand that data conversion isn't without risk. If you attempt to type something other than a number, you get an error message, as shown in Figure 7-8. Chapter 10 helps you understand how to detect and fix errors before they cause the program to crash.

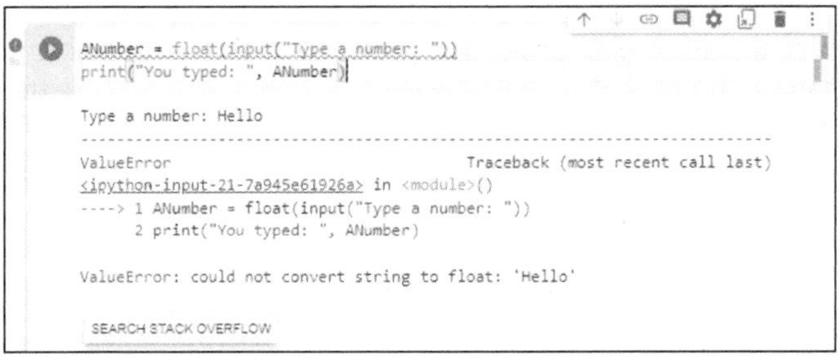

FIGURE 7-8:
Data conversion changes the input type to whatever you need, but could cause errors.

```
ANumber = float(input("Type a number: "))
print("You typed: ", ANumber)

Type a number: Hello
--------------------------------------------------------------
ValueError                                Traceback (most recent call last)
<ipython-input-21-7a945e61926a> in <module>()
----> 1 ANumber = float(input("Type a number: "))
      2 print("You typed: ", ANumber)

ValueError: could not convert string to float: 'Hello'

SEARCH STACK OVERFLOW
```

Chapter **8**

Making Decisions

T he ability to make a decision, to take one path or another, is an essential element of performing useful work. Math gives the computer the capability to obtain useful information. Decisions enable you to do something with the information after obtaining it. Without the capability to make decisions, a computer would be useless. So any language you use will include the capability to make decisions in some manner. This chapter explores the techniques that Python uses to make decisions.

REMEMBER

Think through the process you use when making a decision. You obtain the actual value of something, compare it to a desired value, and then act accordingly. For example, when you see a signal light and see that it's red, you compare the red light to the desired green light, decide that the light isn't green, and then stop (well, you stop if you aren't being chased by someone). Most people don't take time to consider the process they use because they use it so many times every day. Decision making comes naturally to humans, but computers must perform the following tasks every time:

1. Obtain the actual or current value of something.

2. Compare the actual or current value to a desired value.

3. Perform an action that corresponds to the desired outcome of the comparison.

You don't have to type the source code for this chapter manually. In fact, using the downloadable source is a lot easier. You can find the source for this chapter in the BPP4D3E; 08; Making Decisions.ipynb file of the downloadable source. See the Introduction for details on how to find these source files.

Making Simple Decisions by Using the if Statement

The if statement is the easiest method for making a decision in Python. It simply states that if something is true, Python should perform the steps that follow. The following sections tell you how you can use the if statement to make decisions of various sorts in Python. You may be surprised at what this simple statement can do for you.

Understanding the if statement

You use if statements regularly in everyday life. For example, you may say to yourself, "If it's Wednesday, I'll eat tuna salad for lunch." The Python if statement is a little less verbose, but it follows precisely the same pattern. Say you create a variable, TestMe, and place a value of 6 in it, like this:

```
TestMe = 6
```

You can then ask the computer to check for a value of 6 in TestMe, like this:

```
if TestMe == 6:
    print("TestMe does equal 6!")
```

Every Python if statement begins, oddly enough, with the word *if*. When Python sees if, it knows that you want it to make a decision. After the word *if* comes a condition. A *condition* simply states what sort of comparison you want Python to make. In this case, you want Python to determine whether TestMe contains the value 6.

Notice that the condition uses the relational equality operator, ==, and not the assignment operator, =. A common mistake that developers make is to use the assignment operator rather than the equality operator. You can see a list of relational operators in Chapter 7.

The condition always ends with a colon (:). If you don't provide a colon, Python doesn't know that the condition has ended and will continue to look for additional conditions on which to base its decision. After the colon come any tasks you want Python to perform. In this case, Python prints a statement saying that TestMe is equal to 6.

Using the if statement in an application

You can use the if statement in a number of ways in Python. However, you immediately need to know about three common ways to use it:

>> Use a single condition to execute a single statement when the condition is true.

>> Use a single condition to execute multiple statements when the condition is true.

>> Combine multiple conditions into a single decision and execute one or more statements when the combined condition is true.

The following sections explore these three possibilities and provide you with examples of their use. You see additional examples of how to use the if statement throughout the book because it's such an important method of making decisions.

Working with relational operators

A *relational operator* determines how a value on the left side of an expression compares to the value on the right side of an expression. After it makes the determination, it outputs a value of true or false that reflects the truth value of the expression. For example, 6 == 6 is true, while 5 == 6 is false. Table 7-3 in Chapter 7 lists the relational operators. The following steps show how to create and use an if statement.

1. **Open a new notebook.**

   You can also use the downloadable source file, BPP4D3E; 08; Making Decisions.ipynb.

2. **Type** TestMe = 6 **and press Enter.**

   This step assigns a value of 6 to TestMe. Notice that it uses the assignment operator and not the equality operator.

3. **Type** `if TestMe == 6:` **and press Enter.**

   This step creates an `if` statement that tests the value of `TestMe` by using the equality operator. You should notice two features of Notebook at this point:

   - The word *if* is highlighted in a different color than the rest of the statement.

   - The next line is automatically indented.

4. **Type** `print("TestMe does equal 6!").`

   Notice that the word *print* appears in a special color because it's a function name. In addition, the text appears in another color to show you that it's a string value. Color coding makes it much easier to see how Python works.

5. **Click Run Cell.**

   Notebook executes the `if` statement, as shown in Figure 8-1. Because `TestMe` contains a value of 6, the `if` statement works as expected.

Performing multiple tasks

Sometimes you want to perform more than one task after making a decision. Python relies on indentation to determine when to stop executing tasks as part of an `if` statement. As long as the next line is indented, it's part of the `if` statement. When the next line is outdented, it becomes the first line of code outside the `if` block. A *code block* consists of a statement and the tasks associated with that statement. The same term is used no matter what kind of statement you're working with, but in this case, you're working with an `if` statement that is part of a code block. The following steps show how to use indentation to execute multiple steps as part of an `if` statement.

1. **Type the following code into a new cell in the notebook — pressing Enter after each line:**

```
TestMe = 6
if TestMe == 6:
    print("TestMe does equal 6!")
    print("All done!")
```

Notice that the shell continues to indent lines as long as you continue to type code. Each line you type is part of the current if statement code block.

2. **Click Run Cell.**

Python executes the entire code block. You see the output shown in Figure 8-2.

```
▼ Performing multiple tasks

   ▶  TestMe = 6
      if TestMe == 6:
         print("TestMe does equal 6!")
         print("All done!")

      TestMe does equal 6!
      All done!
```

Making multiple comparisons by using logical operators

So far, the examples have all shown a single comparison. Real life often requires that you make multiple comparisons to account for multiple requirements. For example, when baking cookies, if the timer has gone off and the edges are brown, it's time to take the cookies out of the oven.

To make multiple comparisons, you create multiple conditions by using relational operators and combine them by using logical operators (see Table 7-4 in Chapter 7). A *logical operator* describes how to combine conditions. For example, you might say x == 6 and y == 7 as two conditions for performing one or more tasks. The and keyword is a logical operator that states that both conditions must be true.

One of the most common uses for making multiple comparisons is to determine when a value is within a certain range. In fact, *range checking*, the act of determining whether data is between two values, is an important part of making your application secure and user friendly. The following steps help you see how to perform this task.

1. **Type the following code into a new cell of the notebook — pressing Enter after each line:**

```
Value = int(input("Type a number between 1 and 10: "))
if (Value > 0) and (Value <= 10):
    print("You typed: ", Value)
```

The example begins by obtaining an input value. You have no idea what the user has typed other than that it's a value of some sort. The use of the int() function means that the user must type a whole number (one without a decimal portion). Otherwise, the application will raise an *exception* (an error indication; Chapter 10 describes exceptions). This first check ensures that the input is at least of the correct type.

The if statement contains two conditions. The first states that Value must be greater than 0. You could also present this condition as Value >= 1. The second condition states that Value must be less than or equal to 10. Only when Value meets both of these conditions will the if statement succeed and print the value the user typed.

2. **Click Run Cell.**

   Python prompts you to type a number between 1 and 10.

3. **Type 5 and press Enter.**

   The application determines that the number is in the right range and outputs the message shown in Figure 8-3.

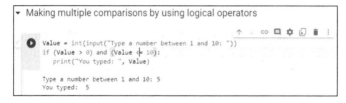

Making multiple comparisons by using logical operators

```
Value = int(input("Type a number between 1 and 10: "))
if (Value > 0) and (Value <= 10):
    print("You typed: ", Value)

Type a number between 1 and 10: 5
You typed:  5
```

4. **Select the cell again. Repeat Steps 2 and 3, but type 22 instead of 5.**

   The application doesn't output anything because the number is in the wrong range. Whenever you type a value that's outside the programmed range, the statements that are part of the if block aren't executed.

REMEMBER

5. **Select the cell again. Repeat Steps 2 and 3, but type 5.5 instead of 5.**

   Python displays the error message shown in Figure 8-4. Even though you may think of 5.5 and 5 as both being numbers, Python sees the first number as a floating-point value and the second as an integer.

6. **Repeat Steps 2 and 3, but type Hello instead of 5.**

   Python displays about the same error message as before. Python doesn't differentiate between types of wrong input. It knows only that the input type is incorrect and therefore unusable.

TIP

The best applications use various kinds of range checking to ensure that the application behaves in a predictable manner. The more predictable an application becomes, the less the user thinks about the application and the more time the user spends on performing useful work. Productive users tend to be a lot happier than those who constantly fight with their applications.

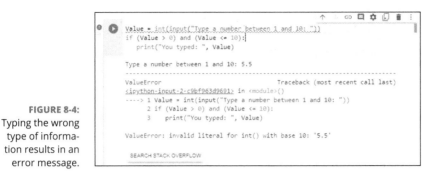

FIGURE 8-4:
Typing the wrong type of information results in an error message.

Choosing Alternatives by Using the if. . .else Statement

Many of the decisions you make in an application fall into a category of choosing one of two options based on conditions. For example, when looking at a signal light, you choose one of two options: Press on the brake to stop or press the accelerator to continue (the assumption is that you won't run the red light). The option you choose depends on the conditions. A green light signals that you can continue on through the light; a red light tells you to stop. The following sections describe how Python makes choosing between two alternatives possible.

Understanding the if. . .else statement

With Python, you choose one of two alternatives by using the else clause of the if statement. A *clause* is an addition to a code block that modifies the way in which it works. Most code blocks support multiple clauses. In this case, the else clause enables you to perform an alternative task, which increases the usefulness of the if statement. Most developers refer to the form of the if statement that has the else clause included as the if...else statement, with the ellipsis implying that something happens between if and else.

WARNING

Sometimes developers encounter problems with the if...else statement because they forget that the else clause always executes when the conditions for the if statement aren't met. Be sure to think about the consequences of always executing a set of tasks when the conditions are false. Sometimes doing so can lead to unintended consequences.

Using the if. . .else statement in an application

The example in the previous section is a little less helpful than it could be when the user enters a value that's outside the intended range. Even entering data of the wrong type produces an error message, but entering the correct type of data outside the range tells the user nothing. In this example, you discover the means for correcting this problem by using an `else` clause. The following steps demonstrate just one reason to provide an alternative action when the condition for an `if` statement is false:

1. **Type the following code into a new cell in the notebook — pressing Enter after each line:**

    ```
    Value = int(input("Type a number between 1 and 10: "))
    if (Value > 0) and (Value <= 10):
        print("You typed: ", Value)
    else:
        print("The value you typed is incorrect!")
    ```

    As before, the example obtains input from the user and then determines whether that input is in the correct range. However, in this case, the `else` clause provides an alternative output message when the user enters data outside the desired range.

    TIP

    Notice that the `else` clause ends with a colon, just as the `if` statement does. Most clauses that you use with Python statements have a colon associated with them so that Python knows when the clause has ended. If you receive a coding error for your application, make sure that you check for the presence of the colon as needed.

2. **Click Run Cell.**

    Python prompts you to type a number between 1 and 10.

3. **Type** 5 **and press Enter.**

    The application determines that the number is in the right range and outputs the message shown previously in Figure 8-3.

4. **Repeat Steps 2 and 3, but type** 22 **instead of 5.**

    This time the application outputs the error message shown in Figure 8-5. The user now knows that the input is incorrect and knows to try entering it again.

FIGURE 8-5:
Providing
feedback for
incorrect input is
always a good
idea.

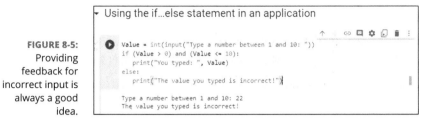

Using the if...else statement in an application

```
Value = int(input("Type a number between 1 and 10: "))
if (Value > 0) and (Value <= 10):
    print("You typed: ", Value)
else:
    print("The value you typed is incorrect!")

Type a number between 1 and 10: 22
The value you typed is incorrect!
```

Using the if. . .elif statement in an application

You go to a restaurant and look at the menu. The restaurant offers eggs, pancakes, waffles, and oatmeal for breakfast. After you choose one of the items, the server brings it to you. Creating a menu selection requires something like an if...else statement, but with a little extra oomph. In this case, you use the elif clause to create another set of conditions. The elif clause is a combination of the else clause and a separate if statement. The following steps describe how to use the if...elif statement to create a menu.

1. **Type the following code into a new cell in the notebook — pressing Enter after each line:**

```
print("1. Red")
print("2. Orange")
print("3. Yellow")
print("4. Green")
print("5. Blue")
print("6. Purple")
Choice = int(input("Select your favorite color: "))
if (Choice == 1):
    print("You chose Red!")
elif (Choice == 2):
    print("You chose Orange!")
elif (Choice == 3):
    print("You chose Yellow!")
elif (Choice == 4):
    print("You chose Green!")
elif (Choice == 5):
    print("You chose Blue!")
elif (Choice == 6):
    print("You chose Purple!")
else:
    print("You made an invalid choice!")
```

The example begins by displaying a menu. The user sees a list of choices for the application. It then asks the user to make a selection, which it places inside Choice. The use of the int() function ensures that the user can't type anything other than a number.

After the user makes a choice, the application looks for it in the list of potential values. In each case, Choice is compared against a particular value to create a condition for that value. When the user types 1, the application outputs the message You chose Red!. If none of the options is correct, the else clause is executed by default to tell the user that the input choice is invalid.

2. **Click Run Cell.**

   Python displays the menu. The application asks you to select your favorite color.

3. **Type 1 and press Enter.**

   The application displays the appropriate output message, as shown in Figure 8-6.

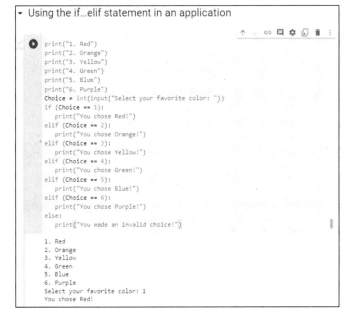

▾ Using the if...elif statement in an application

```
print("1. Red")
print("2. Orange")
print("3. Yellow")
print("4. Green")
print("5. Blue")
print("6. Purple")
Choice = int(input("Select your favorite color: "))
if (Choice == 1):
    print("You chose Red!")
elif (Choice == 2):
    print("You chose Orange!")
elif (Choice == 3):
    print("You chose Yellow!")
elif (Choice == 4):
    print("You chose Green!")
elif (Choice == 5):
    print("You chose Blue!")
elif (Choice == 6):
    print("You chose Purple!")
else:
    print("You made an invalid choice!")

1. Red
2. Orange
3. Yellow
4. Green
5. Blue
6. Purple
Select your favorite color: 1
You chose Red!
```

FIGURE 8-6: Menus let you choose one option from a list of options.

4. **Repeat Steps 3 and 4, but type 5 instead of 1.**

The application displays a different output message — the one associated with the requested color.

5. **Repeat Steps 3 and 4, but type 8 instead of 1.**

The application tells you that you made an invalid choice.

6. **Repeat Steps 3 and 4, but type Red instead of 1.**

The application displays the expected error message, as shown in Figure 8-7. Any application you create should be able to detect errors and incorrect inputs. Chapter 10 shows you how to handle errors so that they're user friendly.

```
print("1. Red")
print("2. Orange")
print("3. Yellow")
print("4. Green")
print("5. Blue")
print("6. Purple")
Choice = int(input("Select your favorite color: "))
if (Choice == 1):
    print("You chose Red!")
elif (Choice == 2):
    print("You chose Orange!")
elif (Choice == 3):
    print("You chose Yellow!")
elif (Choice == 4):
    print("You chose Green!")
elif (Choice == 5):
    print("You chose Blue!")
elif (Choice == 6):
    print("You chose Purple!")
else:
    print("You made an invalid choice!")

1. Red
2. Orange
3. Yellow
4. Green
5. Blue
6. Purple
Select your favorite color: Red
-----------------------------------------------------------
ValueError                          Traceback (most recent call last)
<ipython-input-3-e5261cca43c4> in <module>()
      5 print("5. Blue")
      6 print("6. Purple")
----> 7 Choice = int(input("Select your favorite color: "))
      8 if (Choice == 1):
      9     print("You chose Red!")

ValueError: invalid literal for int() with base 10: 'Red'

SEARCH STACK OVERFLOW
```

FIGURE 8-7: Every application you create should include some means of detecting errant input.

Using Nested Decision Statements

The decision-making process often happens in levels. For example, when you go to the restaurant and choose eggs for breakfast, you have made a first-level decision. Now the server asks you what type of toast you want with your eggs. The server wouldn't ask this question if you had ordered pancakes, so the selection of toast becomes a second-level decision. When the breakfast arrives, you decide whether you want to use jelly on your toast. This is a third-level decision. If you had selected a kind of toast that doesn't work well with jelly, you might not have had to make this decision at all. This process of making decisions in levels, with each level reliant on the decision made at the previous level, is called *nesting.* Developers often use nesting techniques to create applications that can make complex decisions based on various inputs. The following sections describe several kinds of nesting you can use within Python to make complex decisions.

Using multiple if or if. . .else statements

The most commonly used multiple selection technique is a combination of if and if...else statements. This form of selection is often called a *selection tree* because of its resemblance to the branches of a tree. In this case, you follow a particular path to obtain a desired result. The following steps show how to create a selection tree:

1. **Type the following code into the notebook — pressing Enter after each line:**

```
One = int(input("Type a number between 1 and 10: "))
Two = int(input("Type a number between 1 and 10: "))
if (One >= 1) and (One <= 10):
    if (Two >= 1) and (Two <= 10):
        print("Your secret number is: ", One * Two)
    else:
        print("Incorrect second value!")
else:
    print("Incorrect first value!")
```

This is simply an extension of the example you see in the "Using the if. . .else statement in an application" section of the chapter. However, notice that the indentation is different. The second if. . .else statement is indented within the first if. . .else statement. The indentation tells Python that this is a second-level statement.

2. **Click Run Cell.**

   You see a Python Shell window open with a prompt to type a number between 1 and 10.

3. **Type 5 and press Enter.**

   The shell asks for another number between 1 and 10.

4. **Type 2 and press Enter.**

   You see the combination (product) of the two numbers as output, as shown in Figure 8-8.

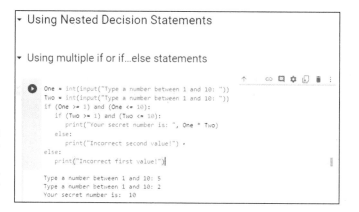

FIGURE 8-8: Adding multiple levels lets you perform tasks with greater complexity.

This example has the same input features as the previous if...else example. For example, if you attempt to provide a value that's outside the requested range, you see an error message. The error message is tailored for either the first or second input value so that the user knows which value was incorrect.

REMEMBER

Providing specific error messages is always useful because users tend to become confused and frustrated otherwise. In addition, a specific error message helps you find errors in your application much faster.

Combining other types of decisions

You can use any combination of if, if...else, and if...elif statements to produce a desired outcome. You can nest the code blocks as many levels deep as needed to perform the required checks. For example, Listing 8-1 shows what you might accomplish for a breakfast menu.

LISTING 8-1: **Creating a Breakfast Menu**

```
print("1. Eggs")
print("2. Pancakes")
print("3. Waffles")
print("4. Oatmeal")
MainChoice = int(input("Choose a breakfast item: "))
if (MainChoice == 2):
   Meal = "Pancakes"
elif (MainChoice == 3):
   Meal = "Waffles"
if (MainChoice == 1):
   print("1. Wheat Toast")
   print("2. Sour Dough")
   print("3. Rye Toast")
   print("4. Pancakes")
   Bread = int(input("Choose a type of bread: "))
   if (Bread == 1):
      print("You chose eggs with wheat toast.")
   elif (Bread == 2):
      print("You chose eggs with sour dough.")
   elif (Bread == 3):
      print("You chose eggs with rye toast.")
   elif (Bread == 4):
      print("You chose eggs with pancakes.")
   else:
      print("We have eggs, but not that kind of bread.")
```

```
elif (MainChoice == 2) or (MainChoice == 3):
    print("1. Syrup")
    print("2. Strawberries")
    print("3. Powdered Sugar")
    Topping = int(input("Choose a topping: "))
    if (Topping == 1):
        print ("You chose " + Meal + " with syrup.")
    elif (Topping == 2):
        print ("You chose " + Meal + " with strawberries.")
    elif (Topping == 3):
        print ("You chose " + Meal + " with powdered sugar.")
    else:
        print ("We have " + Meal + ", but not that topping.")
elif (MainChoice == 4):
    print("You chose oatmeal.")
else:
    print("We don't serve that breakfast item!")
```

This example has some interesting features. For one thing, you might assume that an if...elif statement always requires an else clause. This example shows a situation that doesn't require such a clause. You use an if...elif statement to ensure that Meal contains the correct value, but you have no other options to consider.

The selection technique is the same as you saw for the previous examples. A user enters a number in the correct range to obtain a desired result. Three of the selections require a secondary choice, so you see the menu for that choice. For example, when ordering eggs, it isn't necessary to choose a topping, but you do want a topping for pancakes or waffles.

Notice that this example also combines variables and text in a specific way. Because a topping can apply equally to waffles or pancakes, you need some method for defining precisely which meal is being served as part of the output. The Meal variable that the application defines earlier is used as part of the output after the topping choice is made.

The best way to understand this example is to play with it. Try various menu combinations to see how the application works.

Chapter **9**

Performing Repetitive Tasks

All the examples in the book so far have performed a series of steps just one time and then stopped. However, the real world doesn't work this way. Many of the tasks that humans perform are repetitious. For example, the doctor might state that you need to exercise more and tell you to do 100 push-ups each day. If you just do one push-up, you won't get much benefit from the exercise and you definitely won't be following the doctor's orders. Of course, because you know precisely how many push-ups to do, you can perform the task a specific number of times. Python allows the same sort of repetition by using the `for` statement.

Unfortunately, you don't always know how many times to perform a task. For example, consider needing to check a stack of coins for one of extreme rarity. Taking just the first coin from the top, examining it, and deciding that it either is or isn't the rare coin doesn't complete the task. Instead, you must examine each coin in turn, looking for the rare coin. Your stack may contain more than one. Only after you have looked at every coin in the stack can you say that the task is complete. However, because you don't know how many coins are in the stack, you don't know how many times to perform the task at the outset. You only know the task is done when the stack is gone. Python performs this kind of repetition by using the `while` statement.

REMEMBER

Most programming languages call any sort of repeating sequence of events a *loop*. The idea is to picture the repetition as a circle, with the code going round and round executing tasks until the loop ends. Loops are an essential part of application elements such as menus. In fact, writing most modern applications without using loops would be impossible.

In some cases, you must create loops within loops. For example, to create a multiplication table, you use a loop within a loop. The inner loop calculates the column values and the outer loop moves between rows. You see such an example later in the chapter, so don't worry too much about understanding precisely how such things work right now.

REMEMBER

You don't have to type the source code for this chapter manually. In fact, using the downloadable source is a lot easier. You can find the source for this chapter in the `BPP4D3E; 09; Performing Repetitive Tasks.ipynb` file of the downloadable source. See the Introduction for details on how to find these source files.

Processing Data Using the for Statement

The first looping code block that most developers encounter is the `for` statement. It's hard to imagine creating a conventional programming language that lacks such a statement. In this case, the loop executes a fixed number of times, and you know the number of times it will execute before the loop even begins. Because everything about a `for` loop is known at the outset, `for` loops tend to be the easiest kind of loop to use. However, in order to use one, you need to know how many times to execute the loop. The following sections describe the `for` loop in greater detail.

RECURSION: ANOTHER WAY TO PERFORM TASKS REPETITIVELY

Recursion provides a method of repeating tasks (a type of loop implementation) by using a function that calls itself until it solves a particular problem by simplifying the original problem. It's sort of like talking to yourself until you've unraveled a problem to its simplest case, and then you notice that people are looking at you quite strangely. Functional programming languages such as Haskell get along just fine without `for` or `while` loops by using recursion; see https://sarakhandaker.medium.com/how-to-code-with-no-loops-8ed815624aae for details. Python also supports recursion as an advanced technique that isn't covered in this book, but you can read about it at https://realpython.com/python-recursion/. For the most part, when working with Python, you want to use `for` and `while` loops to keep things simple and easy to debug.

Understanding the for statement

A for loop begins with a for statement. The for statement describes how to perform the loop. The Python for loop works through a sequence of some type. It doesn't matter whether the sequence is a series of letters in a string or items within a collection. You can even specify a range of values to use by specifying the range() function. Here's a simple for statement.

```
for Letter in "Howdy!":
```

The statement begins with the keyword for. The next item is a variable that holds a single element of a sequence. In this case, the variable name is Letter. The in keyword tells Python that the sequence comes next. In this case, the sequence is the string "Howdy". The for statement always ends with a colon, just as the decision-making statements described in Chapter 8 do.

Indented under the for statement are the tasks you want performed within the for loop. Python considers every following indented statement part of the code block that composes the for loop. Again, the for loop works just like the decision-making statements in Chapter 8.

Creating a basic for loop

The best way to see how a for loop actually works is to create one. In this case, the example uses a string for the sequence. The for loop processes each of the characters in the string in turn until it runs out of characters.

1. **Open a new notebook.**

    You can also use the downloadable source file, BPP4D3E; 09; Performing Repetitive Tasks.ipynb.

2. **Type the following code into the notebook — pressing Enter after each line:**

    ```
    LetterNum = 1
    for Letter in "Howdy!":
        print("Letter ", LetterNum, " is ", Letter)
        LetterNum += 1
    ```

    The example begins by creating a variable, LetterNum, to track the number of letters that have been processed. Every time the loop completes, LetterNum is updated (incremented) by 1.

The `for` statement works through the sequence of letters in the string "Howdy!". It places each letter, in turn, in `Letter`. The code that follows displays the current `LetterNum` value and its associated character found in `Letter`.

3. **Click Run Cell.**

The application displays the letter sequence along with the letter number, as shown in Figure 9-1.

▾ Processing Data Using the for Statement

▾ Creating a basic for loop

```
LetterNum = 1
for Letter in "Howdy!":
    print("Letter ", LetterNum, " is ", Letter)
    LetterNum+=1

Letter  1  is  H
Letter  2  is  o
Letter  3  is  w
Letter  4  is  d
Letter  5  is  y
Letter  6  is  !
```

FIGURE 9-1:
Use the for loop to process the characters in a string one at a time.

Controlling execution with the break statement

Life is often about exceptions to the rule. For example, you might want an assembly line to produce a number of clocks. However, at some point, the assembly line runs out of a needed part. If the part isn't available, the assembly line must stop in the middle of the processing cycle. The count hasn't completed, but the line must be stopped anyway until the missing part is restocked.

Interruptions also occur in computers. You might be streaming data from an online source when a network glitch occurs and breaks the connection; the stream temporarily runs dry, so the application runs out of things to do even though the set number of tasks isn't completed.

REMEMBER

The `break` clause makes breaking out of a loop possible. However, you don't simply place the `break` clause in your code — you surround it with an `if` statement that defines the condition for issuing a `break`. The statement might say something like this: If the data stream runs dry, then break out of the loop.

In this example, you see what happens when the count reaches a certain level when processing a string. The example is a little contrived in the interest of keeping things simple, but it reflects what could happen in the real world when a data element is too long to process (possibly indicating an error condition).

1. **Type the following code into a new cell in the notebook — pressing Enter after each line:**

```
Value = input("Type less than 6 characters: ")
LetterNum = 1
for Letter in Value:
    print("Letter ", LetterNum, " is ", Letter)
    LetterNum += 1
    if LetterNum > 6:
        print("The string is too long!")
        break
```

This example builds on the one found in the previous section. However, it lets the user provide a variable-length string. When the string is longer than six characters, the application stops processing it.

The if statement contains the conditional code. When LetterNum is greater than 6, it means that the string is too long. Notice the second level of indentation used for the if statement. In this case, the user sees an error message stating that the string is too long, and then the code executes a break to end the loop.

2. **Click Run Cell.**

Python displays a prompt asking for input.

3. **Type Hello and press Enter.**

The application lists each character in the string.

4. **Perform Steps 2 and 3 again, but type I am too long. instead of Hello.**

The application displays the expected error message and stops processing the string at character 6, as shown in Figure 9-2.

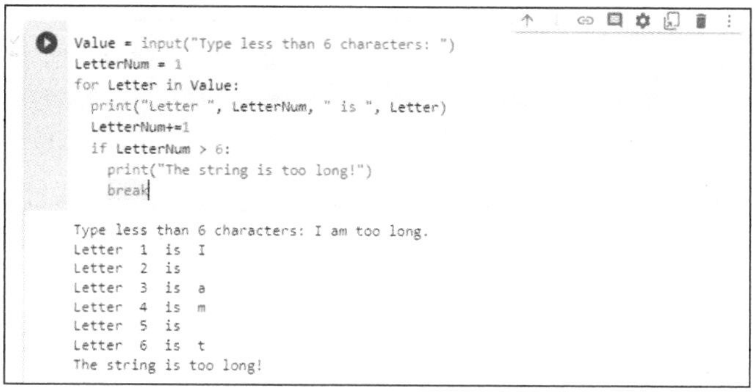

FIGURE 9-2: Long strings are truncated to ensure that they remain a certain size.

TIP

This example adds *length checking* to your repertoire of application data error checks. Chapter 8 shows how to perform range checks, which ensure that a value meets specific value limits. The length check is necessary to ensure that data, especially strings, aren't going to overrun the size of data fields. In addition, a small input size makes it harder for intruders to perform certain types of hacks (such as script injection, as described at `https://www.stackhawk.com/blog/command-injection-python/`) on your system, which makes your system more secure.

Controlling execution with the continue statement

Sometimes you want to check every element in a sequence, but don't want to process certain elements. For example, you might decide that you want to process all the information for every car in a database except brown cars. Perhaps you simply don't need the information about that particular color of car. The break clause simply ends the loop, so you can't use it in this situation. Otherwise, you won't see the remaining elements in the sequence.

REMEMBER

The break clause alternative that many developers use is the continue clause. As with the break clause, the continue clause appears as part of an if statement. However, processing continues with the next element in the sequence rather than ending completely.

The following steps help you see how the continue clause differs from the break clause. In this case, the code refuses to process the letter *w*, but will process every other letter in the alphabet.

1. **Type the following code into a new cell in the notebook — pressing Enter after each line:**

```
LetterNum = 1
for Letter in "Howdy!":
    if Letter == "w":
        continue
        print("Encountered w, not processed.")
    print("Letter ", LetterNum, " is ", Letter)
    LetterNum += 1
```

This example is based on the one found in the "Creating a basic for loop" section, earlier in this chapter. However, this example adds an if statement with the continue clause in the if code block.

WARNING

Notice the `print()` function call that is part of the `if` code block. You never see this string printed because the current loop iteration ends immediately. This kind of unreachable code is often called *dead code* by developers because it just sort of sits there like a couch potato doing nothing at all. Avoid dead code because it complicates the debugging process and makes code harder to read and understand.

2. **Click Run Cell.**

   Python displays the letter sequence along with the letter number, as shown in Figure 9-3. However, notice the effect of the `continue` clause — the letter *w* isn't processed.

▾ Controlling execution with the continue statement

```
LetterNum = 1
for Letter in "Howdy!":
    if Letter == "w":
        continue
        print("Encountered w, not processed.")
    print("Letter ", LetterNum, " is ", Letter)
    LetterNum+=1

Letter  1  is  H
Letter  2  is  o
Letter  3  is  d
Letter  4  is  y
Letter  5  is  !
```

FIGURE 9-3:
Use the
`continue`
clause to avoid
processing
specific elements.

Doing nothing with the pass statement

The Python language includes something not commonly found in other languages: a pass clause. The pass clause tells Python to do nothing. You might wonder why a language would include a clause that does nothing at all. Mostly, the pass clause is used when you're developing the logic for your application and you don't quite know what you're going to do inside an `if`, `for`, `while`, or other statement that isn't complete without code to execute. The pass clause allows you to execute your code so that you can see the logic work without having to deal with error messages. The following steps use an example that is similar to the one found in the previous section, "Controlling execution with the continue statement," except that it uses a pass clause instead.

1. **Type the following code into a new cell in the notebook — pressing Enter after each line:**

```
LetterNum = 1
for Letter in "Howdy!":
    if Letter == "w":
        pass # Add some code here later to process w
    print("Letter ", LetterNum, " is ", Letter)
    LetterNum += 1
```

2. **Click Run Cell.**

The output is similar to that shown in Figure 9-1. The pass clause simply makes the if statement complete in this case.

TIP

Notice how the pass clause makes it possible for this example to run even though the if statement would normally be considered incomplete. Using the pass clause provides you with these advantages during development:

>> Allows you to work on the overall application first, without worrying about details

>> Enables you to run the code in a scaffolded form so that you can verify its overall operation

>> Reduces development time because you don't get involved in the detailed work of writing the application too soon

Validating input with the else statement

Python has another loop clause that you won't find with other languages: else. The else clause makes executing code possible even if you have no elements to process in a sequence. For example, you might need to convey to the user that there simply isn't anything to do. The else clause is always partnered with an if statement that's part of the loop and matched with a break clause in this case, so it's an extension of the example in the "Controlling execution with the break statement" section of the chapter. In fact, that's what the following example does.

1. **Type the following code into the notebook — pressing Enter after each line:**

```
Value = input("Type less than 6 characters: ")
LetterNum = 1
for Letter in Value:
    print("Letter ", LetterNum, " is ", Letter)
    LetterNum += 1
    if (Letter == "" or Letter == Value[-1]):
        break
else:
    print("The string is blank.")
```

Notice the indentation levels in this case. The `if` statement is indented below the `for` statement, but the `else` clause appears at the same level of indentation as the `for` statement. Using the correct indentation is essential in this situation.

The `if` statement also has to check for two conditions in this example:

- The string is empty because the user pressed Enter.

- The processing has reached the end of the string and is complete. (You find the end of a string by using `Value[−1]` in this case; the "Selecting Individual Characters" section of Chapter 12 tells you more about string indexes.)

2. **Click Run Cell.**

   Python displays a prompt asking for input.

3. **Type** Hello **and press Enter.**

   The application lists each character in the string, as shown previously in Figure 9-1.

4. **Repeat Steps 2 and 3. However, simply press Enter instead of entering any sort of text.**

   You see the alternative message shown in Figure 9-4 that tells you the string is blank.

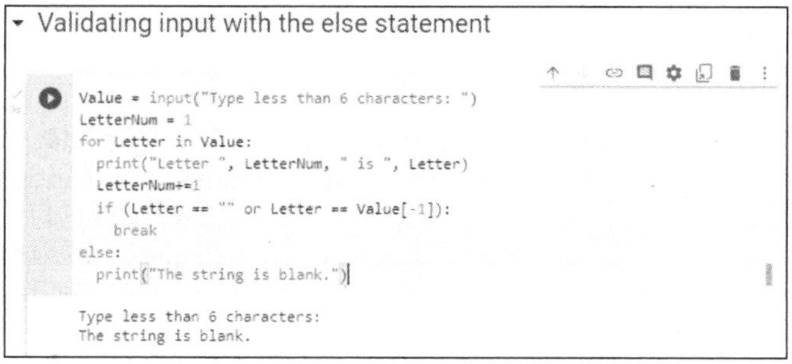

FIGURE 9-4:
The `else` clause enables you to perform tasks based on an empty sequence.

You can easily misuse the `else` clause because an empty sequence doesn't always signify a simple lack of input. An empty sequence can also signal an application error or other conditions that need to be handled differently from a simple omission of data. Make sure you understand how the application works with data to ensure that the `else` clause doesn't end up hiding potential error conditions, rather than making them visible so that they can be fixed.

Processing Data by Using the while Statement

You use the while statement for situations when you're not sure how much data the application will have to process. Instead of instructing Python to process a static number of items, you use the while statement to tell Python to continue processing items until it runs out of items. This kind of loop is useful when you need to perform tasks such as downloading files of unknown size or streaming data from a source such as a radio station. Any situation in which you can't define at the outset how much data the application will process is a good candidate for the while statement, which the following sections describe more fully.

Understanding the while statement

The while statement works with a condition rather than a sequence. The condition states that the while statement should perform a task until the condition is no longer true. For example, imagine a deli with a number of customers standing in front of the counter. The salesperson continues to service customers until no more customers are left in line. The line could (and probably will) grow as the other customers are handled, so it's impossible to know at the outset how many customers will be served. All the salesperson knows is that continuing to serve customers until no more are left is important. Here is how a while statement might look:

```
while Sum < 5:
```

The statement begins with the while keyword. It then adds a condition. In this case, a variable, Sum, must be less than 5 for the loop to continue. Nothing specifies the current value of Sum, nor does the code define how the value of Sum will change. The only thing that is known when Python executes the statement is that Sum must be less than 5 for the loop to continue performing tasks. The statement ends with a colon and the tasks are indented below the statement.

WARNING

Because the while statement doesn't perform a series of tasks a set number of times, creating an *endless loop* is possible, meaning that the loop never ends. For example, say that Sum is set to 0 when the loop begins, and the ending condition is while Sum < 5. If the value of Sum never increases, the loop will continue executing forever (or at least until the computer is shut down). Endless loops can cause all sorts of bizarre problems on systems, such as slowdowns and even computer freezes, so it's best to avoid them. You must always provide a method for the loop to end when using a while loop (contrasted with the for loop, in which the end of the sequence determines the end of the loop). So, when working with the while statement, you must perform three tasks:

1. Create the environment for the condition (such as setting Sum to 0).

2. State the condition within the while statement (such as Sum < 5).

3. Update the condition as needed to ensure that the loop eventually ends (such as adding Sum+=1 to the while code block).

REMEMBER

As with the for statement, you can modify the default behavior of the while statement. In fact, you have access to the same four clauses to modify the while statement behavior:

>> break: Ends the current loop.

>> continue: Immediately ends processing of the current element, but continues on with the next element.

>> pass: Acts as a placeholder for future code.

>> else: Provides an alternative processing technique when conditions aren't met for the loop.

Using the while statement in an application

You can use the while statement in many ways, but this first example is straightforward. It simply displays a count based on the starting and ending condition of a variable named Sum. The following steps help you create and test the example code.

1. **Type the following code into a new cell in the notebook — pressing Enter after each line:**

```
Sum = 0
while Sum < 5:
    print(Sum)
    Sum += 1
```

The example code demonstrates the three tasks you must perform when working with a while loop in a straightforward manner. It begins by setting Sum to 0, which is the first step of setting the condition environment. The condition itself appears as part of the while statement. The end of the while code block accomplishes the third step. Of course, the code displays the current value of Sum before it updates the value of Sum.

REMEMBER

A while statement provides flexibility that you don't get with a for statement. This example shows a relatively straightforward way to update Sum. However, you can use any update method required to meet the goals of the application. Nothing says that you have to update Sum in a specific manner. In addition, the condition can be as complex as you want it to be. For example, you can track the current value of three or four variables if you want. Of course, the more complex you make the condition, the more likely you are to create an endless loop, so you have a practical limit as to how complex you should make the while loop condition.

2. **Click Run Cell.**

   Python executes the while loop and displays the numeric sequence shown in Figure 9-5.

FIGURE 9-5:
The simple while loop displays a sequence of numbers.

Nesting Loop Statements

In some cases, you can use either a for loop or a while loop to achieve the same effect. The loop statements work differently, but the effect is the same. In this example, you create a multiplication table generator by nesting a while loop within a for loop. Because you want the output to look nice, you use a little formatting as well. (Chapter 12 gives you the details.)

1. **Type the following code into a new cell in the notebook — pressing Enter after each line:**

```
X = 1
Y = 1
print ('{:>4}'.format(' '), end= ' ')
for X in range(1, 11):
    print('{:>4}'.format(X), end=' ')
```

```
print()
for X in range(1,11):
    print('{:>4}'.format(X), end=' ')
    while Y <= 10:
        print('{:>4}'.format(X * Y), end=' ')
        Y += 1
    print()
    Y=1
```

This example begins by creating two variables, X and Y, to hold the row and column values of the table. X is the row variable and Y is the column variable.

To make the table readable, this example must create a heading at the top and another along the side. When users see a 1 at the top and a 1 at the side, and follow these values to where they intersect in the table, they can see the value of the two numbers when multiplied.

The first print() statement adds a space (because nothing appears in the corner of the table; see Figure 9-6 to more easily follow this discussion). All the formatting statement says is to create a space 4 characters wide and place a space within it. The {:>4} part of the code determines the size of the column. The format(' ') function determines what appears in that space. The end attribute of the print() statement changes the ending character from a carriage return to a simple space.

The first for loop displays the numbers 1 through 10 at the top of the table. The range() function creates the sequence of numbers for you. When using the range() function, you specify the starting value, which is 1 in this case, and one more than the ending value, which is 11 in this case.

At this point, the cursor is sitting at the end of the heading row. To move it to the next line, the code issues a print() call with no other information.

Even though the next bit of code looks quite complex, you can figure it out if you look at it a line at a time. The multiplication table shows the values from 1 * 1 to 10 * 10, so you need ten rows and ten columns to display the information. The for statement tells Python to create ten rows.

Look again at Figure 9-6 to note the row heading. The first print() call displays the row's label on the left. Of course, you have to format this information, and the code uses a space of four characters that end with a space, rather than a carriage return, in order to continue printing information in that row.

The while loop comes next. This loop prints the columns in an individual row. The column values are the multiplied values of X * Y. Again, the output is formatted to take up four spaces. The while loop ends when Y is updated to the next value by using Y+=1.

Now you're back into the for loop. The print() statement ends the current row. In addition, Y must be reset to 1 so that it's ready for the beginning of the next row, which begins with 1.

2. **Click Run Cell.**

   You see the multiplication table shown in Figure 9-6.

▼ Nesting Loop Statements

```
X = 1
Y = 1
print ('{:>4}'.format(' '), end= ' ')
for X in range(1, 11):
    print('{:>4}'.format(X), end=' ')
print()
for X in range(1,11):
    print('{:>4}'.format(X), end=' ')
    while Y <= 10:
        print('{:>4}'.format(X * Y), end=' ')
        Y+=1
    print()
    Y=1
```

```
       1    2    3    4    5    6    7    8    9   10
  1    1    2    3    4    5    6    7    8    9   10
  2    2    4    6    8   10   12   14   16   18   20
  3    3    6    9   12   15   18   21   24   27   30
  4    4    8   12   16   20   24   28   32   36   40
  5    5   10   15   20   25   30   35   40   45   50
  6    6   12   18   24   30   36   42   48   54   60
  7    7   14   21   28   35   42   49   56   63   70
  8    8   16   24   32   40   48   56   64   72   80
  9    9   18   27   36   45   54   63   72   81   90
 10   10   20   30   40   50   60   70   80   90  100
```

FIGURE 9-6:
The multiplication table is pleasing to the eye thanks to its formatting.

Chapter **10**

Dealing with Errors

ost application code of any complexity has errors in it. When your application suddenly freezes for no apparent reason, that's an error. Seeing one of those obscure message dialog boxes is another kind of error. However, errors can occur that don't provide you with any sort of notification. An application might perform the wrong computation on a series of numbers you provide, resulting in incorrect output that you may never know about unless someone tells you that something is wrong or you check for the issue yourself. Errors need not be consistent, either. You may see them on some occasions and not on others. For example, an error can occur only when the weather is bad or the network is overloaded. In short, errors occur in all sorts of situations and for all sorts of reasons. The big thing to remember is that the computer hasn't personally targeted you and has nothing against you — computers don't have emotions. This chapter is designed to alleviate any computer-related angst you might have about errors.

It shouldn't surprise you that errors occur. Applications are written by humans, and humans make mistakes. Most developers call application errors *exceptions*, meaning that they're the exception to the rule. Because exceptions do occur in applications, you need to detect and do something about them whenever possible. The act of detecting and processing an exception is called *error handling* or *exception handling*. To properly detect errors, you need to know about error sources and why errors occur in the first place. When you do detect the error, you must process it by *catching* the exception. Catching an exception means examining it and possibly doing something about it. So, another part of this chapter is about discovering how to perform exception handling in your own application.

Sometimes your code detects an error in the application. When this happens, you need to *raise* or *throw* an exception. You see both terms used for the same thing, which simply means that your code encountered an error it couldn't handle, so it passed the error information onto another piece of code to *handle* (interpret, process, and, with luck, fix the exception). In some cases, you use custom error message objects to pass on the information. Even though Python has a wealth of generic message objects that cover most situations, some situations are special. For example, you might want to provide special support for a database application, and Python doesn't normally cover that contingency with a generic message object. You need to know when to handle exceptions locally, when to send them to the code that called your code, and when to create special exceptions so that every part of the application knows how to handle the exception — all of which are topics covered by this chapter.

REMEMBER

You don't have to type the source code for this chapter manually. In fact, using the downloadable source is a lot easier. You can find the source for this chapter in the `BPP4D3E; 10; Dealing with Errors.ipynb` file of the downloadable source. See the Introduction for details on how to find these source files.

Knowing Why Python Doesn't Understand You

Developers often get frustrated with programming languages and computers because they seemingly go out of their way to cause communication problems. Of course, programming languages and computers are both inanimate — they don't "want" anything. Programming languages and computers also don't think; they literally accept whatever the developer says. Therein lies the problem.

REMEMBER

Neither Python nor the computer will "know what you mean" when you type instructions as code. Both follow whatever instructions you provide to the letter and literally as you provide them. You may not have meant to tell Python to delete a data file unless some absurd condition occurred. However, if you don't make the conditions clear, Python will delete the file whether the condition exists or not. When an error of this sort happens, people commonly say that the application has a *bug* in it. Bugs are simply coding errors that you can remove by using a debugger. (A *debugger* is a special kind of tool that lets you stop or pause application execution, examine the content of variables, and generally dissect the application to see what makes it tick.)

Errors occur in many cases when the developer makes assumptions that simply aren't true. Of course, this includes assumptions about the application user, who probably doesn't care about the extreme level of care you took when crafting your application. The user will enter bad data. Again, Python won't know or care that the data is bad and will process it even when your intent was to disallow the bad input. Python doesn't understand the concepts of good or bad data; it simply processes incoming data according to any rules you set, which means that you must set rules to protect users from themselves.

Python isn't proactive or creative — those qualities exist only in the developer. When a network error occurs or the user does something unexpected, Python doesn't create a solution to fix the problem. It only processes code. If you don't provide code to handle the error, the application is likely to fail and crash ungracefully — possibly taking all the user's data with it. Of course, the developer can't anticipate every potential error situation, either, which is why most complex applications have errors in them — errors of omission, in this case.

WARNING

Some developers out there think they can create bulletproof code, despite the absurdity of thinking that such code is even possible. Smart developers assume that some number of bugs will get through the code-screening process, that nature and users will continue to perform unexpected actions, and that even the smartest developer can't anticipate every possible error condition. Always assume that your application is subject to errors that will cause exceptions; that way, you'll have the mindset required to actually make your application more reliable. Keeping Murphy's Law, "If anything can go wrong, it will" in mind will help more than you think. (See more about Murphy's laws at `https://people.howstuffworks.com/murphys-law.htm`.) In addition, you must consider that some low-probability events can have a high impact on your software. They're called black-swan events (`https://betterprogramming.pub/the-black-swan-events-in-distributed-systems-d6a5d51adddf`), and you need to be prepared for them as well.

Considering the Sources of Errors

You might be able to divine the potential sources of error in your application by reading tea leaves, but that's hardly an efficient way to do things. Errors actually fall into well-defined categories that help you predict (to some degree) when and where they'll occur. By thinking about these categories as you work through your application, you're far more likely to discover potential error sources before they occur and cause potential damage. The two principle categories are

>> Errors that occur at a specific time

>> Errors that are of a specific type

The following sections discuss these two categories in greater detail. The overall concept is that you need to think about error classifications in order to start finding and fixing potential errors in your application before they become a problem.

Classifying when errors occur

Errors occur at specific times. The two major time frames are

» Compile time

» Runtime

No matter when an error occurs, it causes your application to misbehave. The following sections describe each time frame.

Compile time

A compile time error occurs when you ask Python to run the application. Before Python can run the application, it must interpret the code and put it into a form that the computer can understand. A computer relies on machine code that is specific to that processor and architecture. If the instructions you write are malformed or lack needed information, Python can't perform the required conversion. It presents an error that you must fix before the application can run.

Fortunately, compile-time errors are the easiest to spot and fix. Because the application won't run with a compile-time error in place, the user never sees this error category. You fix this sort of error as you write your code.

TIP

The appearance of a compile-time error should tell you that other typos or omissions could exist in the code. It always pays to check the surrounding code to ensure that no other potential problems exist that might not show up as part of the compile cycle.

CONSIDERING THE EFFECTS OF LIBRARY/ PACKAGE UPDATES ON YOUR CODE

Python relies on a huge number of third-party libraries to perform tasks. A *library* is code that someone else puts together and then you use it with your application so that you don't have to write so much code. These libraries are put into a convenient form called a *package,* as sort of a gift from one programmer to another. As of this writing, there are 3,409,411 released packages listed at https://pypi.org/ for use with the Python programming language. There are 659 packages available for use with email projects (see Chapter 17) alone. So before you write extensive code to perform a specific task, consider the fact that someone else has probably already written the code for you.

Libraries are usually a good addition to your programming toolbox because someone else debugs them for you, so you have fewer errors to worry about. However, it's this whole debugging thing that causes some problems. The code that worked fine with library version 1.0 may not work with library version 2.0 because the updated library fixed problems that your code depends on to work. A fix of this sort is called a *breaking change* because it breaks existing code and causes it to malfunction. Consequently, your code can work one day, but not the next, when something you install updates the libraries to the new version for you without your knowledge. Yes, other programmers can ruin your day by doing the right thing and fixing bugs in their code. Chapter 11 tells you about importing packages (libraries) into your code and using them.

TECHNICAL STUFF

Some update errors also occur in the Python language itself. For example, when working with Python 2, you could create a statement that uses the statement version of `print` like this: `print "Hello World"`. In Python 3, you must use the function version of `print()`, like this: `print("Hello World")`. The update information at `https://docs.python.org/3/whatsnew/3.0.html` tells you more about this change (and others).

Runtime

A runtime error occurs after Python compiles the code you write and the computer begins to execute it. Runtime errors come in several different types, and some are harder to find than others. You know you have a runtime error when the application suddenly stops running and displays an exception dialog box or when the user complains about erroneous output (or at least instability).

REMEMBER

Not all runtime errors produce an exception. Some runtime errors cause instability (the application freezes), errant output, or data damage. Runtime errors can affect other applications or create unforeseen damage to the platform on which the application is running. In short, runtime errors can cause you quite a bit of grief, depending on precisely the kind of error you're dealing with at the time.

Many runtime errors are caused by errant code. For example, you can misspell the name of a variable, preventing Python from placing information in the correct variable during execution. Leaving out an optional (it's not absolutely required in most cases) but necessary (it is required in this specific instance) argument when calling a method can also cause problems. These are examples of *errors of commission*, which are specific errors associated with your code. In general, you can find these kinds of errors by using a debugger or by simply reading your code line by line to check for errors.

Runtime errors can also be caused by external sources not associated with your code (see the "Considering the effects of library/package updates on your code" sidebar for additional information about third-party code). For example, the user can input incorrect information that the application isn't expecting, causing an exception. A network error can make a required resource inaccessible. Sometimes even the computer hardware has a glitch that causes a nonrepeatable application error. These are all examples of *errors of omission*, from which the application might recover if your application has error-trapping code in place. It's important that you consider both kinds of runtime errors — errors of commission and omission — when building your application.

Distinguishing error types

You can distinguish errors by type, that is, by how they're made. Knowing the error types helps you understand where to look in an application for potential problems. Exceptions work like many other things in life. For example, you know that electronic devices don't work without power. So, when you try to turn your television on and it doesn't do anything, you might look to ensure that the power cord is firmly seated in the socket.

TIP

Understanding the error types helps you locate errors faster, earlier, and more consistently, resulting in fewer misdiagnoses. The best developers know that fixing errors while an application is in development is always easier than fixing it when the application is in production because users are inherently impatient and want errors fixed immediately and correctly. In addition, fixing an error earlier in the development cycle is always easier than fixing it when the application nears completion because less code exists to review.

The trick is to know where to look. With this in mind, Python (and most other programming languages) breaks errors into the following types:

>> Syntactical

>> Semantic

>> Logical

The following sections examine each of these error types in more detail. I've arranged the sections in order of difficulty, starting with the easiest to find. A syntactical error is generally the easiest; a logical error is generally the hardest.

Syntactical

Whenever you make a typo of some sort, you create a syntactical error. Some Python syntactical errors are quite easy to find because the application simply doesn't run. The interpreter may even point out the error for you by highlighting the errant code and displaying an error message. However, some syntactical errors are quite hard to find. Python is case sensitive, so you may use the wrong case for a variable in one place and find that the variable isn't quite working as you thought it would. Finding the one place where you used the wrong capitalization can be quite challenging.

REMEMBER

Most syntactical errors occur at compile time and the interpreter points them out for you. Fixing the error is made easy because the interpreter generally tells you what to fix, and with considerable accuracy. Even when the interpreter doesn't find the problem, syntactical errors prevent the application from running correctly, so any errors the interpreter doesn't find show up during the testing phase. Few syntactical errors should make it into production as long as you perform adequate application testing.

Semantic

When you create a loop that executes one too many times, you don't generally receive any sort of error information from the application. The application will happily run because it thinks that it's doing everything correctly, but that one additional loop can cause all sorts of data errors. When you create an error of this sort in your code, it's called a *semantic error.*

REMEMBER

Semantic errors occur because the meaning behind a series of steps used to perform a task is wrong — the result is incorrect even though the code apparently runs precisely as it should. Semantic errors are tough to find, and you sometimes need some sort of debugger to find them. (Chapter 20 provides a discussion of tools that you can use with Python to perform tasks such as debugging applications. You can also find blog posts about debugging on my blog at http://blog. johnmuellerbooks.com.)

Logical

Some developers don't create a division between semantic and logical errors, but they are different. A semantic error occurs when the code is essentially correct but the implementation is wrong (such as having a loop execute once too often). Logical errors occur when the developer's thinking is faulty. In many cases, this sort of error happens when the developer uses a relational or logical operator incorrectly. However, logical errors can happen in all sorts of other ways, too. For example, a developer might think that data is always stored on the local hard drive, which means that the application may behave in an unusual manner when it attempts to load data from a network drive instead.

REMEMBER

Logical errors are quite hard to fix because the problem isn't with the actual code, yet the code itself is incorrectly defined. The thought process that went into creating the code is faulty; therefore, the developer who created the error is less likely to find it. Smart developers use a second pair of eyes to help spot logical errors. Having a formal application specification also helps because the logic behind the tasks the application performs is usually given a formal review.

Catching Exceptions

Generally speaking, a user should never see an exception dialog box. Your application should always catch the exception and handle it before the user sees it. Of course, the real world is different — users do see unexpected exceptions from time to time. However, catching every potential exception is still the goal when developing an application. The following sections describe how to catch exceptions and handle them.

UNDERSTANDING THE BUILT-IN EXCEPTIONS

Python comes with a host of built-in exceptions — far more than you might think possible. You can see a list of these exceptions at https://docs.python.org/3.10/library/exceptions.html. The documentation breaks the exception list down into categories (see the exception hierarchy at https://docs.python.org/3.10/library/exceptions.html#exception-hierarchy). Here is a brief overview of the Python exception categories that you work with regularly:

- **Base classes:** The base classes provide the essential building blocks (such as the Exception exception) for other exceptions. However, you might actually see some of these exceptions, such as the ArithmeticError exception, when working with an application.

- **Concrete exceptions:** Applications can experience hard errors — errors that are hard to overcome because there really isn't a good way to handle them or they signal an event that the application must handle. For example, when a system runs out of memory, Python generates a MemoryError exception. Recovering from this error is hard because it isn't always possible to release memory from other uses. When the user presses an interrupt key (such as Ctrl+C or Delete), Python generates a KeyboardInterrupt exception. The application must handle this exception before proceeding with any other tasks.

- **OS exceptions:** The operating system can generate errors that Python then passes along to your application. For example, if your application tries to open a file that doesn't exist, the operating system generates a FileNotFoundError exception.

- **Warnings:** Python tries to warn you about unexpected events or actions that could result in errors later. For example, if you try to inappropriately use a resource, such as an icon, Python generates a ResourceWarning exception. You want to remember that this particular category is a warning and not an actual error: Ignoring it can cause you woe later, but you can ignore it.

Basic exception handling

To handle exceptions, you must tell Python that you want to do so and then provide code to perform the handling tasks. You have a number of ways in which you can perform this task. The following sections start with the simplest method first and then move on to more complex methods that offer added flexibility.

Handling a single exception

In Chapter 8, the various examples have a terrible habit of spitting out exceptions when the user inputs unexpected values. Part of the solution is to provide range checking. However, range checking doesn't overcome the problem of a user typing text such as Hello in place of an expected numeric value. Exception handling provides a more complex solution to the problem, as described in the following steps.

1. **Open a new notebook.**

    You can also use the downloadable source file, BPP4D3E; 10; Dealing with Errors.ipynb.

2. **Type the following code into the notebook — pressing Enter after each line:**

```
try:
    Value = int(input("Type a number between 1 and 10: "))
except ValueError:
    print("You must type a number between 1 and 10!")
else:
    if (Value > 0) and (Value <= 10):
        print("You typed: ", Value)
    else:
        print("The value you typed is incorrect!")
```

The code within the try block has its ValueError exception handled. In this case, handling the exception means getting input from the user by using the int(input()) calls. If an exception occurs outside this block, the code doesn't handle it. With reliability in mind, the temptation might be to enclose all the executable code in a try block so that every exception would be handled. However, you want to keep your exception handling small and specific to make locating the problem easier.

REMEMBER

The except block looks for a specific exception in this case: ValueError. When the user creates a ValueError exception by typing Hello instead of a numeric value, this particular exception block is executed. If the user were to generate some other exception, this except block wouldn't handle it.

The else block contains all the code that is executed when the try block code is successful (doesn't generate an exception). The remainder of the code is in this block because you don't want to execute it unless the user does provide valid input. When the user provides a whole number as input, the code can then range check it to ensure that it's correct.

3. **Click Run Cell.**

Python asks you to type a number between 1 and 10.

4. **Type Hello and press Enter.**

The application displays an error message, as shown in Figure 10-1.

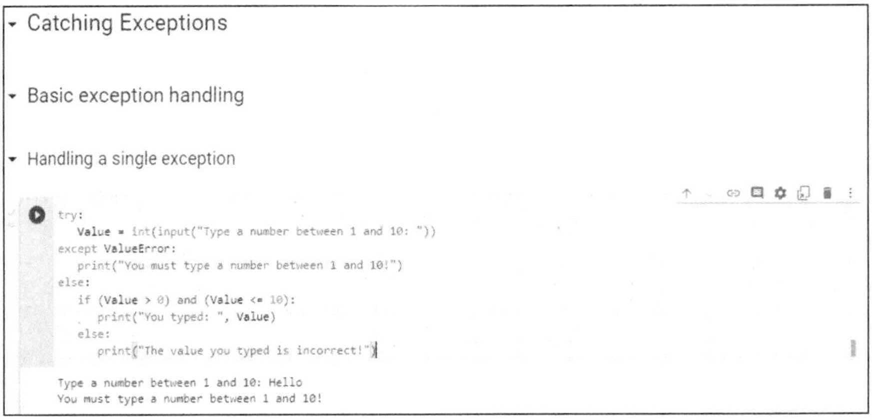

FIGURE 10-1:
Typing the wrong input type generates an error message instead of an exception.

```
try:
    Value = int(input("Type a number between 1 and 10: "))
except ValueError:
    print("You must type a number between 1 and 10!")
else:
    if (Value > 0) and (Value <= 10):
        print("You typed: ", Value)
    else:
        print("The value you typed is incorrect!")

Type a number between 1 and 10: Hello
You must type a number between 1 and 10!
```

5. **Perform Steps 3 and 4 again, but type 5.5 instead of Hello.**

The application generates the same error message, as shown in Figure 10-1.

6. **Perform Steps 3 and 4 again, but type 22 instead of Hello.**

The application outputs the expected range error message, as shown in Figure 10-2. Exception handling doesn't weed out range errors. You must still check for them separately.

```
try:
    Value = int(input("Type a number between 1 and 10: "))
except ValueError:
    print("You must type a number between 1 and 10!")
else:
    if (Value > 0) and (Value <= 10):
        print("You typed: ", Value)
    else:
        print("The value you typed is incorrect!")

Type a number between 1 and 10: 22
The value you typed is incorrect!
```

7. **Perform Steps 3 and 4 again, but type 7 instead of Hello.**

This time, the application finally reports that you've provided a correct value of 7. Even though it seems like a lot of work to perform this level of checking, you can't really be certain that your application is working correctly without it.

Using the except clause without an exception

You can create an exception handling block in Python that's generic because it doesn't look for a specific exception. In most cases, you want to provide a specific exception when performing exception handling for these reasons:

» To avoid hiding an exception you didn't consider when designing the application

» To ensure that others know precisely which exceptions your application will handle

» To handle the exceptions correctly by using specific code for that exception

However, sometimes you may need a generic exception-handling capability, such as when you're working with third-party libraries or interacting with an external service. The following steps demonstrate how to use an except clause without a specific exception attached to it.

1. **Type the following code into a new cell of the notebook — pressing Enter after each line:**

```
try:
    Value = int(input("Type a number between 1 and 10: "))
```

```
except:
    print("This is the generic error!")
except ValueError:
    print("You must type a number between 1 and 10!")
else:
    if (Value > 0) and (Value <= 10):
        print("You typed: ", Value)
    else:
        print("The value you typed is incorrect!")
```

The only difference between this example and the previous example is that the except clause doesn't have the ValueError exception specifically associated with it. The result is that this except clause will also catch any other exception that occurs.

2. **Click Run Cell.**

You see the error message shown in Figure 10-3. Python automatically detects that you have placed the exception handlers in the wrong order. (You discover more about this issue in the "Handling more specific to less specific exceptions" section, later in the chapter.) Notice that the errant lines have red, squiggly lines under them in Colab so that you can see the error with less effort.

Type the following code in a new cell to reverse the order of the two exceptions so that they appear like this:

```
try:
    Value = int(input("Type a number between 1 and 10: "))
except ValueError:
    print("You must type a number between 1 and 10!")
except:
    print("This is the generic error!")
```

```
else:
    if (Value > 0) and (Value <= 10):
        print("You typed: ", Value)
    else:
        print("The value you typed is incorrect!")
```

3. **Click Run Cell.**

   Python asks you to type a number between 1 and 10.

4. **Type** Hello **and press Enter.**

   The application displays an error message (refer to Figure 10-1). When the exceptions are in the right order, the code detects specific errors first and then uses less specific handlers only when necessary.

5. **Click Run Cell.**

   Python asks you to type a number between 1 and 10.

6. **Choose Runtime ⇨ Interrupt Execution (when using Colab) or Kernel ⇨ Interrupt (when using Jupyter Notebook).**

   This act is akin to pressing Ctrl+C or Cmd+C in other IDEs. However, nothing actually appears to happen. If you're working with Jupyter Notebook, you can look at the server window to see a Kernel Interrupted message. In addition, you see the generic error message. Python is still waiting for you to enter a value in the input( ) textbox.

7. **Select the input() textbox (if necessary), type** 5.5, **and press Enter.**

   You still see the generic error message as before, now shown in Figure 10-4 because Notebook is reacting to the interrupt, rather than the incorrect input; the reason is that the interrupt came first. Python queues errors in the order in which it receives them. Consequently, you may find that an application outputs what appears to be the wrong error message at times.

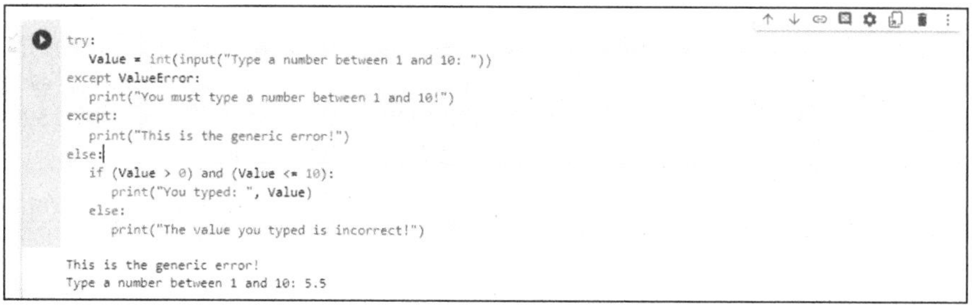

FIGURE 10-4: Generic exception handling traps the KeyboardInterrupt exception.

8. **Perform Steps 3 and 4 again, but type** 5.5 **instead of Hello.**

The application generates the same error message as before (again, refer to Figure 10-1). In this case, no interrupt occurred, so you see the error message you expected.

Working with exception arguments

Most exceptions don't provide arguments (a list of values that you can check for additional information). The exception either occurs or it doesn't. However, a few exceptions do provide arguments, and you see them used later in the book. The arguments tell you more about the exception and provide details that you need to correct it.

TECHNICAL STUFF

For the sake of completeness, this chapter includes a simple example that generates an exception with an argument. You can safely skip the remainder of this section if desired because the information is covered in more detail later in the book.

1. **Type the following code into a new cell in the notebook — pressing Enter after each line:**

```python
import sys
try:
    File = open("myfile.txt")
except IOError as e:
    print("Error opening file!\r\n" +
        "Error Number: {0}\r\n".format(e.errno) +
        "Error Text: {0}".format(e.strerror))
else:
    print("File opened as expected.")
    File.close()
```

This example uses some advanced features. The import statement obtains code from another file. Chapter 11 tells you how to use this Python feature.

The open( ) function opens a file and provides access to the file through the File variable. Chapter 16 tells you how file access works. Given that myfile. txt doesn't exist in the application directory, the operating system can't open it and will tell Python that the file doesn't exist.

Trying to open a nonexistent file generates an IOError exception. This particular exception provides access to two arguments:

- errno: Provides the operating system error number as an integer

- strerror: Contains the error information as a human-readable string

The as clause places the exception information into a variable, e, that you can access as needed for additional information. The except block contains a print() call that formats the error information into an easily read error message.

If you should decide to create the my file.txt file, the else clause executes. In this case, you see a message stating that the file opened normally. The code then closes the file without doing anything with it.

2. **Click Run Cell.**

The application displays the Error opening file information, as shown in Figure 10-5.

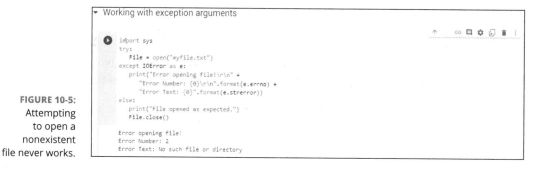

FIGURE 10-5:
Attempting
to open a
nonexistent
file never works.

OBTAINING A LIST OF EXCEPTION ARGUMENTS

The list of arguments supplied with exceptions varies by exception and by what the sender provides. It isn't always easy to figure out what you can hope to obtain in the way of additional information. One way to handle the problem is to simply print everything by using code like this:

```
import sys
try:
    File = open("myfile.txt")
except IOError as e:
    for Arg in e.args:
        print(Arg)
else:
    print("File opened as expected.")
    File.close()
```

(continued)

(continued)

The args property always contains a list of the exception arguments in string format as shown in the following screenshot. You can use a simple for loop to print each of the arguments. The only problem with this approach is that you're missing the argument names, so you know the output information (which is obvious in this case), but you don't know what to call it.

```
In [5]: import sys
        try:
            File = open("myfile.txt")
        except IOError as e:
            for Arg in e.args:
                print(Arg)
        else:
            print("File opened as expected.")
            File.close()

        2
        No such file or directory
```

A more complex method of dealing with the issue is to print both the names and the contents of the arguments. The following code displays both the names and the values of each of the arguments:

```
import sys
try:
    File = open("myfile.txt")
except IOError as e:
    for Entry in dir(e):
        if (not Entry.startswith("_")):
            try:
                print(Entry, " = ", e.__getattribute__(Entry))
            except AttributeError:
                print("Attribute ", Entry, " not accessible.")
else:
    print("File opened as expected.")
    File.close()
```

In this case, you begin by getting a listing of the attributes associated with the error argument object using the dir() function. The output of the dir() function is a list of strings containing the names of the attributes that you can print as shown in the following screenshot. Only those arguments that don't start with an underscore (_) contain useful information about the exception. However, even some of those entries are inaccessible, so you must encase the output code in a second try ... except block (see the "Nested exception handling" section, later in the chapter, for details).

```
In [6]: import sys
        try:
            File = open("myfile.txt")
        except IOError as e:
            for Entry in dir(e):
                if (not Entry.startswith("_")):
                    try:
                        print(Entry, " = ", e.__getattribute__(Entry))
                    except AttributeError:
                        print("Attribute ", Entry, " not accessible.")
        else:
            print("File opened as expected.")
            File.close()

args = (2, 'No such file or directory')
Attribute  characters_written  not accessible.
errno  =  2
filename  =  myfile.txt
filename2  =  None
strerror  =  No such file or directory
winerror  =  None
with_traceback  =  <built-in method with_traceback of FileNotFoundError object
at 0x000001EA39EE0440>
```

The attribute name is easy because it's contained in Entry. To obtain the value associated with that attribute, you must use the __getattribute() function and supply the name of the attribute you want. When you run this code, you see both the name and the value of each of the attributes supplied with a particular error argument object. In this case, the actual output is as follows:

```
args  =  (2, 'No such file or directory')
Attribute  characters_written  not accessible.
errno  =  2
filename  =  myfile.txt
filename2  =  None
strerror  =  No such file or directory
with_traceback  =  <built-in method with_traceback of
    FileNotFoundError object at 0x7f52bf07f5f0>
```

Handling multiple exceptions with a single except clause

Most applications can generate multiple exceptions for a single line of code. This fact is demonstrated in the "Using the except clause without an exception" section of the chapter. How you handle the multiple exceptions depends on your goals for the application, the types of exceptions, and the relative skill of your users. Sometimes when working with a less skilled user, it's simply easier to say that the application experienced a nonrecoverable error and then log the details into a log file in the application directory or a central location.

Using a single except clause to handle multiple exceptions works only when a common action fulfills the needs of all the exception types. Otherwise, you need to handle each exception individually. The following steps show how to handle multiple exceptions by using a single except clause.

1. **Type the following code into a new cell of the notebook — pressing Enter after each line:**

```
try:
    Value = int(input("Type a number between 1 and 10: "))
except (ValueError, KeyboardInterrupt):
    print("You must type a number between 1 and 10!")
else:
    if (Value > 0) and (Value <= 10):
        print("You typed: ", Value)
    else:
        print("The value you typed is incorrect!")
```

Note that the except clause now sports both a ValueError and a KeyboardInterrupt exception. These exceptions appear within parentheses and are separated by commas.

2. **Click Run Cell.**

Python asks you to type a number between 1 and 10.

3. **Type** Hello **and press Enter.**

The application displays an error message (refer to Figure 10-1).

4. **Click Run Cell.**

Python asks you to type a number between 1 and 10.

5. **Choose Runtime ⇨ Interrupt Execution for Colab or Kernel ⇨ Interrupt for Jupyter Notebook.**

This act is akin to pressing Ctrl+C or Cmd+C in other IDEs.

6. **Click Run Cell, type** 5.5, **and press Enter.**

The application displays an error message (refer to Figure 10-1).

7. **Perform Steps 2 and 3 again, but type** 7 **instead of Hello.**

This time, the application finally reports that you've provided a correct value of 7.

Handling multiple exceptions with multiple except clauses

When working with multiple exceptions, it's usually a good idea to place each exception in its own except clause. This approach allows you to provide custom handling for each exception and makes it easier for the user to know precisely what went wrong. Of course, this approach is also a lot more work. The following steps demonstrate how to perform exception handling by using multiple except clauses.

1. **Type the following code into a new cell of the notebook — pressing Enter after each line:**

```python
try:
    Value = int(input("Type a number between 1 and 10: "))
except ValueError:
    print("You must type a number between 1 and 10!")
except KeyboardInterrupt:
    print("You pressed Ctrl+C!")
else:
    if (Value > 0) and (Value <= 10):
        print("You typed: ", Value)
    else:
        print("The value you typed is incorrect!")
```

REMEMBER

Notice the use of multiple except clauses in this case. Each except clause handles a different exception. You can use a combination of techniques, with some except clauses handling just one exception and other except clauses handling multiple exceptions. Python lets you use the approach that works best for the error-handling situation.

2. **Click Run Cell.**

    Python asks you to type a number between 1 and 10.

3. **Type** Hello **and press Enter.**

    The application displays an error message (refer to Figure 10-1).

4. **Perform Steps 2 and 3 again, but type** 22 **instead of Hello.**

    The application outputs the expected range error message (refer to Figure 10-2).

5. **Perform Steps 2 and 3 again, but choose Runtime ⇨ Interrupt Execution for Colab or Kernel ⇨ Interrupt for Jupyter Notebook.**

    The application outputs a specific message, You pressed Ctrl+C, that tells the user what went wrong.

6. **Perform Steps 2 and 3 again, but type 7 instead of Hello.**

This time, the application finally reports that you've provided a correct value of 7.

Handling more specific to less specific exceptions

One strategy for handling exceptions is to provide specific except clauses for all known exceptions and generic except clauses to handle unknown exceptions. You can see the exception hierarchy that Python uses at https://docs.python. org/3/library/exceptions.html#exception-hierarchy. When viewing this chart, BaseException is the uppermost exception. Most exceptions are derived from Exception. When working through math errors, you can use the generic ArithmeticError or a more specific ZeroDivisionError exception.

Python evaluates except clauses in the order in which they appear in the source code file. The first clause is examined first, the second clause is examined second, and so on. The following steps help you examine an example that demonstrates the importance of using the correct exception order. In this case, you perform tasks that result in math errors.

1. **Type the following code into a new cell of the notebook — pressing Enter after each line:**

```
try:
    Value1 = int(input("Type the first number: "))
    Value2 = int(input("Type the second number: "))
    Output = Value1 / Value2
except ValueError:
    print("You must type a whole number!")
except KeyboardInterrupt:
    print("You pressed Ctrl+C!")
except ArithmeticError:
    print("An undefined math error occurred.")
except ZeroDivisionError:
    print("Attempted to divide by zero!")
else:
    print(Output)
```

The code begins by obtaining two inputs: Value1 and Value2. The first two except clauses handle unexpected input. The second two except clauses handle math exceptions, such as dividing by zero. If everything goes well with the application, the else clause executes, which prints the result of the operation.

2. Click Run Cell.

Python asks you to type the first number.

3. Type Hello and press Enter.

As expected, Python displays the ValueError exception message. However, it always pays to check for potential problems.

4. Click Run Cell again.

Python asks you to type the first number.

5. Type 8 and press Enter.

The application asks you to enter the second number.

6. Type 0 and press Enter.

You see the error message for the ArithmeticError exception, as shown in Figure 10-6. What you should actually see is the ZeroDivisionError exception because it's more specific than the ArithmeticError exception.

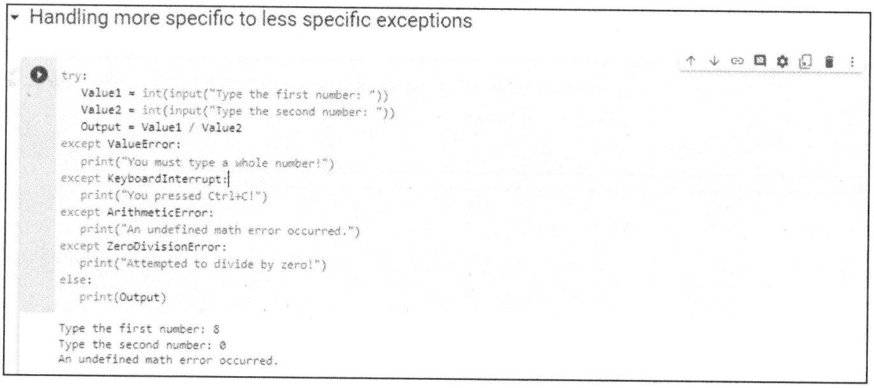

FIGURE 10-6: The order in which Python processes exceptions is important.

```
▼ Handling more specific to less specific exceptions

try:
    Value1 = int(input("Type the first number: "))
    Value2 = int(input("Type the second number: "))
    Output = Value1 / Value2
except ValueError:
    print("You must type a whole number!")
except KeyboardInterrupt:
    print("You pressed Ctrl+C!")
except ArithmeticError:
    print("An undefined math error occurred.")
except ZeroDivisionError:
    print("Attempted to divide by zero!")
else:
    print(Output)

Type the first number: 8
Type the second number: 0
An undefined math error occurred.
```

7. Reverse the order of the two exceptions so that they look like this:

```
except ZeroDivisionError:
    print("Attempted to divide by zero!")
except ArithmeticError:
    print("An undefined math error occurred.")
```

8. Perform Steps 4 through 6 again.

This time, you see the ZeroDivisionError exception message because the exceptions appear in the correct order.

9. **Perform Steps 4 through 5 again, but type 2 for the second number instead of 0.**

This time, the application finally reports an output value of 4.0.

Notice that the output is a floating-point value. Division results in a floating-point value unless you specify that you want an integer output by using the floor division operator (//).

REMEMBER

Nested exception handling

Sometimes you need to place one exception-handling routine within another in a process called *nesting.* When you nest exception-handling routines, Python tries to find an exception handler in the nested level first and then moves to the outer layers. You can nest exception-handling routines as deeply as needed to make your code safe.

One of the more common reasons to use a dual layer of exception-handling code is when you want to obtain input from a user and need to place the input code in a loop to ensure that you actually get the required information. The following steps demonstrate how this sort of code might work.

1. **Type the following code into a new cell of the notebook — pressing Enter after each line:**

```
TryAgain = True
while TryAgain:
    try:
        Value = int(input("Type a whole number. "))
    except ValueError:
        print("You must type a whole number!")
        try:
            DoOver = input("Try again (y/n)? ")
        except:
            print("OK, see you next time!")
            TryAgain = False
        else:
            if (str.upper(DoOver) == "N"):
                TryAgain = False
    except KeyboardInterrupt:
        print("You pressed Ctrl+C!")
        print("See you next time!")
        TryAgain = False
    else:
        print(Value)
        TryAgain = False
```

The code begins by creating an input loop. Using loops for this type of purpose is actually quite common in applications because you don't want the application to end every time an input error is made. This is a simplified loop, and normally you create a separate function to hold the code.

When the loop starts, the application asks the user to type a whole number. It can be any integer value. If the user types any non-integer value or presses Ctrl+C, Cmd+C, or another interrupt key combination, the exception-handling code takes over. Otherwise, the application prints the value that the user supplied and sets `TryAgain` to `False`, which causes the loop to end.

A `ValueError` exception can occur when the user makes a mistake. Because you don't know why the user input the wrong value, you have to ask if the user wants to try again. Of course, getting more input from the user could generate another exception. The inner `try...except` code block handles this secondary input.

TIP

Notice the use of the `str.upper()` function when getting character input from the user. This function makes it possible to receive y or Y as input and accept them both. Whenever you ask the user for character input, converting lowercase characters to uppercase is a good idea so that you can perform a single comparison (reducing the potential for error).

REMEMBER

The `KeyboardInterrupt` exception displays two messages and then exits automatically by setting `TryAgain` to `False`. The `KeyboardInterrupt` occurs only when the user presses a specific key combination designed to end the application. The user is unlikely to want to continue using the application at this point.

2. **Click Run Cell.**

    Python asks the user to input a whole number.

3. **Type** Hello **and press Enter.**

    The application displays an error message and asks whether you want to try again.

4. **Type** Y **and press Enter.**

    The application asks you to input a whole number again, as shown in Figure 10-7.

5. **Type** 5.5 **and press Enter.**

    The application again displays the error message and asks whether you want to try again.

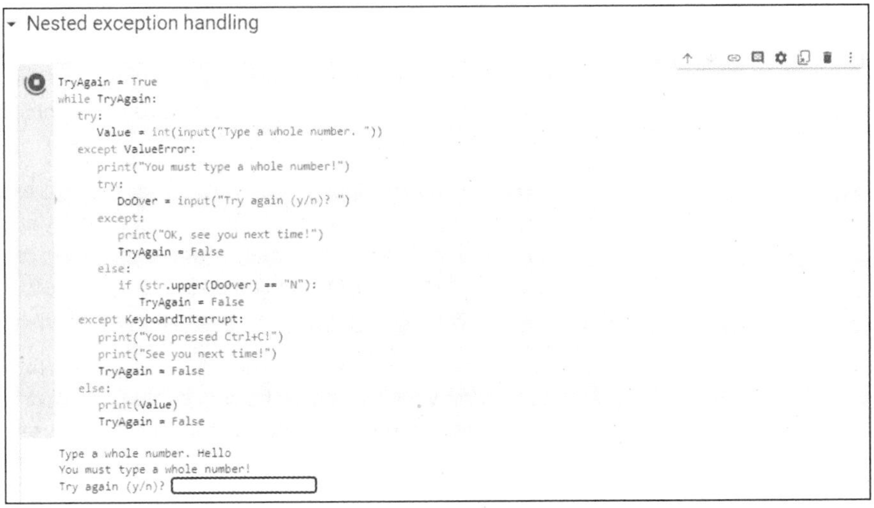

FIGURE 10-7:
Using a loop means that the application can recover from the error.

```
Nested exception handling

TryAgain = True
while TryAgain:
    try:
        Value = int(input("Type a whole number. "))
    except ValueError:
        print("You must type a whole number!")
        try:
            DoOver = input("Try again (y/n)? ")
        except:
            print("OK, see you next time!")
            TryAgain = False
        else:
            if (str.upper(DoOver) == "N"):
                TryAgain = False
    except KeyboardInterrupt:
        print("You pressed Ctrl+C!")
        print("See you next time!")
        TryAgain = False
    else:
        print(Value)
        TryAgain = False

Type a whole number. Hello
You must type a whole number!
Try again (y/n)?
```

6. **Choose Runtime ⇨ Interrupt Execution for Colab or Kernel ⇨ Interrupt for Jupyter Notebook to interrupt the application.**

   The application ends by displaying OK, see you next time!. Notice that the message is the one from the inner exception. The application never gets to the outer exception because the inner exception handler provides generic exception handling.

7. **Click Run Cell.**

   Python asks the user to input a whole number.

8. **Choose Kernel ⇨ Interrupt to interrupt the application, type** 5.5, **and then press Enter.**

   The application ends by displaying You pressed Ctrl+C!. Notice that the message is the one from the outer exception. In Steps 6 and 8, the user ends the application by pressing an interrupt key. However, the application uses two different exception handlers to address the problem.

Raising Exceptions

So far, the examples in this chapter have reacted to exceptions. Something happens and the application provides error-handling support for that event. However, situations arise for which you may not know how to handle an error event during the application design process. Perhaps you can't even handle the error at a particular level and need to pass it up to some other level to handle. In short, in some situations, your application must generate an exception. This act is called *raising* (or sometimes *throwing*) the exception. The following sections describe common scenarios in which you raise exceptions in specific ways.

Raising exceptions during exceptional conditions

The example in this section demonstrates how you raise a simple exception — that it doesn't require anything special. The following steps simply create the exception and then handle it immediately.

1. **Type the following code into a new cell of the notebook — pressing Enter after each line:**

    ```
    try:
        raise ValueError
    except ValueError:
        print("ValueError Exception!")
    ```

    You wouldn't ever actually create code that looks like this, but it shows you how raising an exception works at its most basic level. In this case, the `raise` call appears within a `try...except` block. A basic raise call simply provides the name of the exception to raise (or throw). You can also provide arguments as part of the output to provide additional information.

    REMEMBER

    Notice that this `try...except` block lacks an `else` clause because there is nothing to do after the call. Although you rarely use a `try...except` block in this manner, you can. You may encounter situations like this one sometimes and need to remember that adding the `else` clause is purely optional. On the other hand, you must add at least one `except` clause.

2. **Click Run Cell.**

    Python displays the expected exception text, `ValueError Exception!`.

Passing error information to the caller

Python provides exceptionally flexible error handling in that you can pass information to the *caller* (the code that is calling your code) no matter which exception you use. Of course, the caller may not know that the information is available, which leads to a lot of discussion on the topic. If you're working with someone else's code and don't know whether additional information is available, you can always use the technique described in the "Obtaining a list of exception arguments" sidebar, earlier in this chapter, to find it.

You may have wondered whether you could provide better information when working with a `ValueError` exception than with an exception provided natively by Python. The following steps show that you can modify the output so that it does include helpful information.

1. **Type the following code into a new cell of the notebook — pressing Enter after each line:**

```
try:
    Ex = ValueError()
    Ex.strerror = "Value must be within 1 and 10."
    raise Ex
except ValueError as e:
    print("ValueError Exception!", e.strerror)
```

   The `ValueError` exception normally doesn't provide an attribute named `strerror` (a common name for string error), but you can add it simply by assigning a value to it as shown. When the example raises the exception, the `except` clause handles it as usual but obtains access to the attributes using `e`. You can then access the `e.strerror` member to obtain the added information.

2. **Click Run Cell.**

   Python displays an expanded `ValueError` exception, as shown in Figure 10-8.

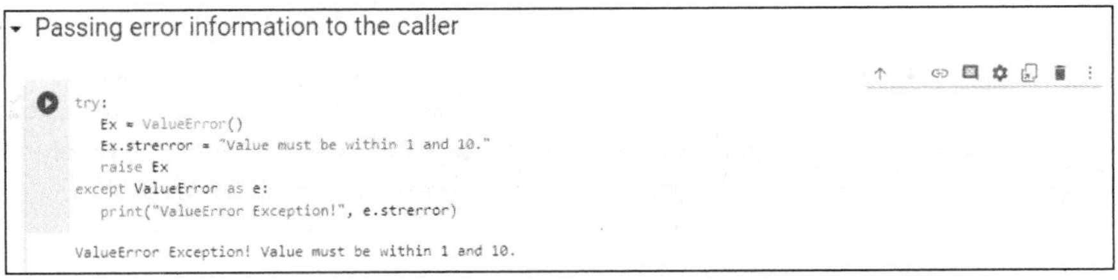

FIGURE 10-8:
You can add error information to any exception.

Deciding to Say "Oops" in Your Own Way: Custom Exceptions

Python provides a wealth of standard exceptions that you should use whenever possible. These exceptions are incredibly flexible, and you can even modify them as needed (within reason) to meet specific needs. For example, the "Passing error information to the caller" section of this chapter demonstrates how to modify a `ValueError` exception to allow for additional data. However, sometimes you simply must create a custom exception because none of the standard exceptions will work. Perhaps the exception name just doesn't tell the viewer the purpose that the exception serves. You may need a custom exception for specialized database work or when working with a service.

WARNING

The example in this section is going to seem a little complicated for now because you haven't worked with classes before. Chapter 15 introduces you to classes and helps you understand how they work. If you want to skip this section until after you read Chapter 15, you can do so without any problem.

The example in this section shows a quick method for creating your own exceptions. To perform this task, you must create a class that uses an existing exception as a starting point. To make things a little easier, this example creates an exception that builds upon the functionality provided by the ValueError exception. The advantage of using this approach rather than the one shown in the preceding section, "Passing error information to the caller," is that this approach tells anyone who follows you precisely what the addition to the ValueError exception is. It also makes the modified exception easier to use.

1. Type the following code into the notebook — pressing Enter after each line:

```
class CustomValueError(ValueError):
    def __init__(self, arg):
        self.strerror = arg
        self.args = {arg}
try:
    raise CustomValueError("Value must be within 1 and 10.")
except CustomValueError as e:
    print("CustomValueError Exception!", e.strerror)
```

This example essentially replicates the functionality of the example in the "Passing error information to the caller" section of the chapter. However, it places the same error in both strerror and args so that the developer has access to either (as would normally happen).

The code begins by creating the CustomValueError class that uses the ValueError exception class as a starting point. The __init__() function provides the means for creating a new instance of that class. Think of the class as a blueprint and the instance as the building created from the blueprint.

REMEMBER

Notice that the strerror attribute has the value assigned directly to it, but args receives it as an array. The args member normally contains an array of all the exception values as strings, so this is standard procedure, even when args contains just one value as it does now.

The code for using the exception is considerably easier than modifying `ValueError` directly. All you do is call `raise` with the name of the exception and the arguments you want to pass, all on one line.

2. **Click Run Cell.**

   The application displays a similar error message to that shown in Figure 10-8, except this time it notes that it's a custom error message by saying, `CustomValueError Exception! Value must be within 1 and 10`.

Using the finally Clause

Normally you want to handle any exception that occurs in a way that doesn't cause the application to crash. However, sometimes you can't do anything to fix the problem, and the application is most definitely going to crash. At this point, your goal is to cause the application to crash gracefully, which means closing files so that the user doesn't lose data and performing other tasks of that nature. Anything you can do to keep damage to data and the system to a minimum is an essential part of handling data for a crashing application.

The `finally` clause is part of the crashing-application strategy. You use this clause to perform any required last-minute tasks. Normally, the `finally` clause is quite short and uses only calls that are likely to succeed without further problem. It's essential to close the files, log the user off, and perform other required tasks, and then let the application crash before something terrible happens (such as a total system failure). With this necessity in mind, the following steps show a simple example of using the `finally` clause:

1. **Type the following code into a new cell in the notebook — pressing Enter after each line:**

```
import sys
try:
    raise ValueError
    print("Raising an exception.")
except ValueError:
    print("ValueError Exception!")
    sys.exit()
finally:
    print("Taking care of last minute details.")
print("This code will never execute.")
```

In this example, the code raises a `ValueError` exception. The `except` clause executes as normal when this happens. The call to `sys.exit()` means that the application exits after the exception is handled. Perhaps the application can't recover in this particular instance, but the application normally ends, which is why the final `print()` function call won't ever execute.

REMEMBER

The `finally` clause code always executes. It doesn't matter whether the exception happens or not. The code you place in this block needs to be common code that you always want to execute. For example, when working with a file, you place the code to close the file into this block to ensure that the data isn't damaged by remaining in memory rather than going to disk.

2. **Click Run Cell.**

   The application displays the `except` clause message and the `finally` clause message, as shown in Figure 10-9. The `sys.exit()` call prevents any other code from executing.

REMEMBER

Note that this isn't a normal exit, so Jupyter Notepad displays additional information for you in the form of a traceback. Colab doesn't display this information, but you can display it by using %tb. Simply type **%tb** in an empty cell and click Run Cell to see the information. When you use some other IDEs, the application may simply exit without displaying any additional information.

3. **Comment out the** `raise ValueError` call **by preceding it with two pound signs, like this:**

   ```
   ## raise ValueError
   ```

▾ Using the finally Clause

```
import sys
try:
    raise ValueError
    print("Raising an exception.")
except ValueError:
    print("ValueError Exception!")
    sys.exit()
finally:
    print("Taking care of last minute details.")
print("This code will never execute.")

ValueError Exception!
Taking care of last minute details.
An exception has occurred, use %tb to see the full traceback.

SystemExit

SEARCH STACK OVERFLOW
/usr/local/lib/python3.7/dist-packages/IPython/core/interactiveshell.py:2890: UserWarning: To exit: use 'exit', 'quit', or
    warn("To exit: use 'exit', 'quit', or Ctrl-D.", stacklevel=1)
```

FIGURE 10-9:
Use the finally clause to ensure that specific actions take place before the application ends.

Removing the exception will demonstrate how the `finally` clause actually works. Using two pound signs will make the commented code stand out and easier to search for.

4. **Click Run Cell.**

   The application displays a series of messages, including the `finally` clause message, as shown in Figure 10-10. This part of the example shows that the `finally` clause always executes, so you need to use it carefully.

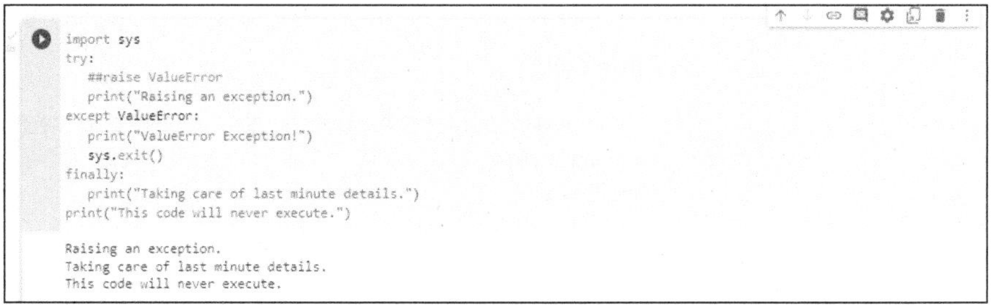

FIGURE 10-10:
Be sure to remember that the finally clause always executes.

```
import sys
try:
    ##raise ValueError
    print("Raising an exception.")
except ValueError:
    print("ValueError Exception!")
    sys.exit()
finally:
    print("Taking care of last minute details.")
print("This code will never execute.")

Raising an exception.
Taking care of last minute details.
This code will never execute.
```

3

Performing Common Tasks

Chapter **11**

Interacting with Packages

The examples in this book are small, but the functionality of the resulting applications is extremely limited as well. Even tiny real-world applications contain thousands of lines of code. In fact, applications that contain millions of lines of code are somewhat common. Imagine trying to work with a file large enough to contain millions of lines of code — you'd never find anything. In short, you need some method to organize code into small pieces that are easier to manage, much like the examples in this book. The Python solution is to place code in separate code groupings called *packages.* Commonly used groupings that contain source code for generic needs and more than one package are called *libraries.*

REMEMBER

Packages are contained in separate files. To use the package, you must tell Python to grab the code and read it into the current application. The process of obtaining code found in external files is called *importing.* You import a package or library to use the code it contains. A few examples in the book have already shown the `import` statement in use, but this chapter explains the `import` statement in detail so that you know how to use it.

The library code is self-contained and well documented (at least in most cases it is). Some developers might feel that they never need to look at the library code, and they're right to some degree — you never have to look at the library code in order to use it. You might want to view the library code, though, to ensure that you understand how the code works. In addition, the library code can teach you new programming techniques that you might not otherwise discover. So, viewing the library code is optional, but it can be helpful.

REMEMBER

You don't have to type the source code for this chapter manually. In fact, using the downloadable source is a lot easier. You can find the source for this chapter in the BPP4D3E; 11; Interacting with Packages.ipynb and BPP4D3E; 11; Packages.ipynb files of the downloadable source. See the Introduction for details on how to find these source files.

Creating Code Groupings

Code groupings in the form of packages and libraries are part of working with even the simplest program in Python. Some libraries are automatically imported for you because you use them for every application. Other libraries require that you import them individually. As part of the initial setup, Python created a pointer to the general-purpose libraries it uses. That's why you can simply add an import statement with the name of the library, and Python can find it. However, it pays to know how to locate the files on disk in case you ever need to update them or want to add your own packages and libraries to the list of files that Python can use.

The one thing you do need to know how to do is obtain and use the Python library documentation. This chapter shows you how to obtain and use the library documentation as part of the application-creation process. In the sections that follow, you discover more about the code groupings that Python uses, including how to interact with them at a basic level.

WARNING

The example in the "Creating your first package" section that follows works well only with Jupyter Notebook. Google Colab users can still follow along, but the act of working online makes this particular example (the only one in the book) quite a challenge to complete. The problems are that you would need to download the file locally, rename it because Colab mangles the name, and then upload it to the correct directory online, which can be insanely difficult to find. Consequently, the steps will focus on Jupyter Notebook use in this one particular case.

I'm confused! Understanding modules versus packages

TECHNICAL STUFF

In some sources, you may see *modules* used in place of packages. People often use the two terms interchangeably because there really isn't much of a difference between them. Most sources define a *module* as a single file containing code with an extension of .py. A *package* is a group of modules often organized in a hierarchical fashion (although, hierarchical organization isn't a language requirement). Even though there are small differences between the two, you can view both as methods of putting code into an easily used container, so this chapter uses "package" throughout because that's the term you see most often in the official documentation. If you want a more detailed view of the differences, you can read about it at https://learnpython.com/blog/python-modules-packages-libraries-frameworks/.

Creating your first package

Grouping like pieces of code together is important to make the code easier to use, modify, and understand. As an application grows, managing the code found in a single file becomes harder and harder. At some point, the code becomes impossible to manage because the file has become too large for anyone to work with.

The term *code* is used broadly in this particular case. Code groupings can include:

>> Classes

>> Functions

>> Variables

>> Runnable code

The collection of classes, functions, variables, and runnable code within a package is known as *attributes.* A package has attributes that you access by that attribute's name. Later sections in this chapter discuss precisely how package access works.

The runnable code can actually be written in a language other than Python. For example, it's somewhat common to find packages that are written in C/C++ instead of Python. The reason that some developers use runnable code is to make the Python application faster, less resource intensive, and better able to use a particular platform's resources. However, using runnable code comes with the downside of making your application less portable (able to run on other platforms) unless you have runnable code packages for each platform that you want to support. In addition, dual-language applications can be harder to maintain because you must have developers who can speak each of the computer languages used in the application.

The most common way to create a package is to define one or more separate files containing the code you want to group separately from the rest of the application. For example, you might want to create a print routine that an application uses in a number of places. The print routine isn't designed to work on its own but is part of the application as a whole. You want to separate it because the application uses it in numerous places and you could potentially use the same code in another application. The ability to reuse code ranks high on the list of reasons to create packages.

To make things easier to understand, the examples in this chapter use a common package. The package doesn't do anything too amazing, but it demonstrates the principles of working with packages. Open a Python 3 Notebook project, name it BPP4D3E; 11; Packages, and create the code shown in Listing 11-1. After you complete this task, download the code as a new Python file named BPP4D3E; 11; Packages1.py by choosing File ⇨ Download As ⇨ Python (.py) in Notebook.

LISTING 11-1: **A Simple Demonstration Package**

```
def SayHello(Name):
    print("Hello ", Name)
    return
def SayGoodbye(Name):
    print("Goodbye ", Name)
    return
```

WARNING

This example specifically uses a Notebook filename that contains special characters and spaces to make a point. Any package you create can't have spaces or special characters in the filename and still work correctly. Consequently, you must rename BPP4D3E; 11; Packages1.py to BPP4D3E_11_Packages.py if you want it to work with the remainder of the example in this chapter.

You may need to copy the resulting file to your existing BPP4D3E folder, depending on where your browser normally downloads files. When done correctly, your Notebook dashboard should contain a copy of the file, as shown in Figure 11-1. Using the Notebook's Import feature makes things considerably easier. Notice that the name of the .py file is BPP4D3E_11_Packages.py.

The example code contains two simple functions named SayHello() and Say-Goodbye(). In both cases, you supply a Name to print and the function prints it onscreen along with a greeting for you. At that point, the function returns control to the caller. Obviously, you normally create more complicated functions, but these functions work well for the purposes of this chapter.

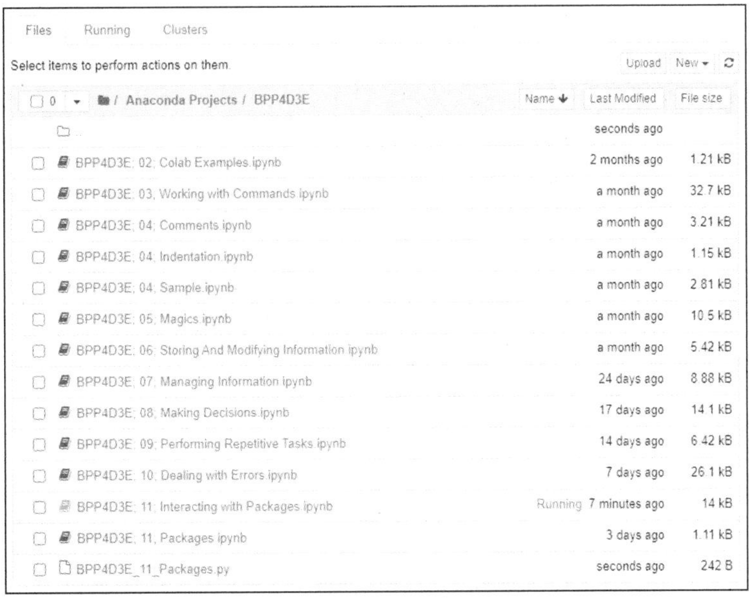

FIGURE 11-1:
Make sure you place a copy of the package in your BPP4D3E folder.

INTERACTING WITH THE CURRENT PYTHON DIRECTORY

The directory that Python is using to access code affects which packages you can load. The Python library files are always included in the list of locations that Python can access, but Python knows nothing of the directory you use to hold your source code unless you tell it to look there. Of course, you need to know how to interact with the directory functions in order to tell Python where to look for specific bits of code.

1. **Open a new notebook.**

   You can also use the downloadable source file, BPP4D3E; 11; Interacting with Packages.ipynb.

2. **Type** import os **and press Enter.**

   This action imports the Python os library. You need to import this library to change the directory (the location Python sees on disk) to the working directory for this book.

3. **Type** print(os.getcwd()) **and click Run Cell.**

   You see the current working directory (CWD) that Python uses to obtain local code.

(continued)

(continued)

4. In a new cell, type for entry in os.listdir(): print(entry) **and click Run Cell.**

You see a listing of the directory entries. The listing lets you determine whether the file you need is in the CWD. If not, you need to change directories to a location that does contain the required file.

To change directories to a new location, you use the os.chdir() method and include the new location as a string, such as os.chdir('C:\MyDir'). However, you normally find with Notebook that the CWD does contain the files for your current project.

TIP

The code in this sidebar works with Google Colab as well as Jupyter Notebook, but the Google Colab results are less useful. The Colab Python executable files are normally located in the /usr/local/bin/python directory, which you can determine using the !which python command, where the ! (bang) operator (https://anaconda.zendesk.com/hc/en-us/articles/360023858254-Executing-Terminal-Commands-in-Jupyter-Notebooks) provides access to the system shell, and the which command (https://linuxize.com/post/linux-which-command/) provides the location of a particular executable, python in this case.

Understanding the package types

The Python support system is immense. In fact, you'll likely never use more than a small fraction of it for even the most demanding applications. It's not that Python itself is all that huge; the language is actually somewhat concise compared to many other languages out there. The immensity comes from the Python system of packages and libraries that perform everything from intense scientific work, to AI, to space exploration, to biologic modeling, to anything else you can imagine and many things you can't. However, not all those packages are available all the time, so you need some idea of what sort of packages Python supports and where you might find them (in order of preference):

» **Built-in:** The built-in packages address most common needs. When working with Jupyter Notebook as part of *Anaconda* (a development package containing multiple tools, including conda, that you can find at https://www.anaconda.com/), you find them in the \Users\<*Username*>\Adaconda3\Lib folder on your system, and all you need to do to use them is import them into your application. Locating them in Google Colab is somewhat more difficult. You may need to do a little searching. However, if you're using Python 3.7, you could use this command (all on one line) in a Colab cell to obtain a listing of the built-in packages (see the "Interacting with the current python directory" sidebar for details on using os commands):

```
for entry in os.listdir("/usr/local/lib/python3.7/
    dist-packages"): print(entry)
```

>> **Custom:** As demonstrated in this chapter, you can create your own packages and use them as needed. They appear on your hard drive, normally in the same directory as your project code, and you simply import them into your application.

>> **Conda:** You can find a wealth of packages specifically designed for Anaconda (Jupyter Notebook). Many of these packages appear at https://anaconda. org/mutirri/repo. Before you can use these packages, you must install them by using the conda utility at the Anaconda command line, as described in the "Installing conda packages" section of this chapter. After you have the package installed, you use it as you would any built-in package. If you are using Colab, you won't have access to the conda utility, which is explained in the "And just why is conda missing in Colab?" section of the chapter.

>> **Non-conda:** Just because a package isn't specifically designed for use with Anaconda doesn't mean that you can't use it. You can find a great wealth of packages from third parties that provide significant functionality. To install these packages, you use the pip utility, as described in the "Installing packages by using pip" and "Installing packages using the %pip magics" sections, later in this chapter. After you have the package installed, you may have to perform additional configuration as described by the party who created the package. Generally, when the package is configured, you use it as you would any built-in package.

Considering the package cache

This section doesn't apply to Google Colab, so you can skip it if you're working online or simply don't want to know about the package cache. Anaconda provides a package cache that resides outside the Python library. This package cache lets you easily interact with the Anaconda-specific packages by using the conda command-line utility. To see how you use this package cache:

1. **Open an Anaconda command prompt or terminal window.**

   You get access to this feature through the Anaconda Prompt entry in the Anaconda3 folder on your system.

2. **Type** conda list **and press Enter.**

   You see a list of the packages that you have installed now.

Note that the output displays the package name as you would access it from within Anaconda, the package version, and the associated Python version. All this information is helpful in managing the packages. The following list provides the essential conda commands for managing your packages:

>> conda clean: Removes packages that you aren't using.

>> conda config: Configures the package cache setup.

>> conda create: Defines a new conda environment that contains a specific list of packages, which makes it easier to manage the packages and can improve application speed.

>> conda help: Displays a complete list of conda commands.

>> conda info: Displays the conda configuration information, which includes details on where conda stores packages and where it looks for new packages.

>> conda install: Installs one or more packages into the default or specified conda environment.

>> conda list: Outputs a list of conda packages with varying levels of detail. You can specify which packages to list and in which environments to look.

>> conda remove: Removes one or more packages from the package cache.

>> conda search: Looks for specific packages by using the search criteria you provide.

>> conda update: Updates some or all of the packages in the package cache.

These commands can do a lot more than you might think. Of course, it's impossible to memorize all that information, so you can rely on the --help command-line switch to obtain full details on using a particular command. For example, to learn more about conda list, type **conda list --help** and press Enter.

Importing Packages

To use a package, you must import it. Python places the package code inline with the rest of your application in memory — as if you had created one huge file. Neither file is changed on disk — they're still separate, but the way Python views the code is different.

You have two ways to import packages. Each technique is used in specific circumstances:

» `import`: You use the `import` statement when you want to import an entire package. This is the most common method that developers use to import packages because it saves time and requires only one line of code. However, this approach also uses more memory resources than does the approach of selectively importing the attributes you need, which the next paragraph describes.

» `from...import`: You use the `from...import` statement when you want to selectively import individual package attributes. This method saves resources, but at the cost of complexity. In addition, if you try to use an attribute that you didn't import, Python registers an error. Yes, the package still contains the attribute, but Python can't see it because you didn't import it.

Now that you have a better idea of how to import packages, it's time to look at them in detail. The following sections help you work through importing packages using the two techniques available in Python.

Using the import statement

The `import` statement is the most common method for importing a package into Python. This approach is fast and ensures that the entire package is ready for use. The following steps get you started using the `import` statement:

1. **Open a new notebook, if you haven't already created one for the code in the "Interacting with the current python directory" sidebar.**

You can also use the downloadable source file, BPP4D3E; 11; Interacting with Packages.ipynb.

2. **Change directories, if necessary, to the downloadable source code directory.**

Generally, Notebook places you in the correct directory to use the source code files, so you won't need to perform this step. See the instructions found in the "Interacting with the current Python directory" sidebar.

3. **In a new cell, type** import BPP4D3E_11_Packages **and press Enter.**

This instruction tells Python to import the contents of the BPP4D3E_11_Packages.py file that you created in the "Creating your first package" section of the chapter. The entire library is now ready for use.

WARNING

It's important to know that Python also creates a cache of the package in the __pycache__ subdirectory of the BPP4D3E folder. If you look into your source code directory after you import BPP4D3E_11_Packages for the first time, you see the new __pycache__ directory. If you want to make changes to your package, you must delete this directory. Otherwise, Python will continue to use the unchanged cache file instead of your updated source code file.

The cached filename includes the version of Python for which it is meant, so it's BPP4D3E_11_Packages.cpython-38.pyc in this case. The 38 in the filename means that this file is Python 3.8 specific. A .pyc file represents a compiled Python file, which is used to improve application speed.

4. **Type** dir(BPP4D3E_11_Packages) **and click Run Cell.**

You see a listing of the package contents, which includes the SayHello( ) and SayGoodbye( ) functions, as shown in Figure 11-2. (A discussion of the other entries appears in the "Viewing the Package Content" section, later in this chapter.)

FIGURE 11-2:
A directory listing
shows that
Python imports
both functions
from the package.

```
                   Using the import statement

In [3]:  import BPP4D3E_11_Packages
         dir(BPP4D3E_11_Packages |

Out[3]:  ['SayGoodbye',
          'SayHello',
          '__builtins__',
          '__cached__',
          '__doc__',
          '__file__',
          '__loader__',
          '__name__',
          '__package__',
          '__spec__']
```

5. **In a new cell, type** BPP4D3E_11_Packages.SayHello("Josh").

Notice that you must precede the attribute name, which is the SayHello( ) function in this case, with the package name, which is BPP4D3E_11_Packages. The two elements are separated by a period (also called a dot). Every call to a package that you import follows the same pattern.

6. **Type** BPP4D3E_11_Packages.SayGoodbye("Sally") **and click Run Cell.**

The SayHello( ) and SayGoodbye( ) functions output the expected text.

Using the from. . .import statement

The from...import statement has the advantage of importing only the attributes you need from a package. This difference means that the package uses less memory and other system resources than using the import statement does. In addition, the from...import statement makes the package a little easier to use because some commands, such as dir(), show less information, or only the information that you actually need. The point is that you get only what you want and not anything else. The following steps demonstrate using the from...import statement. However, before you can import BPP4D3E_11_Packages selectively, you must remove it from the environment, which is the first part of the following process.

1. **Type the following code into a new cell in the Notebook:**

```
import sys
del sys.modules["BPP4D3E_11_Packages"]
del BPP4D3E_11_Packages
dir(BPP4D3E_11_Packages)
```

2. **Click Run Cell.**

You see the error message shown in Figure 11-3. Listing the content of the BPP4D3E_11_Packages package isn't possible anymore because it's no longer loaded.

FIGURE 11-3:
Removing a
package from the
environment
requires two
steps.

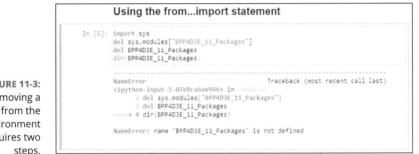

3. **In a new cell, type** from BPP4D3E_11_Packages import SayHello **and press Enter.**

Python imports the SayHello( ) function from BPP4D3E_11_Packages. Only this specific function is now ready for use.

REMEMBER

To import both functions you need, you create a list of attributes to import; the names can be separated by commas, such as from BPP4D3E_11_Packages import SayHello, SayGoodbye.

4. **Type** dir(BPP4D3E_11_Packages) **and click Run Cell.**

Python displays an error message, as shown previously in Figure 11-3. Python imports only the attributes that you specifically request. This means that the BPP4D3E_11_Packages package isn't in memory — only the attributes that you requested are in memory.

5. **In a new cell, type** dir(SayHello) **and click Run Cell.**

You see a listing of attributes that are associated with the SayHello( ) function, as shown in Figure 11-4 (which is only a partial list). You don't need to know how these attributes work just now, but you'll use some of them later in the book.

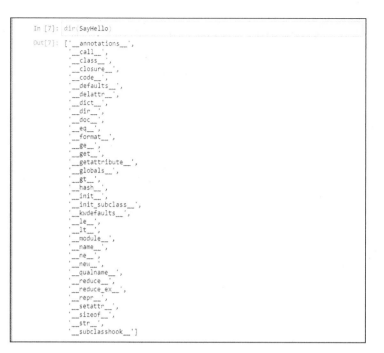

```
In [7]: dir(SayHello)
Out[7]: ['__annotations__',
         '__call__',
         '__class__',
         '__closure__',
         '__code__',
         '__defaults__',
         '__delattr__',
         '__dict__',
         '__dir__',
         '__doc__',
         '__eq__',
         '__format__',
         '__ge__',
         '__get__',
         '__getattribute__',
         '__globals__',
         '__gt__',
         '__hash__',
         '__init__',
         '__init_subclass__',
         '__kwdefaults__',
         '__le__',
         '__lt__',
         '__module__',
         '__name__',
         '__ne__',
         '__new__',
         '__qualname__',
         '__reduce__',
         '__reduce_ex__',
         '__repr__',
         '__setattr__',
         '__sizeof__',
         '__str__',
         '__subclasshook__']
```

FIGURE 11-4:
Use the dir()
function to obtain
information
about the specific
attributes you
import.

6. **In a new cell, type** SayHello("Angie") **and click Run Cell.**

   The SayHello() function outputs the expected text.

   REMEMBER

   When you import attributes by using the from...import statement, you don't need to precede the attribute name with a package name. This feature makes the attribute easier to access.

   WARNING

   Using the from...import statement can also cause problems. If attributes from two different packages have the same name, you can import only one of them using this approach. Using the import statement form prevents name collisions, which is important when you have a large number of attributes to import. In sum, you must exercise care when using the from...import statement.

7. **In a new cell, type** SayGoodbye("Harold") **and click Run Cell.**

   You imported only the SayHello() function, so Python knows nothing about SayGoodbye() and displays an error message. The selective nature of the from...import statement can cause problems when you assume that an attribute is present when it really isn't.

Using the import. . .as statement

Having to precede every attribute name with the BPP4D3E_11_Packages name will cause severe finger cramping after a while, and no one wants that! Of course, such a long name can also cause steaming-brain syndrome as you attempt to remember what the package name is. Fortunately, Python is concerned about your health and provides an alternative to finger cramping and a steaming brain in the form of the import...as statement. The as part of the statement gives the package a shorter, easier-to-remember name that won't cause finger problems or that other thing. The following steps show how to use this approach.

1. **Type the following code into a new cell in the Notebook:**

```
import BPP4D3E_11_Packages as BPP
dir(BPP)
```

2. **Click Run Cell.**

You see the same listing of package contents as that shown in Figure 11-2, but you had to type less code to get it.

3. **Type the following code into a new cell in the Notebook:**

```
BPP.SayHello("Albert")
BPP.SayGoodbye("Daphne")
```

4. **Click Run Cell.**

The two functions output the expected text. However, you typed a lot less code to obtain the results.

Finding Packages

To use the code in a package, Python must be able to locate the package and load it into memory, so you need to know where the package resides. When working with Jupyter Notebook, the packages reside on your hard drive. If you don't find them on your hard drive, you can download what you need. Colab stores its files in the /usr/local/lib/python3.7/dist-packages folder (with the 3.7 indicating the Python version you're using) online. Anything on your local disk is inaccessible. The following sections discuss how to find packages that are already available to Python in more detail. (The "Downloading Packages from Other Sources" section, later in the chapter, tells how to obtain packages that you can't already access.)

Locating packages on disk

Some of the information in this section works only with Jupyter Notebook; it may not work with any browser-based IDE you use (such as Google Colab). The location information is stored as paths within Python. Whenever you request that Python import a package, Python looks at all the files in its list of paths to find it. The path information comes from three sources:

>> **Environment variables:** Environment variables, such as PYTHONPATH, tell Python where to find packages on disk (see the "Using environment variables with Python" sidebar for details).

>> **Current directory:** Earlier in this chapter, you discover that you can change the current Python directory so that it can locate any packages used by your application.

>> **Default directories:** Even when you don't define any environment variables and the current directory doesn't yield any usable packages, Python can still find its own libraries in the set of default directories that are included as part of its own path information.

Knowing the current path information is helpful because the lack of a path can cause your application to fail. To obtain path information, type **for p in sys.path: print(p)** in a new cell and click Run Cell. You see a listing of the path information, as shown in Figure 11-5. Your listing may be different from the one shown in Figure 11-5, depending on your platform, the version of Python you have installed, and the Python features you have installed.

FIGURE 11-5:
The sys.path attribute contains a listing of the individual paths for your system.

The `sys.path` attribute is reliable but may not always contain every path that Python can see. If you don't see a needed path, you can always check in another place that Python looks for information. The following steps show how to perform this task:

1. **Type the following code into a new cell in the Notebook:**

```
import os
os.environ['PYTHONPATH'].split(os.pathsep)
```

When you have a PYTHONPATH environment variable defined, you see a list of one or more paths, such as ['C:\\BP4D'] or ['/env/python']. However, if you don't have the environment variable defined, you see an error message instead.

You must provide split() with a value to look for in splitting a list of items. The os.pathsep *constant* (a variable that has one, unchangeable, defined value) defines the path separator for the current platform so that you can use the same code on any platform that supports Python.

2. **Click Run Cell.**

You see the listing of paths for your platform and setup.

TIP

You can also add and remove items from `sys.path`. For example, if you want to add the current working directory to the list of packages, you type **sys.path. append(os.getcwd())** in the Notebook cell and click Run Cell. When you list the `sys.path` contents again, you see that the new entry is added to the end of the list. Likewise, when you want to remove an entry, you type **sys.path.remove(os. getcwd())** in the Notebook cell and click Run Cell. The addition is present only during the current session.

WARNING

If you change an environment variable while the Jupyter Notebook server is running, you won't see any changes within the Notebook. To see the changes, you must restart Jupyter Notebook completely from scratch.

Locating packages online

When working with a browser-based IDE, you often see the results of using a virtual environment, the platform that the host has chosen to use, or simply find the information you need in a location other than what you expected. Consequently, the code in the "Locating packages on disk" section may work, but may not provide what you need. For example, to ensure that you can actually find the Python path, you need to use the `!echo $PYTHONPATH` command for Linux and macOS, or `!echo %PYTHONPATH%` for Windows (see the article at https://www3.ntu.edu.sg/home/ehchua/programming/howto/Environment_Variables.html for details on how environment variables work on different operating systems). Using the wrong form of the command for a particular host doesn't do anything terrible; you just won't see the path to Python (assuming that the host actually defines the `PYTHONPATH` environment variable).

In many situations, you must rely more heavily on magics (as discussed in Chapter 5) when working with packages and attempting to perform other tasks when using a browser-based IDE. For example, when working with Colab, every `!` operator command you use creates an entirely new subshell, which means that the changes made by each statement may be lost. Consequently, if you wanted to do something like change directories to load a package, you'd need to use the `%cd` magics command rather than the `!cd` operator command, even though it seems as if both should work. The result of the `!cd` operator command would go away as soon as the command completed, but the `%cd` magics command is permanent for a particular session. Note that the functions in the `os` package (as used in the previous section) are often effective when working with browser-based IDEs. For example, you may be able to use `os.chdir()`, rather than rely on the `%cd` magics.

Downloading Packages from Other Sources

Your copy of Python and the associated Jupyter Notebook component of Anaconda or Google Colab come with a wide assortment of packages that fulfill many common needs. In fact, for experimentation purposes, you seldom have to go beyond these packages because they are already installed as part of your IDE. Of course, someone is always thinking of some new way to do things, which requires new code and packages to store the code. In addition, some coding techniques are so esoteric that including the packages to support them with a default install would consume space that most people will never use. Consequently, you may have to install packages from online or other sources from time to time.

The two most common methods of obtaining new packages are to use the conda (which you find only in Jupyter Notebook) or pip (also known by the recursive acronym Pip Installs Packages) utilities. However, you may find packages that use other installation methods with varying degrees of success. You use conda and pip for different purposes:

>> conda: Provides general-purpose package management for a wide range of languages with special needs in the conda environment.

>> pip: Provides services specifically for Python in any environment. When you need a Python-specific package, look to pip first. For example, pip gives you access to the Python Package Index (PyPI) found at https://pypi.org/.

TIP

You can read more about the differences between conda and pip at https:// jakevdp.github.io/blog/2016/08/25/conda-myths-and-misconceptions/ and https://docs.conda.io/projects/conda/en/latest/commands.html#conda-vs-pip-vs-virtualenv-commands. The following sections discuss these two methods.

Opening the Anaconda Prompt

Before you can do much in the way of managing packages in Jupyter Notebook, you must open the Anaconda Prompt. The Anaconda Prompt is just like any other command prompt or terminal window, but it provides special configuration features to make working with the various command-line utilities supplied with Anaconda easier. To open the prompt, locate its icon in the Anaconda3 folder on your machine. For example, when using a Windows system, you can open the Anaconda Prompt by choosing Start ▷ All Programs ▷ Anaconda3 ▷ Anaconda Prompt. The Anaconda Prompt may take a moment or two to appear onscreen because of its configuration requirements.

Working with conda packages

When working with Jupyter Notebook, you can perform a wide range of tasks using conda, but some tasks are more common than others. The following sections describe how to perform five essential tasks using conda. You can obtain additional information about this utility at https://docs.conda.io/projects/conda/en/latest/commands.html. Typing **conda --help** at the Anaconda Prompt or terminal window and pressing Enter also yields an overview of help information.

Viewing conda packages

You can view conda packages in two ways. The first is to create a list of available packages, while the second is to search for a specific package. Listing helps you discover whether a package is already installed. Searching helps you discover the details about the installed package.

You can perform searching and listing in a general way to locate everything installed on a particular system. In this case, you use the commands by themselves:

```
conda list
conda search
```

The output of these commands is lengthy and might scroll right off the end of the screen buffer (making it impossible to scroll back and view all of the results). You can use conda list | more to display the output one page at a time on some platforms.

Note that the output shows the package name, version, and associated version of Python. You can use this output to determine whether a package is installed on your system. However, sometimes you need more, which requires a search. For example, say that you want to know what you have installed from the scikit-learn package for the Windows 64-bit platform. In this case, you type **conda search --platform win-64 scikit-learn** and press Enter.

TIP

A number of flags exist to greatly increase the amount of information you receive. For example, when you use the --json flag, you obtain details such as a complete list of dependencies for the package, whether the package is completely installed, and a URL containing the location of the packages online. You can learn more about conda searches at https://docs.conda.io/projects/conda/en/latest/commands/search.html.

Installing conda packages

The lists of conda packages appear at https://docs.anaconda.com/anaconda/packages/pkg-docs/. The lists are grouped by Python version number and platform. To determine whether a package is available for your version of Python on a particular platform, simply click the associated link. You can use conda to install a package using the conda install command documented at https://docs.conda.io/projects/conda/en/latest/commands/install.html. For example, to install SciPy, you type **conda install scipy** and press Enter at the Anaconda Prompt.

Updating conda packages

The packages you use to develop applications can become outdated with time. The
developers who maintain them might add new features or apply bug fixes. The
problem with updates is that they can cause your application to work incorrectly, or
sometimes not at all if you're depending on a broken behavior. However, it's generally
a good idea to keep packages updated if for no other reason than to apply security-
related bug fixes. Of course, you need to know that the package requires updating. To
find outdated packages, you use the conda search --outdated --names-only
command, followed by the name of the package you want to check.

After you know what you need to update, you can use the conda update command
to perform the task. For example, you might want to update the NumPy package,
which means typing **conda update numpy** and pressing Enter. Few packages are
stand-alone, so conda will present a list of items that you need to update along
with NumPy. Type **y** and press Enter to proceed. Figure 11-6 shows a typical
sequence of events during the update process.

WARNING

You do have the option of updating all packages at one time. Simply type **conda
update --all** and press Enter to get started. However, you may find that interactions between packages make the update less successful than it could be if you
performed the updates individually. In addition, the update can take a long time,
so be sure to have plenty of coffee and a copy of *War and Peace* on hand. You can
learn more about conda updates at https://docs.conda.io/projects/conda/
en/latest/commands/update.html.

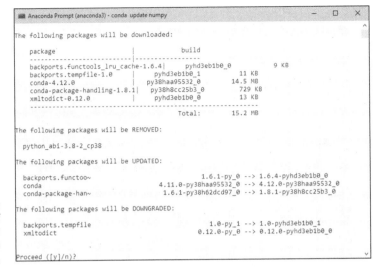

FIGURE 11-6:
You see a lot of
information
during the update
process.

Removing conda packages

At some point, you might decide that you no longer need a conda package. The only problem is that you don't know whether other packages depend on the package in question. Because package dependencies can become quite complex, and you want to be sure that your applications will continue to run, you need to check which other packages depend on this particular package. Unfortunately, the conda info command (described at https://docs.conda.io/projects/conda/en/latest/commands/info.html) tells you only about the package requirements — that is, what it depends on. Best practice is to not uninstall packages after you've installed them.

REMEMBER

However, assuming that you really must remove the package, you use the conda remove command described at https://docs.conda.io/projects/conda/en/latest/commands/remove.html. This command removes the package that you specify, along with any packages that depend on this package. In this case, best practice is to use the --dry-run command-line switch first to ensure that you really do want to remove the package. For example, you may decide that you want to remove NumPy. In this case, you type **conda remove --dry-run numpy** and press Enter. The command won't actually execute; conda simply shows what would happen if you actually did run the command.

And just why is conda missing in Colab?

Colab doesn't come with conda because it isn't part of the Anaconda suite of tools. Unfortunately, a number of tools recommend using conda, especially those associated with data science and statistics. Consequently, you may actually want to install conda into your Colab environment. Installing conda as part of Colab can become a complex undertaking and is well outside the scope of this book. However, you can find help for installing conda in Colab online in articles like the one at https://towardsdatascience.com/conda-google-colab-75f7c867a522, and there is even a YouTube video showing the process at https://www.youtube.com/watch?v=Rm2ak31u1us. The video actually tells you how to access a script that can reduce the complexity of the task.

Installing packages by using pip

Oddly enough, working with pip is much like working with conda. They both need to perform essentially the same tasks, so if you know how to use one, you know how to use the other. The reference at https://pip.pypa.io/en/stable/cli/ shows that pip does support essentially the same commands (with a few wording differences). For example, if you want to find a list of outdated packages, you type **pip list --outdated** and press Enter. Here is a list of the common commands that pip supports:

>> check: Verify that the installed packages have compatible dependencies.

>> download: Download the specified packages for later installation.

>> freeze: Output installed packages in requirements format.

>> help: Display a help screen listing an overview of the commands.

>> install: Install the specified packages.

>> list: List the installed packages.

>> search: Search online at PyPI for packages.

>> show: Show information about the installed packages.

>> uninstall: Uninstall the specified packages.

TIP

When working with either Jupyter Notebook or Google Colab, you can use the ! operator to work with pip. Consequently, typing **!pip list --outdated** in a cell and then clicking Run Cell produces a list of outdated packages on your system. The advantage of this approach is that you can create a notebook that contains information about your setup that you can refer to as needed when working on projects.

Installing packages using the %pip magics

There is a magics version of the pip command that is accessible from within Colab and Jupyter Notebook. It works just like the ! operator version, except you use %pip instead. You use this approach when you need to work with pip within the current kernel so that the result of a `pip` command doesn't just evaporate when the command completes. This technique allows you to execute a number of `pip` commands in sequence and know that they'll work as expected.

TIP

It shouldn't surprise you to know that a `%conda` magics command exists for Jupyter Notebook users. As with `%pip`, `%conda` works the same as the command-line version.

Viewing the Package Content

Python gives you several different ways to view package content. The method that most developers use is to work with the `dir()` function, which tells you about the attributes that the package provides.

Look at Figure 11-2, earlier in the chapter. In addition to the `SayGoodbye()` and `SayHello()` function entries discussed previously, the list has other entries. These attributes are automatically generated by Python for you. These attributes perform the following tasks or contain the following information:

» `__builtins__`: Contains a listing of all the built-in attributes that are accessible from the package. Python adds these attributes automatically for you.

» `__cached__`: Tells you the name and location of the cached file that is associated with the package. The location information (path) is relative to the current Python directory.

» `__doc__`: Outputs help information for the package, assuming that you've actually filled it in. For example, if you type **print(os.__doc__)** and press Enter, Python will output the help information associated with the os library. (Using the `print()` function ensures that the output is nicely formatted.)

» `__file__`: Tells you the name and location of the package. The location information (path) is relative to the current Python directory.

» `__initializing__`: Determines whether the package is in the process of initializing itself. Normally this attribute returns a value of `False`. This attribute is useful when you need to wait until one package is done loading before you import another package that depends on it.

» `__loader__`: Outputs the loader information for this package. The *loader* is a piece of software that gets the package and puts it into memory so that Python can use it. This is one attribute you rarely (if ever) use.

» `__name__`: Tells you just the name of the package.

» __package__: This attribute is used internally by the import system to make it easier to load and manage packages. You don't need to worry about this particular attribute.

It may surprise you to find that you can drill down even further into the attributes. Type **dir(BPPD_11_Packages.SayHello)** and press Enter. You see the attributes associated with the SayHello() function.

Some of these entries, such as __name__, also appeared in the package listing. However, you might be curious about some of the other entries. For example, you might want to know what __sizeof__ is all about. One way to get additional information is to type **help("__sizeof__")** and press Enter. You see some scanty (but useful) help information, such as "Size of object in memory, in bytes."

Python won't blow up if you try the attribute. Even if the notebook does experience problems, you can always restart the kernel (or simply restart the environment as a whole). Another way to check out a package is to simply try the attributes. For example, if you type **BPPD_11_Packages.SayHello.__sizeof__()** and press Enter, you see the size of the SayHello() function in bytes, which is 120 bytes in this case.

Viewing Package Documentation

You can use the doc() function whenever needed to get quick help. However, you have a better way to study the packages and libraries located in the Python path — the Python Package Documentation. This feature often appears as Package Docs in the Python folder on your system. It's also referred to as PyDoc. Whatever you call it, the Python Package Documentation makes life a lot easier for developers. The following sections describe how to work with this feature.

Using !pydoc to access PyDoc

You can access a command-line version of PyDoc from the Anaconda Prompt when working with Jupyter Notebook, but the best and easiest way to use PyDoc is within a notebook cell using the ! operator. This approach works equally well in Colab and Jupyter Notebook, so you can use the same techniques even if you switch between the two IDEs. If you type **!pydoc** and click Run Cell, you see the output shown in Figure 11-7, which describes how to use PyDoc from within your IDE.

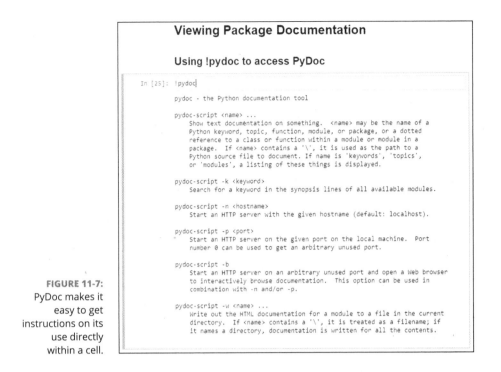

FIGURE 11-7:
PyDoc makes it
easy to get
instructions on its
use directly
within a cell.

Typing a search term

To search for a particular Python keyword, function, or other attribute using PyDoc, simply add a search term after the !pydoc command. For example, if you want to learn more about the print() function, type **!pydoc print** and click Run Cell. You see output similar to that shown in Figure 11-8.

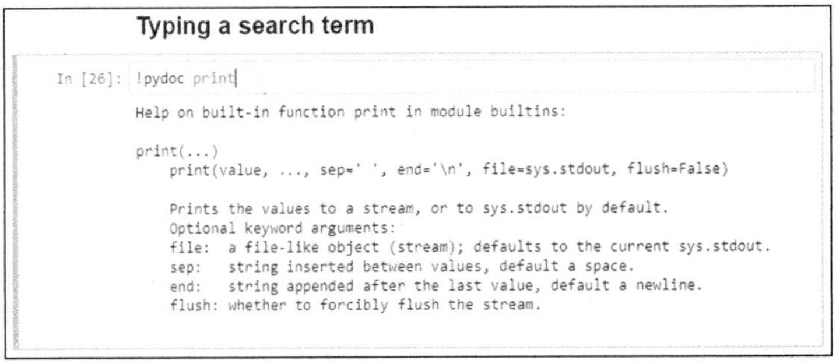

FIGURE 11-8:
PyDoc will tell you
all about the
print()
function if
you ask.

When working with Jupyter Notebook, you can perform keyword searches using the –k switch. A *keyword search* helps you locate features that could be helpful, but that you don't necessarily know about when you start the search. Keyword searches don't work in Colab (you get an error instead). Note that keyword searches can take a long time to run and produce copious results. For example, type **!pydoc -k stream** and click Run Cell to see a long list of packages, functions, and other features that work with streams. (The size of this list will amaze you.) Figure 11-9 shows a sampling of what you might see when executing this command.

FIGURE 11-9:
Keyword searches help you locate items that you may not know how to reference otherwise.

Chapter **12**

Working with Strings

Your computer doesn't understand strings. It's a basic fact. Computers understand numbers, not letters. When you see a string on the computer screen, the computer actually sees a series of numbers. However, humans understand strings quite well, so applications need to be able to work with them. Fortunately, Python makes working with strings relatively easy. It translates the string you understand into the numbers the computer understands, and vice versa.

To make strings useful, you need to be able to manipulate them. Of course, that means taking strings apart and using just the pieces you need or searching the string for specific information. This chapter describes how you can build strings by using Python, dissect them as needed, and use just the parts you want after you find what's required. String manipulation is an important part of applications because humans depend on computers performing that sort of work for them (even though the computer has no idea of what a string is).

After you have the string you want, you need to present it to the user in an eye-pleasing manner. The computer doesn't really care how it presents the string, so often you get the information, but it lacks pizzazz. In fact, it may be downright difficult to read. Knowing how to format strings so that they look nice onscreen is important because users need to see information in a form they understand. By the time you complete this chapter, you know how to create, manipulate, and format strings so that the user sees precisely the right information.

You don't have to type the source code for this chapter manually. In fact, using the downloadable source is a lot easier. You can find the source for this chapter in the `BPP4D3E; 12; Working with Strings.ipynb` file of the downloadable source. See the Introduction for details on how to find these source files.

Understanding That Strings Are Different

Most aspiring developers (and even a few who have written code for a long time) really have a hard time understanding that computers truly do only understand 0s and 1s. Even larger numbers are made up of 0s and 1s. Comparisons take place with 0s and 1s. Data is moved by using 0s and 1s. In short, strings don't exist for the computer (and numbers just barely exist). Although grouping 0s and 1s to make numbers is relatively easy, strings are a lot harder because now you're talking about information that the computer must manipulate as numbers but present as characters.

There are no strings in computer science. Strings are made up of characters, and individual characters are actually numeric values. When you work with strings in Python, what you're really doing is creating an assembly of characters that the computer sees as numeric values. That's why the following sections are so important. They help you understand why strings are so special. Understanding this material will save you a lot of headaches later.

Defining a character by using numbers

To create a character, you must first define a relationship between that character and a number. More important, everyone must agree that when a certain number appears in an application and is viewed as a character by that application, the number is translated into a specific character. One of the most common ways to perform this task is to use the American Standard Code for Information Interchange (ASCII). Python uses ASCII to translate the number 65 to the letter A. The chart at `https://www.asciitable.com/` shows the various numeric values and their character equivalents.

Every character you use must have a different numeric value assigned to it. The letter A uses a value of 65. To create a lowercase a, you must assign a different number, which is 97. The computer views A and a as completely different characters, even though people view them as uppercase and lowercase versions of the same character.

The numeric values used in this chapter are in decimal. However, the computer still views them as 0s and 1s. For example, the letter A is really the value 01000001 and the letter *a* is really the value 01100001. When you see an *A* onscreen, the computer sees a binary value instead.

TECHNICAL
STUFF

Having just one character set to deal with would be nice. However, not everyone could agree on a single set of numeric values to equate with specific characters. Part of the problem is that ASCII doesn't support characters used by other languages; also, it lacks the capability to translate special characters into an onscreen presentation. In fact, character sets abound. You can see a number of them at http://www.i18nguy.com/unicode/codepages.html. Click one of the character set entries to see how it assigns specific numeric values to each character. Most characters sets do use ASCII as a starting point.

Using characters to create strings

Python doesn't make you jump through hoops to create strings. However, the term *string* should actually give you a good idea of what happens. Think about beads or anything else you might string. You place one bead at a time onto the string. Eventually you end up with some type of ornamentation — perhaps a necklace or tree garland. The point is that these items are made up of individual beads.

The same concept used for necklaces made of beads holds true for strings in computers. When you see a sentence, you understand that the sentence is made up of individual characters that are strung together by the programming language you use. The language creates a structure that holds the individual characters together. So, the language, not the computer, knows that so many numbers in a row (each number being represented as a character) defines a string such as a sentence.

REMEMBER

You may wonder why it's important to even know how Python works with characters. The reason is that many of the functions and special features that Python provides work with individual characters, and you need to know that Python sees the individual characters. Even though you see a sentence, Python sees a specific number of characters.

Unlike most programming languages, strings in Python can use either single quotes or double quotes. For example, `"Hello There!"` with double quotes is a string, as is `'Hello There!'` with single quotes. Python also supports triple double and single quotes that let you create strings spanning multiple lines. The following steps help you create an example that demonstrates some of the string features that Python provides.

1. **Open a new notebook.**

   You can also use the downloadable source file, BPP4D3E ; 12 ; Working with Strings.ipynb.

2. **Type the following code into the notebook — pressing Enter after each line:**

```
print('Hello There (Single Quote)!')
print("Hello There (Double Quote)!")
print("""This is a multiple line
string using triple double quotes.
You can also use triple single quotes.""")
```

Each of the three `print()` function calls demonstrates a different principle in working with strings. Equally acceptable is to enclose the string in either single or double quotes. When you use a triple quote (either single or double), the text can appear on multiple lines.

3. **Click Run Cell.**

Python outputs the expected text. Notice that the multiline text appears on three lines (see Figure 12-1), just as it does in the source code file, so this is a kind of formatting. You can use multiline formatting to ensure that the text breaks where you want it to onscreen.

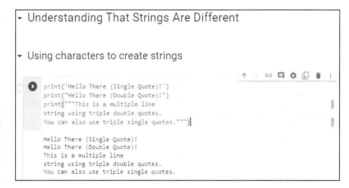

FIGURE 12-1: Strings consist of individual characters that are linked together.

Creating Stings with Special Characters

Some strings include special characters. These characters are different from the alphanumeric and punctuation characters that you're used to using. In fact, they fall into these categories:

>> **Control:** An application requires some means of determining that a particular character isn't meant to be displayed but rather to control the display. All the control movements are based on the *insertion pointer,* the line you see when

you type text on the screen. For example, you don't see a tab character. The tab character provides a space between two elements, and the size of that space is controlled by a tab stop. Likewise, when you want to go to the next line, you use a carriage return (which returns the insertion pointer to the beginning of the line) and linefeed (which places the insertion pointer on the next line) combination.

TECHNICAL
STUFF

To add spice to your life and make things completely confusing, some platforms use just a carriage return to advance to the next line, and other platforms use just the linefeed to advance to the next line. If you encounter problems in certain situations with too many lines or an unexpected result, try using just a carriage return or a linefeed in place of the combination of the two. The computer knows what it's doing; the humans don't.

» **Accented:** Characters that have accents, such as the acute ('), grave (`), circumflex (^), umlaut or diaeresis (¨), tilde (~), or ring (°), represent emphasis or special spoken sounds, in most cases. You must use special characters to create alphabetical characters with these accents included.

» **Drawing:** You can create rudimentary art with some characters. You can see examples of the box-drawing characters at `http://jrgraphix.net/r/Unicode/2500-257F`. Some people actually create art by using ASCII characters as well (`http://www.asciiworld.com/`).

» **Typographical:** A number of typographical characters, such as the pilcrow (¶), are used when displaying certain kinds of text onscreen, especially when the application acts as an editor.

» **Other:** Depending on the character set you use, the selection of characters is nearly endless. Need a smile? Well, there is a smiley face character for that need (☺). You can find a character for just about any need. The point is that you need some means of telling Python how to present these special characters.

A common need when working with strings, even strings from simple console applications, is control characters. With this in mind, Python provides escape sequences that you use to define control characters directly (and a special escape sequence for other characters).

REMEMBER

An *escape sequence* literally escapes the common meaning of a letter, such as *a*, and gives it a new meaning (such as the ASCII bell or beep). The combination of the backslash (\) and a letter (such as *a*) is commonly viewed as a single letter by developers — an *escape character* or *escape code*. Table 12-1 provides an overview of these escape sequences.

TABLE 12-1

Python Escape Sequences

Escape Sequence	Meaning
\newline	Ignored
\\	Backslash (\)
\'	Single quote (')
\"	Double quote (")
\a	ASCII Bell (BEL)
\b	ASCII Backspace (BS)
\f	ASCII Formfeed (FF)
\n	ASCII Linefeed (LF)
\r	ASCII Carriage Return (CR)
\t	ASCII Horizontal Tab (TAB)
\u*hhhh*	Unicode character (a specific kind of character set with broad appeal across the world) with a hexadecimal value that replaces *hhhh*
\v	ASCII Vertical Tab (VT)
ooo	ASCII character with octal numeric value that replaces *ooo*
\x*hh*	ASCII character with hexadecimal value that replaces *hh*

The best way to see how the escape sequences work is to try them. The following steps help you create an example that tests various escape sequences so that you can see them in action.

1. **Type the following code into a new cell in the notebook — pressing Enter after each line:**

```
print("Part of this text\r\nis on the next line.")
print("This is an A with a grave accent: \xC0.")
print("This is a drawing character: \u2562.")
print("This is a pilcrow: \266.")
print("This is a division sign: \xF7.")
```

The example code uses various techniques to achieve the same end — to create a special character. Of course, you can use control characters directly, as shown in the first line. Many special letters are accessible by using a hexadecimal number that has two digits (as in the second and fifth lines). However, some require that you rely on Unicode numbers (which always require four digits), as shown in the third line. Octal values use three digits and have no special character associated with them, as shown in the fourth line.

2. **Click Run Cell.**

   Python outputs the expected text and special characters, as shown in Figure 12-2.

```
Creating Stings with Special Characters

print("Part of this text\r\nis on the next line.")
print("This is an A with a grave accent: \xC0.")
print("This is a drawing character: \u2562.")
print("This is a pilcrow: \266.")
print("This is a division sign: \xF7.")

Part of this text
is on the next line.
This is an A with a grave accent: À.
This is a drawing character: ╢.
This is a pilcrow: ¶.
This is a division sign: ÷.
```

WARNING

Notebook uses a standard character set across platforms, so you should see the same special characters no matter which platform you test. However, when creating your application, make sure to test it on various platforms to see how the application will react. A character set on one platform may use different numbers for special characters than another platform does. In addition, user selection of character sets could have an impact on how special characters displayed by your application appear. When working on applications that will see use with multiple languages, the chance of having problems between character sets is much higher. Always make sure that you test special character usage completely.

Selecting Individual Characters

Earlier in the chapter, you discover that strings are made up of individual characters. They are, in fact, just like beads on a necklace — with each bead being an individual element of the whole string.

Python makes it possible to access individual characters in a string. This is an important feature because you can use it to create new strings that contain only part of the original. In addition, you can combine strings to create new results.

The secret to this feature is the square bracket. You place a square bracket with a number in it after the name of the variable. Here's an example:

```
MyString = "Hello World"
print(MyString[0])
```

In this case, the output of the code is the letter *H*. Python strings are zero-based, which means they start with the number *o* and proceed from there. For example, if you were to type `print(MyString[1])`, the output would be the letter *e*.

You can also obtain a range of characters from a string. Simply provide the beginning and ending letter count separated by a colon in the square brackets. For example, `print(MyString[6:11])` would output the word `World`. The output would begin with letter 6 and end with letter 10 (remember that the index is zero based). The following steps demonstrate some basic tasks that you can perform by using Python's character-selection technique.

1. **Type the following code into a new cell in the notebook — pressing Enter after each line.**

    ```
    String1 = "Hello World"
    String2 = "Python is Fun!"
    print(String1[0])
    print(String1[0:5])
    print(String1[:5])
    print(String1[6:])
    String3 = String1[:6] + String2[:6]
    print(String3)
    print(String2[:7]*5)
    ```

    The example begins by creating two strings. It then demonstrates various methods for using the index on the first string. Notice that you can leave out the beginning or ending number in a range if you want to work with the remainder of that string.

    The next step is to combine two substrings. In this case, the code combines the beginning of String1 with the beginning of String2 to create String3.

    The use of the + sign to combine two strings is called *concatenation*. This sign is one of the handier operators to remember when you're working with strings in an application.

    The final step is to use a Python feature called *repetition*. You use repetition to make a number of copies of a string or substring.

2. **Click Run Cell.**

    Python outputs a series of substrings and string combinations, as shown in Figure 12-3.

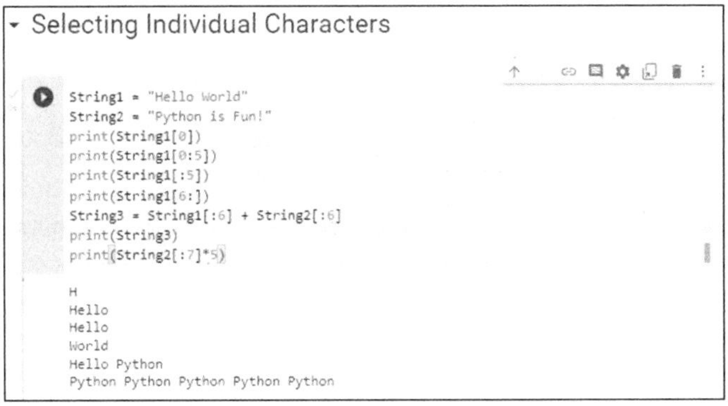

FIGURE 12-3:
You can select individual pieces of a string.

Slicing and Dicing Strings

Working with ranges of characters provides some degree of flexibility, but it doesn't provide you with the capability to actually manipulate the string content or discover anything about it. For example, you might want to change the characters to uppercase or determine whether the string contains all letters. Fortunately, Python has functions that help you perform tasks of this sort. Here are the most commonly used functions:

» `capitalize()`: Capitalizes the first letter of a string.

» `center(width, fillchar=" ")`: Centers a string so that it fits within the number of spaces specified by *width*. If you supply a character for *fillchar*, the function uses that character. Otherwise, `center()` uses spaces to create a string of the desired width.

» `expandtabs(tabsize=8)`: Expands tabs in a string by replacing the tab with the number of spaces specified by *tabsize*. The function defaults to 8 spaces per tab when *tabsize* isn't provided.

» `isalnum()`: Returns `True` when the string has at least one character and all characters are alphanumeric (letters or numbers).

» `isalpha()`: Returns `True` when the string has at least one character and all characters are alphabetic (letters only).

» `isdecimal()`: Returns `True` when a string contains only decimal (base 10) characters. For example, `'100'` would return `True` because the string can represent a decimal value of 100. The string `'0xF'` would return `False` because it represents a base 16 number, not a base 10 number. Likewise, `'10.55'` would return `False` because this is a floating-point value, not a decimal number.

» `isdigit()`: Returns True when a string contains only digits (numbers and not letters).

» `islower()`: Returns True when a string has at least one alphabetic character and all alphabetic characters are in lowercase.

» `isnumeric()`: Returns True when a string contains only numeric characters.

» `isspace()`: Returns True when a string contains only whitespace characters (which includes spaces, tabs, carriage returns, linefeeds, form feeds, and vertical tabs, but not the backspace).

» `istitle()`: Returns True when a string is cased for use as a title, such as `'Hello World'`. However, the function requires that even little words have the title case. For example, `'Follow a Star'` returns False, even though it's properly cased, but `'Follow A Star'` returns True.

» `isupper()`: Returns True when a string has at least one alphabetic character and all alphabetic characters are in uppercase.

» `join(seq)`: Creates a string in which the base string is separated in turn by each character in *seq* in a repetitive fashion. For example, if you start with `MyString = "Hello"` and type `print(MyString.join("!*!"))`, the output is `!Hello*Hello!`.

TIP

The `join()` function is also used to join lists of characters. For example, `print('-'.join(['a', 'b', 'c']))` would result in an output of a–b–c. It can also be used with tuples, where `print(', '.join(('apples', 'cherries', 'and peaches')))` outputs apples, cherries, and peaches and sets, such as `print(', '.join({'apples', 'cherries', 'and peaches'}))`.

» `len(str)`: Obtains the length of *str*.

» `ljust(width, fillchar=" ")`: Left justifies a string so that it fits within the number of spaces specified by *width*. If you supply a character for *fillchar*, the function uses that character. Otherwise, `ljust()` uses spaces to create a string of the desired width.

» `lower()`: Converts all uppercase letters in a string to lowercase letters.

» `lstrip()`: Removes all leading whitespace characters in a string.

» `max(str)`: Returns the character that has the maximum numeric value in *str*. For example, a would have a larger numeric value than A.

» `min(str)`: Returns the character that has the minimum numeric value in *str*. For example, A would have a smaller numeric value than a.

» `rjust(width, fillchar=" ")`: Right justifies a string so that it fits within the number of spaces specified by *width*. If you supply a character for *fillchar*, the function uses that character. Otherwise, `rjust()` uses spaces to create a string of the desired width.

>> `rstrip()`: Removes all trailing whitespace (right side of the string) characters in a string.

>> `split(str=" ", num=string.count(str))`: Splits a string into substrings using the delimiter specified by `str` (when supplied). The default is to use a space as a delimiter. Consequently, if your string contains `'A Fine Day'`, the output would be three substrings consisting of A, Fine, and Day. You use *num* to define the number of substrings to return. The default is to return every substring that the function can produce.

>> `splitlines(num=string.count('\n'))`: Splits a string that contains newline (\n) characters into individual strings. Each break occurs at the newline character. The output has the newline characters removed. You can use *num* to specify the number of strings to return.

>> `strip()`: Removes all leading and trailing whitespace characters in a string.

>> `swapcase()`: Inverts the case for each alphabetic character in a string.

>> `title()`: Returns a string in which the initial letter in each word is in upper-case and all remaining letters in the word are in lowercase.

>> `upper()`: Converts all lowercase letters in a string to uppercase letters.

>> `zfill(width)`: Returns a string that is left-padded with zeros so that the resulting string is the size of *width*. This function is designed for use with strings containing numeric values. It retains the original sign information (if any) supplied with the number.

Playing with these functions a bit can help you understand them better. The following steps create an example that demonstrates some of the tasks you can perform by using these functions.

1. **Type the following code into a new cell in the notebook — pressing Enter after each line:**

```
MyString = " Hello World "
print(MyString.upper())
print(MyString.strip())
print(MyString.center(21, "*"))
print(MyString.strip().center(21, "*"))
print(MyString.isdigit())
print(MyString.istitle())
print(max(MyString))
print(MyString.split())
print(MyString.split()[0])
```

The code begins by creating MyString, which includes spaces before and after the text so that you can see how space-related functions work. The initial task is to convert all the characters to uppercase.

Removing extra space is a common task in application development. The strip() function performs this task well. The center() function lets you add padding to both the left and right side of a string so that it consumes a desired amount of space. When you combine the strip() and center() functions, the output is different from when you use the center() function alone.

REMEMBER

You can combine functions to produce a desired result. Python executes each of the functions one at a time from left to right. The order in which the functions appear will affect the output, and developers commonly make the mistake of putting the functions in the wrong order. If your output is different from what you expected, try changing the function order.

Some functions work on the string as an input rather than on the string instance. The max() function falls into this category. If you had typed MyString.max(), Python would have displayed an error. The bulleted list that appears earlier in this section shows which functions require this sort of string input by including a *str* input as part of the function declaration.

When working with functions that produce a list as an output, you can access an individual member by providing an index to it. The example shows how to use split() to split the string into substrings. It then shows how to access just the first substring in the list. You find out more about working with lists in Chapter 13.

2. **Click Run Cell.**

Python outputs a number of modified strings, as shown in Figure 12-4.

```
▾ Slicing and Dicing Strings

    MyString = " Hello World "
    print(MyString.upper())
    print(MyString.strip())
    print(MyString.center(21, "*"))
    print(MyString.strip().center(21, "*"))
    print(MyString.isdigit())
    print(MyString.istitle())
    print(max(MyString))
    print(MyString.split())
    print(MyString.split()[0])

     HELLO WORLD
    Hello World
    **** Hello World ****
    *****Hello World*****
    False
    True
    r
    ['Hello', 'World']
    Hello
```

FIGURE 12-4:
Using functions makes string manipulation a lot more flexible.

Locating a Value in a String

Sometimes you need to locate specific information in a string. For example, you may want to know whether a string contains the word Hello in it. One of the essential purposes behind creating and maintaining data is to be able to search it later to locate specific bits of information. Strings are no different — they're most useful when you can find what you need quickly and without any problems. Python provides a number of functions for searching strings. Here are the most commonly used functions:

» count(*str*, *beg=* 0, *end=*len(*string*)): Counts how many times *str* occurs in a string. You can limit the search by specifying a beginning index using *beg* or an ending index using *end*.

» endswith(*suffix*, *beg=0*, *end=*len(*string*)): Returns True when a string ends with the characters specified by *suffix*. You can limit the check by specifying a beginning index using *beg* or an ending index using *end*.

» find(*str*, *beg=0*, *end=*len(*string*)): Determines whether *str* occurs in a string and outputs the index of the location. You can limit the search by specifying a beginning index using *beg* or an ending index using *end*. This function returns a value of –1 when the target isn't present.

» index(*str*, *beg=0*, *end=*len(*string*)): Provides the same functionality as find(), but raises an exception when *str* isn't found.

» replace(*old, new* [, *max*]): Replaces all occurrences of the character sequence specified by *old* in a string with the character sequence specified by *new*. You can limit the number of replacements by specifying a value for *max*.

» rfind(*str*, *beg=0*, *end=*len(*string*)): Provides the same functionality as find(), but searches backward from the end of the string instead of the beginning.

» rindex(*str*, *beg=0*, *end=*len(*string*)): Provides the same functionality as index(), but searches backward from the end of the string instead of the beginning.

» startswith(*prefix*, *beg=0*, *end=*len(string)): Returns True when a string begins with the characters specified by *prefix*. You can limit the check by specifying a beginning index using *beg* or an ending index using *end*.

Finding the data that you need is an essential programming task — one that is required no matter what kind of application you create. The following steps help you create an example that demonstrates the use of search functionality within strings.

1. **Type the following code into a new cell in the notebook — pressing Enter after each line:**

```
SearchMe = "The apple is red and the berry is blue!"
print(SearchMe.find("is"))
print(SearchMe.rfind("is"))
print(SearchMe.count("is"))
print(SearchMe.startswith("The"))
print(SearchMe.endswith("The"))
print(SearchMe.replace("apple", "car")
     .replace("berry", "truck"))
```

The example begins by creating SearchMe, a string with two instances of the word is. The two instances are important because they demonstrate how searches differ depending on where you start. When using find(), the example starts from the beginning of the string. By contrast, rfind() starts from the end of the string.

Of course, you won't always know how many times a certain set of characters appears in a string. The count() function lets you determine this value.

Depending on the kind of data you work with, sometimes the data is heavily formatted and you can use a particular pattern to your advantage. For example, you can determine whether a particular string (or substring) ends or begins with a specific sequence of characters. You could just as easily use this technique to look for a part number.

The final bit of code replaces apple with car and berry with truck. Notice the technique used to place the code on two lines. In some cases, your code will need to appear on multiple lines to make it more readable.

2. **Click Run Cell.**

Python displays the output shown in Figure 12-5. Notice especially that the searches returned different indexes based on where they started in the string. Using the correct function when performing searches is essential to ensure that you get the results you expected.

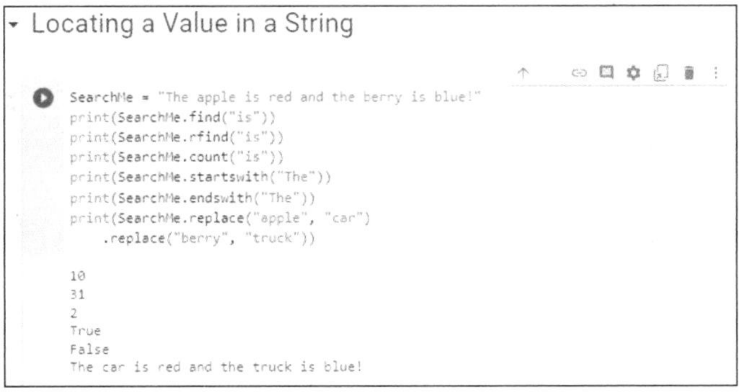

FIGURE 12-5:
Using string
search features
correctly is
essential.

Using String Interpolation

You can format strings in a number of ways using Python. The main emphasis of formatting is to present the string in a form that is both pleasing to the user and easy to understand. Formatting doesn't mean adding special fonts or effects in this case, but refers merely to the presentation of the data. For example, the user might want a fixed-point number rather than a decimal number as output. The following sections discuss and demonstrate various techniques for formatting strings, a process known as *string interpolation* (just so that programmers can sound fancy).

Employing the % (modulo) approach

In some cases, all you really need is simple information replacement in a string. The % (modulo) operator approach is the simplest form of formatting that Python provides, but it also sees less use in new applications because it's extremely limited and there are better methods (as explored in the sections that follow this one). Even so, if you're in a hurry and need something quite simple and easy to troubleshoot, the % operator may be the way to go.

When using the % operator, you place the % operator in every location where you want to see some information appear, along with the type of that information, as shown in the following table:

Operator	Description	Operator	Description	Operator	Description
%c	Character	%d	Decimal integer	%e	Float exponent (lowercase)
%E	Float exponent (uppercase)	%f	Float (lowercase)	%F	Float (uppercase)

Operator	Description	Operator	Description	Operator	Description
%g	General format (lowercase)	%G	General format (uppercase)	%i	Integer
%o	Octal integer	%s	String	%u	Unsigned integer
%x	Hexadecimal integer				

The % operator also allows the addition of some formatting information, as described in the next section of the chapter for the format() function, but this formatting information is generally limited to number of decimal places. The following steps show how to use the % operator in various ways:

1. **Type the following code into a new cell in the notebook — pressing Enter after each line:**

```
print("%c is lowercase %c" %('a', 65))
print("%s are %s" %("Violets", "Blue"))
print("%d is %#x hexadecimal" %(60, 60))
```

In each case, you see a print() function that uses one of the % operator replacements, such as %c in the first case. Notice that when using %c you can use either a character, 'a', or an ASCII number, 65. The values you want to substitute for each of the % operator entries appear in a tuple (a series of values enclosed in paretheses and delimited by commas) with the % operator outside of it. The values are always replaced sequentially, and you must provide enough values for each of the % operator entries in the string.

The % operator handles characters differently from strings. When working with strings, you use the %s operator.

The third print() function call is for the integer value 60. Notice that you must provide 60 twice, once for each % operator entry. In this case, the values are output the first time as a decimal integer and the second time as a hexadecimal integer. The # in the %#x operator tells Python to place a 0x in front of the output. The # character is one of a number of *format flags:*

● #: Adds 0x in front of hexadecimal output.

● +: Adds a plus sign in front of positive values.

● –: Left justifies the output, rather than using the default right justification.

● " ": Inserts spaces before a numeric output.

● 0: Inserts zeros before the numeric output.

2. **Click Run Cell.**

   Python outputs data in various forms:

   ```
   a is lowercase A
   Violets are Blue
   60 is 0x3c hexadecimal
   ```

   at the next step results in some examples of numeric formatting.

3. **Type the following code into a new cell in the notebook — pressing Enter after each line:**

   ```
   Value1 = 100
   Value2 = float('inf')
   print('% e is smaller than %E.' %(Value1, Value2))
   print("%.3F is smaller than %.2f." %(Value1,
                                        Value2))
   print("%05d" %Value1)
   ```

   This part of the example focuses on an integer value of 100 and a float value of infinity. The code formats the two values in various ways. Notice the use of uppercase and lowercase % operators. In addition, there is a space between the % and the e in the third line, which adds a space in front of the output value. (Adding more spaces won't add more spaces to the output.) The fourth line has a .3 in front of the F that controls the number of digits after the decimal point. The last line shows how to add zeros in front of the number.

4. **Click Run Cell.**

   Python outputs data in various forms:

   ```
    1.000000e+02 is smaller than INF.
   100.000 is smaller than inf.
   00100
   ```

   The final part of the example shows a special use for % operator formatting when working with a dictionary.

5. **Type the following code into a new cell in the notebook — pressing Enter after each line:**

   ```
   Employees = {
       'Monica': {
           'Occupation': "Designer",
           'Name': "Monica",
           'Department': "Engineering"
       },
   ```

```
    'Sam': {
        'Occupation': "Programmer",
        'Name': "Sam",
        'Department': "Software"
    }
}

for Item in Employees:
    print("%(Name)s is a %(Occupation)s in " \
        "%(Department)s." %Employees[Item])
```

This example uses a nested dictionary. Don't worry too much about the precise use of dictionaries for now; you discover how to use them in Chapter 14. For now, think about this code as being a kind of database. It contains two employees, Monica and Sam. There are entries for each employee: Occupation, Name, and Department.

A for loop comes next. It gets the name of an employee (not the actually employee information) from Employees and uses that name to access a particular employee record using %Employees[Item]. Now you have a single employee record, and you can access the information by name using the % and enclosing the information you want within a tuple, such as %(Name). As always, you must tell Python what kind of data format to use, so the entire operator would be %(Name)s.

TIP

Notice the use of the line-continuation character, \, in this part of the example. Whenever your code becomes too long, you can use a line-continuation character to continue the code on the next line.

6. **Click Run Cell.**

Python outputs data in various forms. Figure 12-6 shows the outputs for this entire example.

Working with the format() function

The format() function provides more functionality and flexibility than using the % operator shown in the previous section. You create a formatting specification as part of the string and then use the format() function to add data to that string. A format specification may be as simple as two curly brackets {} that specify a placeholder for data. You can number the placeholder to create special effects. For example, {0} would contain the first data element in a string. When the data elements are numbered, you can even repeat them so that the same data appears more than once in the string.

FIGURE 12-6:
The % operator is
good for simple
output needs.

The formatting specification follows a colon. When you want to create just a for-matting specification, the curly brackets contain just the colon and whatever for-matting you want to use. For example, {:f} would create a fixed-point number as output. If you want to number the entries, the number that precedes the colon: {0:f} creates a fixed-point number output for data element one. The formatting specification follows this form, with the italicized elements serving as placehold-ers here:

```
[[fill]align][sign][#][0][width][,][.precision][type]
```

The specification at https://docs.python.org/3/library/string.html pro-vides you with the in-depth details, but here's an overview of what the various entries mean:

» **fill:** Defines the fill character used when displaying data that is too small to fit within the assigned space.

>> **align:** Specifies the alignment of data within the display space. You can use these alignments:

- <: Left aligned

- >: Right aligned

- ^: Centered

- =: Justified

>> **sign:** Determines the use of signs for the output:

- +: Positive numbers have a plus sign and negative numbers have a minus sign.

- −: Negative numbers have a minus sign.

- *<space>*: Positive numbers are preceded by a space and negative numbers have a minus sign.

>> **#:** Specifies that the output should use the alternative display format for numbers. For example, hexadecimal numbers will have a 0x prefix added to them.

>> **0:** Specifies that the output should be sign aware and padded with zeros as needed to provide consistent output.

>> **width:** Determines the full width of the data field (even if the data won't fit in the space provided).

>> **,:** Specifies that numeric data should have commas as a thousands separator.

>> **.precision:** Determines the number of characters after the decimal point.

>> **type:** Specifies the output type, even if the input type doesn't match. The types are split into three groups:

- *String:* Use an s or nothing at all to specify a string.

- *Integer:* The integer types are as follows: b (binary); c (character); d (decimal); o (octal); x (hexadecimal with lowercase letters); X (hexadecimal with uppercase letters); and n (locale-sensitive decimal that uses the appropriate characters for the thousands separator).

- *Floating point:* The floating-point types are as follows: e (exponent using a lowercase e as a separator); E (exponent using an uppercase E as a separator); f (lowercase fixed point); F (uppercase fixed point); g (lowercase general format); G (uppercase general format); n (locale-sensitive general format that uses the appropriate characters for the decimal and thousands separators); and % (percentage).

The formatting specification elements must appear in the correct order or Python won't know what to do with them. If you specify the alignment before the fill character, Python displays an error message rather than performing the required formatting. The following steps help you see how the formatting specification works and demonstrate the order you need to follow in using the various formatting specification criteria.

1. **Type the following code into a new cell in the notebook — pressing Enter after each line:**

```
Formatted = "{:d}"
print(Formatted.format(7000))
Formatted = "{:,d}"
print(Formatted.format(7000))
Formatted = "{:^15,d}"
print(Formatted.format(7000))
Formatted = "{:*^15,d}"
print(Formatted.format(7000))
Formatted = "{:*^15.2f}"
print(Formatted.format(7000))
Formatted = "{:*>15X}"
print(Formatted.format(7000))
Formatted = "{:*<#15x}"
print(Formatted.format(7000))
Formatted = "A {0} {1} and a {0} {2}."
print(Formatted.format("blue", "car", "truck"))
```

The example starts simply with a field formatted as a decimal value. It then adds a thousands separator to the output. The next step is to make the field wider than needed to hold the data and to center the data within the field. Finally, the field has an asterisk added to pad the output.

Of course, the example contains other data types. The next step is to display the same data in fixed-point format. The example also shows the output in both uppercase and lowercase hexadecimal format. The uppercase output is right aligned and the lowercase output is left aligned.

Finally, the example shows how you can use numbered fields to your advantage. In this case, it creates an interesting string output that repeats one of the input values.

2. **Click Run Cell.**

Python outputs data in various forms, as shown in Figure 12-7.

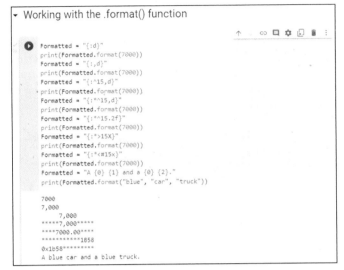

FIGURE 12-7:
Use formatting to
present data in
precisely the
form you want.

Simplifying things using f-string

Most developers today use the f-string because it emcompasses all the functionality of earlier Python string formatting and adds a few new tricks to it. An *f-string*
is simply a string that is preceded by the lowercase letter *f*. In many respects, it
looks like a less complicated version of the format() method demonstrated in the
previous section. With this similarity in mind, it's time to look at an example.

1. **Type the following code into a new cell in the notebook — pressing Enter
after each line:**

```
Value1 = 22
Value2 = 33
print(f"Value1 has a value of {Value1}.")
print(f"{Value1} + {Value2} = {Value1 + Value2}.")
print(f"This value: {str(Value1).center(8)}" \
      " is centered.")
print(f"Value1 as a hexadecimal value of " \
      f"{Value1:x}.")
```

This example starts with two values: Value1 and Value2. The first print() call
shows how you begin the string with the lowercase letter f and then add the
content within single or double quotes. Notice how the use of a variable name
within the curly braces ({}) makes reading the statement easy.

Unlike other forms of string formatting, an f-string can contain expressions,
such as {Value1 + Value2}. In fact, you can make function calls and perform
data conversion as part of an f-string like this: {str(Value1).center(8)}.

You still have the ability to use all the formatting functionality offered by the `format()` method, so f-strings can have formatting instructions like this: `{Value1:x}`, which produces hexadecimal output.

REMEMBER

Notice that if you have a line-contuation character but the next line doesn't contain a variable or expression, you don't need to preced it with an `f`. However, if the next line does contain replaceable content, you must include the `f` or Python won't know how to interpret the content.

2. **Click Run Cell.**

   Python outputs data in various forms, as shown in Figure 12-8.

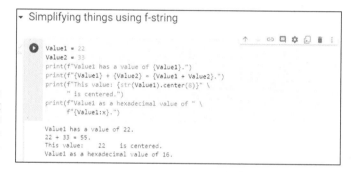

FIGURE 12-8: The f-string approach is simpler than other methods, yet quite flexible.

Creating and using string templates

String templates are for those times when you repeat the same information in different places in your application, but with different data. The template is simply a string, but it uses a $ in front of the replaceable values instead of the other methods shown in previous sections. The best way to see how a string template works is to see it in action, which you can do by following these steps:

1. **Type the following code into a new cell in the notebook — pressing Enter after each line:**

```
from string import Template

X = 1
Y = 2

Sums = Template("$Value1 + $Value2 = $Value3")
print(Sums.substitute(Value1 = X, Value2 = Y,
                      Value3 = X + Y))
```

To use a string template, you must import `Template` from the `string` package using the `import` statement shown. (Chapter 11 tells you how packages work and how to use `import` statements.)

The code begins by creating a variable, Sums, as a template that contains three replacement values: $Value1, $Value2, and $Value3. You can replace these values with anything and in any order, as shown in the next line.

2. **Click Run Cell.**

   Python outputs the expected templated string, as shown in Figure 12-9.

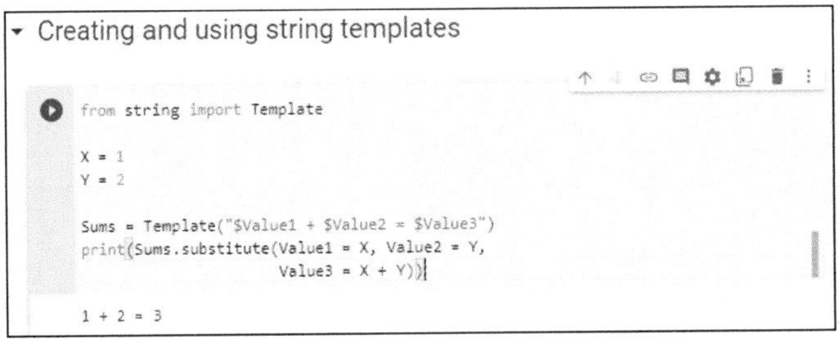

FIGURE 12-9:
String templates
enable you to
create reusable
content with
ease.

Creating and using string templates

```
from string import Template

X = 1
Y = 2

Sums = Template("$Value1 + $Value2 = $Value3")
print(Sums.substitute(Value1 = X, Value2 = Y,
                      Value3 = X + Y))

1 + 2 = 3
```

REMEMBER

The replaceable values can literally be anything. For example, you could just as easily replace the preceding `print()` call with `print(Sums.substitute(Value1 = 'A', Value2 = "{:x}".format(90), Value3 = True))`. The output would be A + 5a = True. Of course, no one ever said that the output has to make sense.

Chapter **13**

Managing Lists

A lot of people lose sight of the fact that most programming techniques are based on the real world. Part of the reason is that programmers often use terms that other people don't to describe these real-world objects. For example, most people would call a place to store something a box or a cupboard — but programmers insist on using the term *variable.* Lists are different. Everyone makes lists and uses them in various ways to perform an abundance of tasks. In fact, you're probably surrounded by lists of various sorts where you're sitting right now as you read this book. So, this chapter is about something you already use quite a lot. The only difference is that you need to think of lists in the same way Python does.

You may read that lists are hard to work with. The reason that some people find working with lists difficult is that they're not used to actually thinking about the lists they create. When you create a list, you simply write items down in whatever order makes sense to you. Sometimes you rewrite the list when you're done to put it in a specific order. In other cases, you use your finger as a guide when going down the list to make looking through it easier. The point is that everything you normally do with lists is also doable within Python. The difference is that you must now actually think about what you're doing in order to make Python understand what you want done.

Lists are incredibly important in Python. This chapter introduces you to the concepts used to create, manage, search, and print lists (among other tasks). When you complete the chapter, you can use lists to make your Python applications more robust, faster, and more flexible. In fact, you'll wonder how you ever got along without using lists in the past. The important thing to keep in mind is that you have already used lists most of your life. There really isn't any difference now except that you must now think about the actions that you normally take for granted when managing your own lists.

REMEMBER

You don't have to type the source code for this chapter manually. In fact, using the downloadable source is a lot easier. You can find the source for this chapter in the BPP4D3E; 13; Managing Lists.ipynb file of the downloadable source. See the Introduction for details on how to find these source files.

Organizing Information in an Application

People create lists to organize information and make it easier to access and change. You use lists in Python for the same reason. In many situations, you really do need some sort of organizational aid to hold data. For example, you might want to create a single place to look for days of the week or months of the year. The names of these items would appear in a list, much as they would if you needed to commit them to paper in the real world. The following sections describe lists and how they work in more detail.

Defining organization using lists

The Python specification defines a list as a kind of sequence. *Sequences* simply provide some means of allowing multiple data items to exist together in a single storage unit, but as separate entities. Think about one of those large mail holders you see in apartment buildings. A single mail holder contains a number of small mailboxes, each of which can contain mail. Python supports other kinds of sequences as well (Chapter 14 discusses a number of these sequences):

>> Tuples

>> Dictionaries

>> Stacks

>> Queues

>> Deques

REMEMBER

Of all the sequences, lists are the easiest to understand and are the most directly related to a real-world object. Working with lists helps you become better able to work with other kinds of sequences that provide greater functionality and improved flexibility. The point is that the data is stored in a list much as you would write it on a piece of paper — one item comes after another. The list has a beginning, a middle, and an end. (Even if you might not normally number them in real life, Python always numbers the items for you.)

Understanding how computers view lists

The computer doesn't view lists in the same way that you do. It doesn't have an internal notepad and use a pen to write on it. A computer has memory. The computer stores each item in a list in a separate memory location. The memory is contiguous, so as you add new items, they're added to the next location in memory. In many respects, the computer uses something like a mailbox to hold your list. The list as a whole is the mail holder. As you add items, the computer places them in the next mailbox within the mail holder.

REMEMBER

Just as the mailboxes are numbered in a mail holder, the memory slots used for a list are numbered. The numbers begin with 0, not with 1 as you might expect. (This is the same numbering system as that used with strings, as explained in the "Selecting Individual Characters" section of Chapter 12.) Each mailbox receives the next number in line. A mail holder with the months of the year would contain 12 mailboxes. The mailboxes would be numbered from 0 to 11 (not 1 to 12, as you might think). Getting the numbering scheme down as quickly as possible is essential because even experienced developers get into trouble by using 1 and not 0 as a starting point at times.

Depending on what sort of information you place in each mailbox, the mailboxes need not be of the same size. Python lets you store a string in one mailbox, an integer in another, and a floating-point value in another. The computer doesn't know what kind of information is stored in each mailbox and it doesn't care. All that the computer sees is slots that could hold anything. Python performs all the work required to treat the data elements according to the right type and to ensure that when you request item five, you actually get item five.

TIP

In general, it's good practice to create lists of like items to make the data easier to manage. When creating a list of all integers, for example, rather than of mixed data, you can make assumptions about the information and don't have to spend nearly as much time checking it. However, in some situations, you might need to mix data. Many other programming languages require that lists have just one type of data, but Python offers the flexibility of using mixed data sorts. Just remember that using mixed data in a list means that you must determine the data type when retrieving the information in order to work with the data correctly. Treating a string as an integer would cause problems in your application.

Creating Lists

As in real life, before you can do anything with a list, you must create it. As previously stated, Python lists can mix types. However, restricting a list to a single type when you can is always the best practice. The following steps demonstrate how to create Python lists.

1. **Open a new notebook.**

   You can also use the downloadable source file, BPP4D3E; 13; Managing Lists.ipynb.

2. **Type the following code into a new cell in the notebook — pressing Enter after each line.**

   ```
   List1 = ["One", 1, "Two", True]
   print(List1)
   ```

   Python creates a list named List1 for you. This list contains two string values ("One" and "Two"), an integer value (1), and a Boolean value (True).

REMEMBER

   Notice that each data type that you type is a different color. The color of an entry is a cue that tells you whether you have typed the entry correctly, which helps reduce errors when creating a list.

3. **Click Run Cell.**

   You see the content of the list as a whole, as shown in Figure 13-1. Notice that the string entries appear in single quotes, even though you typed them using double quotes. Strings can appear in either single quotes or double quotes in Python.

▾ Creating Lists

```
List1 = ["One", 1, "Two", True]
print(List1)

['One', 1, 'Two', True]
```

FIGURE 13-1:
Python displays
the content of
List1.

4. **In a new cell in the notebook, type** dir(List1) **and click Run Cell.**

   Python displays a list of actions that you can perform using lists. Notice that the output is actually a list. So, you're using a list to determine what you can do with another list.

REMEMBER

As you start working with objects of greater complexity, you need to remember that the dir() command always shows what tasks you can perform using that object. The actions that appear without underscores are the main actions that you can perform using a list. These actions are the following:

- append
- clear
- copy
- count
- extend
- index
- insert
- pop
- remove
- reverse
- sort

Accessing Lists

After you create a list, you want to access the information it contains. An object isn't particularly useful if you can't at least access the information it contains. The previous section shows how to use the print() and dir() functions to interact with List1, but other ways exist to perform the task, as described in the following steps.

1. **In a new cell in the notebook, type** List1[1] **and click Run Cell.**

   You see the value 1 as output. The use of a number within a set of square brackets is called an *index*. Python always uses zero-based indexes, so asking for the element at index 1 means getting the second element in the list.

2. **In a new cell in the notebook, type** List1[1:3] **and click Run Cell.**

   You see a range of values that includes two elements. When typing a range, the end of the range is always one greater than the number of elements returned. In this case, that means that you get elements 1 and 2, not elements 1 through 3 as you might expect.

3. **In a new cell in the notebook, type** List1[1:] **and click Run Cell.**

You see all the elements, starting from element 1 to the end of the list. A range can have a blank ending number, which simply means to print the rest of the list.

4. **In a new cell in the notebook, type** List1[:3] **and click Run Cell.**

Python displays the elements from 0 through 2. Leaving the start of a range blank means that you want to start with element 0. Figure 13-2 shows the result of the various list-indexing tasks you've performed so far.

```
▾ Accessing Lists

[3]  List1[1]

     1

[4]  List1[1:3]

     [1, 'Two']

[5]  List1[1:]

     [1, 'Two', True]

⏵  List1[:3]

     ['One', 1, 'Two']
```

FIGURE 13-2: Knowing the correct indexing operation to perform is important.

TECHNICAL STUFF

Even though doing so is really confusing, you can use negative indexes with Python. Instead of working from the left, Python will work from the right and backward. For example, if you have List1 = ["One", 1, "Two", True] and type List1[-2], you get Two as output. Likewise, typing List1[-3] results in an output of 1. The rightmost element is element –1 in this case.

Looping through Lists

To automate the processing of list elements, you need some way to loop through the list. The easiest way to perform this task is to rely on a for statement, as described in the following steps.

1. **Type the following code into a new cell in the notebook — pressing Enter after each line.**

```
List1 = [0, 1, 2, 3, 4, 5]
for Item in List1:
    print(Item)
```

The example begins by creating a list consisting of numeric values. It then uses a `for` loop to obtain each element in turn and print it onscreen.

2. **Click Run Cell.**

   Python shows the individual values in the list, one on each line, as shown in Figure 13-3.

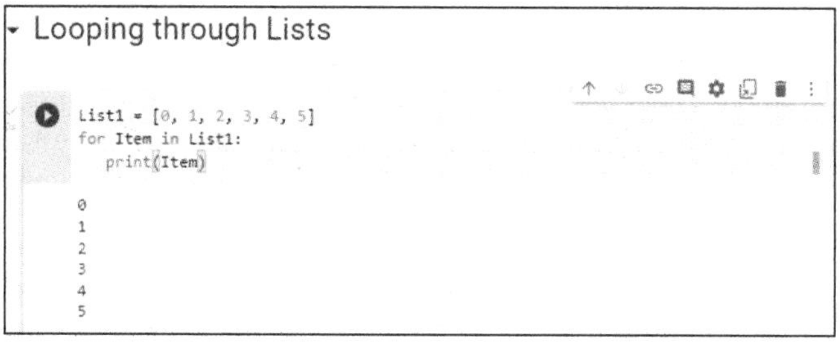

FIGURE 13-3:
A loop makes it easy to obtain a copy of each item and process it as needed.

FIGURE 13-3: A loop makes it easy to obtain a copy of each item and process it as needed.

Modifying Lists

You can modify the content of a list as needed. Modifying a list means to change a particular entry, add a new entry, or remove an existing entry. To perform these tasks, you must sometimes read an entry. The concept of modification is found within the acronym CRUD, which stands for Create, Read, Update, and Delete. Here are the list functions associated with CRUD:

>> `append()`: Adds a new entry to the end of the list.

>> `clear()`: Removes all entries from the list.

>> `copy()`: Creates a copy of the current list and places it in a new list.

>> `extend()`: Adds items from an existing list and into the current list.

>> `insert()`: Adds a new entry to the position specified in the list.

>> `pop()`: Removes an entry from the end of the list.

>> `remove()`: Removes an entry from the specified position in the list.

The following steps show how to perform modification tasks with lists. This is a hands-on exercise. As the book progresses, you see these same functions used within application code. The purpose of this exercise is to help you gain a feel for how lists work.

1. **Type the following code into a new cell in the notebook — pressing Enter after each line.**

```
List2 = []
len(List2)
```

Python creates a list named List2 for you. Notice that the square brackets are empty. List2 doesn't contain any entries. You can create empty lists that you fill with information later. In fact, this is precisely how many lists start because you usually don't know what information they will contain until the user interacts with the list.

2. **Click Run Cell.**

The len() function outputs 0. When creating an application, you can check for an empty list by using the len() function. If a list is empty, you can't perform tasks such as removing elements from it because there is nothing to remove.

3. **Type the following code into a new cell in the notebook — pressing Enter after each line.**

```
List2.append(1)
len(List2)
```

4. **Click Run Cell.**

The len() function now reports a length of 1.

5. **In a new cell in the notebook, type** List2[0] **and click Run Cell.**

You see the value of 1 stored in element 0 of List2.

6. **Type the following code into a new cell in the notebook — pressing Enter after each line.**

```
List2.insert(0, 2)
List2
```

The insert() function requires two arguments. The first argument is the index of the insertion, which is element 0 in this case. The second argument is the object you want inserted at that point, which is 2 in this case.

7. **Click Run Cell.**

Python has added another element to List2. However, using the insert() function lets you add the new element before the first element, so the output is now [2, 1].

8. **Type the following code into a new cell in the notebook — pressing Enter after each line.**

```
List3 = List2.copy()
List2.extend(List3)
List2
```

The new list, List3, is a precise copy of List2. Copying is often used to create a temporary version of an existing list so that a program can make temporary modifications to it rather than to the original list. When the user is done, the application can either delete the temporary list or copy it to the original list.

Python copies all the elements in List3 to the end of List2. Extending is commonly used to consolidate two lists.

9. **Click Run Cell.**

You see that the copy and extend processes have worked. List2 now contains the values [2, 1, 2, 1].

10. **Type** List2.pop() **into a new cell of the notebook and click Run Cell.**

Python displays a value of 1. The 1 was stored at the end of the list, and pop( ) always removes values from the end.

USING OPERATORS WITH LISTS

Lists can also rely on operators to perform certain tasks. For example, if you want to create a list that contains four copies of the word *Hello*, you could use MyList = ["Hello"] * 4 to fill it. A list allows repetition as needed. The multiplication operator (*) tells Python how many times to repeat a given item. You need to remember that every repeated element is separate, so what MyList contains is ['Hello', 'Hello', 'Hello', 'Hello'].

You can also use concatenation to fill a list. For example, using MyList = ["Hello"] + ["World"] + ["!"] * 4 creates six elements in MyList. The first element is Hello, followed by World and ending with four elements with one exclamation mark (!) in each element.

The membership operator (in) also works with lists. This chapter uses a straightforward and easy-to-understand method of searching lists (the recommended approach). However, you can use the membership operator to make things shorter and simpler by using "Hello" in MyList. Assuming that you have your list filled with ['Hello', 'World', '!', '!', '!', '!'], the output of this statement is True.

11. **Type** List2.remove(1) **into a new cell of the notebook and click Run Cell.**

This time, Python removes the item at element 1. Unlike the pop( ) function, the remove( ) function doesn't display the value of the item it removed.

12. **Type the following code into a new cell in the notebook — pressing Enter after each line.**

```
List2.clear()
len(List2)
```

Using clear( ) means that the list shouldn't contain any elements now. The len( ) function will affirm that List2 is definitely empty.

13. **Click Run Cell.**

You see that the output is 0. List2 is definitely empty. At this point, you've tried all the modification methods that Python provides for lists as shown in Figure 13-4. Work with List2 some more using these various functions until you feel comfortable making changes to the list.

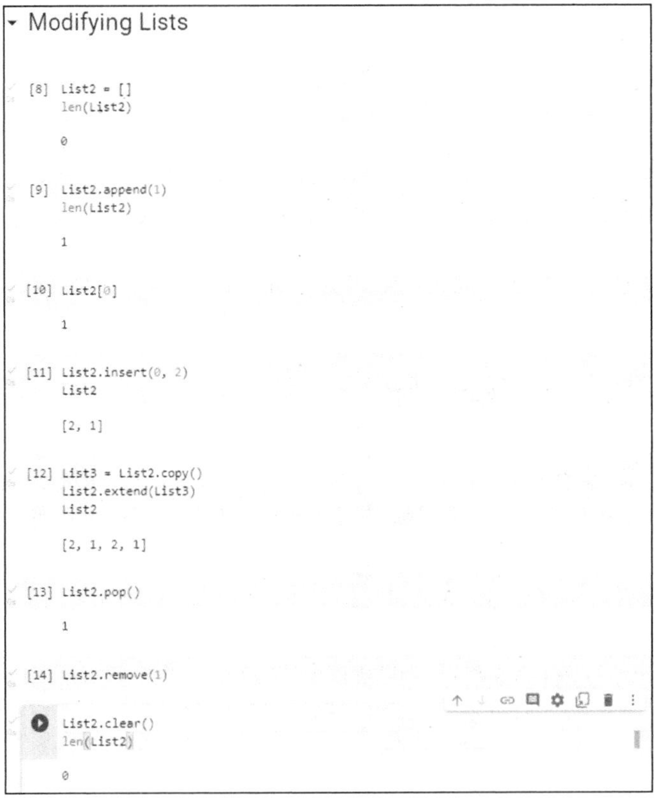

FIGURE 13-4: Python provides a wide range of actions you can perform using lists.

Searching Lists

Modifying a list isn't very easy when you don't know what the list contains. The ability to search a list is essential if you want to make maintenance tasks easier. The following steps help you create an application that demonstrates the ability to search a list for specific values.

1. **Type the following code into a new cell in the notebook — pressing Enter after each line:**

```
Colors = ["Red", "Orange", "Yellow", "Green", "Blue"]
ColorSelect = ""
while str.upper(ColorSelect) != "QUIT":
    ColorSelect = input("Please type a color name: ")
    if (Colors.count(ColorSelect) >= 1):
        print("The color exists in the list!")
    elif (str.upper(ColorSelect) != "QUIT"):
        print("The list doesn't contain the color.")
```

The example begins by creating a list named Colors that contains color names. It also creates a variable named ColorSelect to hold the name of the color that the user wants to find. The application then enters a loop where the user is asked for a color name that is placed in ColorSelect. As long as this variable doesn't contain the word QUIT, the application continues a loop that requests input.

Whenever the user inputs a color name, the application asks the list to count the number of occurrences of that color. When the value is equal to or greater than one, the list does contain the color and an appropriate message appears onscreen. On the other hand, when the list doesn't contain the requested color, an alternative message appears onscreen.

TIP

Notice how this example uses an elif clause to check whether ColorSelect contains the word QUIT. This technique of including an elif clause ensures that the application doesn't output a message when the user wants to quit the application. You need to use similar techniques when you create your applications to avoid potential user confusion or even data loss (when the application performs a task the user didn't actually request).

2. **Click Run Cell.**

Python asks you to type a color name.

3. **Type** Blue **and press Enter.**

You see a message telling you that the color does exist in the list.

4. **Type** Purple **and press Enter.**

You see a message telling you that the color doesn't exist.

5. **Type** Quit **and press Enter.**

The application ends. Notice that the application displays neither a success nor a failure message. Figure 13-5 shows the results of the various inputs.

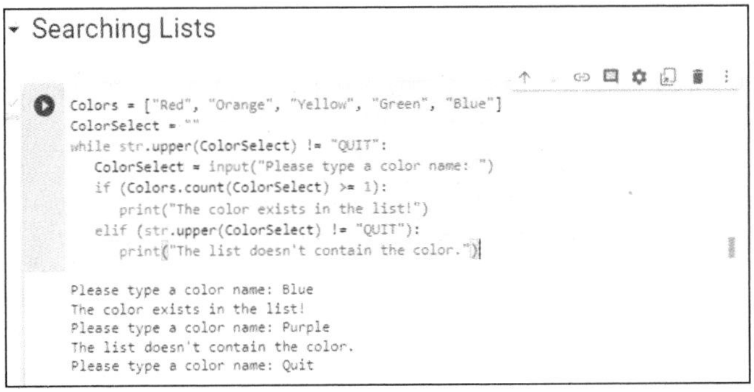

FIGURE 13-5:
Combining loops with conditional code allows multiple selection entries.

```
▼ Searching Lists

  ▶  Colors = ["Red", "Orange", "Yellow", "Green", "Blue"]
     ColorSelect = ""
     while str.upper(ColorSelect) != "QUIT":
         ColorSelect = input("Please type a color name: ")
         if (Colors.count(ColorSelect) >= 1):
             print("The color exists in the list!")
         elif (str.upper(ColorSelect) != "QUIT"):
             print("The list doesn't contain the color.")

     Please type a color name: Blue
     The color exists in the list!
     Please type a color name: Purple
     The list doesn't contain the color.
     Please type a color name: Quit
```

Sorting Lists

The computer can locate information in a list no matter what order it appears in. It's a fact, though, that longer lists are easier to search when you put them in sorted order. However, the main reason to put a list in sorted order is to make it easier for the human user to actually see the information the list contains. People work better with sorted information. This example begins with an unsorted list. It then sorts the list and outputs it to the display. The following steps demonstrate how to perform this task.

1. **Type the following code into a new cell in the notebook — pressing Enter after each line:**

```
Colors = ["Red", "Orange", "Yellow", "Green", "Blue"]
for Item in Colors:
    print(Item, end=" ")
print()
Colors.sort()
for Item in Colors:
    print(Item, end=" ")
print()
```

The example begins by creating an array of colors. The colors are currently in unsorted order. The example then prints the colors in the order in which they appear. Notice the use of the end=" " argument for the print() function to ensure that all color entries remain on one line (making them easier to compare).

Sorting the list is as easy as calling the sort() function. After the example calls the sort() function, it prints the list again so that you can see the result.

REMEMBER

2. **Click Run Cell.**

Python outputs both the unsorted and sorted lists, as shown in Figure 13-6.

FIGURE 13-6:
Sorting a list is as easy as calling the sort() function.

```
Colors = ["Red", "Orange", "Yellow", "Green", "Blue"]
for Item in Colors:
    print(Item, end=" ")
print()
Colors.sort()
for Item in Colors:
    print(Item, end=" ")
print()

Red Orange Yellow Green Blue
Blue Green Orange Red Yellow
```

You may need to sort items in reverse order at times. To accomplish this task, you use the reverse() function. The function must appear on a separate line. So the previous example would look like this if you wanted to sort the colors in reverse order:

TIP

```
Colors = ["Red", "Orange", "Yellow", "Green", "Blue"]
for Item in Colors:
    print(Item, end=" ")
print()
Colors.sort()
Colors.reverse()
for Item in Colors:
    print(Item, end=" ")
print()
```

Printing Lists

Python provides myriad ways to output information. In fact, the number of ways would amaze you. This chapter has shown just a few of the most basic methods for outputting lists so far, using the most basic methods. Real-world printing can become more complex, so you need to know a few additional printing techniques to get you started. Using these techniques is actually a lot easier if you play with them as you go along.

1. **Type the following code into a new cell in the notebook — pressing Enter after each line:**

```
Colors = ["Red", "Orange", "Yellow", "Green", "Blue"]
print(*Colors, sep='\n')
```

This example begins by using the same list of colors in the previous section. In that section, you use a `for` loop to print the individual items. This example takes another approach. It uses the splat (∗) operator, also called the positional expansion operator (and an assortment of other interesting terms), to unpack the list and send each element to the `print()` method one item at a time. The `sep` argument tells how to separate each of the printed outputs, relying on a newline character in this case.

2. **Click Run Cell.**

   Python outputs the list one item at a time.

3. **Type the following code into a new cell in the notebook and click Run Cell.**

```
for Item in Colors: print(Item.rjust(8), sep='\n')
```

Code doesn't have to appear on multiple lines. This example takes two lines of code and places them on just a single line. However, it also demonstrates the use of the `rjust()` method, which right justifies the string. Numerous methods of this sort are described at `https://docs.python.org/3.8/library/string.html`.

4. **Type the following code into a new cell in the notebook and click Run Cell.**

```
print('\n'.join(Colors))
```

Python provides more than one way to perform any task. In this case, the code uses the `join()` method to join the newline character with each member of `Colors`. The output is the same as that shown in Step 3, even though the approach is different. The point is to use the approach that best suits a particular need.

5. **Type the following code into a new cell in the notebook and click Run Cell.**

```
print('First: {0}\nSecond: {1}'.format(*Colors))
```

In this case, the output is formatted in a specific way with accompanying text, and the result doesn't include every member of Colors. The {0} and {1} entries represent placeholders for the values supplied from *Colors. Figure 13-7 shows the output from all of the techniques demonstrated in these steps. You can read more about this approach (the topic is immense) at https://docs.python.org/3/tutorial/inputoutput.html.

```
  Printing Lists

[23] Colors = ["Red", "Orange", "Yellow", "Green", "Blue"]
    print(*Colors, sep='\n')

    Red
    Orange
    Yellow
    Green
    Blue

[24] for Item in Colors: print(Item.rjust(8), sep='/n')

         Red
      Orange
      Yellow
       Green
        Blue

[25] print('\n'.join(Colors))

    Red
    Orange
    Yellow
    Green
    Blue

    print('First: {0}\nSecond: {1}'.format(*Colors))

    First: Red
    Second: Orange
```

FIGURE 13-7: Python provides a lot of different ways to print lists.

REMEMBER This section touches on only some of the common techniques used to format output in Python. There are lots more. You see many of these approaches demonstrated in the chapters that follow. Chapter 12 also demonstrates a number of ways to work with strings. These techniques are also useful when working with lists. The essential goal is to use a technique that's easy to read, works well with all anticipated inputs, and doesn't paint you into a corner when you're creating additional output later.

Working with the Counter Object

Sometimes you have a data source and you simply need to know how often things happen (such as the appearance of a certain item in the list). When you have a short list, you can simply count the items. However, when you have a really long list, getting an accurate count is nearly impossible. For example, consider what it would take if you had a really long novel like *War and Peace* in a list and wanted to know the frequency of the words the novel used. The task would be nearly impossible without a computer. (Some people would insist on counting those words one by one, using 3-x-5 cards to record the result — you know who you are.)

REMEMBER

The Counter object lets you count items quickly. In addition, it's incredibly easy to use. This book shows the Counter object in use a number of times, but this chapter shows how to use it specifically with lists. The example in this section creates a list with repetitive elements and then counts how many times those elements actually appear.

1. **Type the following code into a new cell in the notebook — pressing Enter after each line:**

```
from collections import Counter

MyList = [1, 2, 3, 4, 1, 2, 3, 1, 2, 1, 5]
ListCount = Counter(MyList)
print(ListCount)
for ThisItem in ListCount.items():
    print("Item: ", ThisItem[0],
            " Appears: ", ThisItem[1])
print("The value 1 appears {0} times."
        .format(ListCount.get(1)))
```

To use the Counter object, you must import it from collections. Of course, if you work with other collection types in your application, you can import the entire collections package by typing **import collections** instead.

The example begins by creating a list, MyList, with repetitive numeric elements. You can easily see that some elements appear more than once. The example places the list into a new Counter object, ListCount. You can create Counter objects in all sorts of ways, but this is the most convenient method when working with a list.

WARNING

The Counter object and the list aren't actually connected in any way. When the list content changes, you must re-create the Counter object because it won't automatically see the change. An alternative to re-creating the counter is to call the clear() method first and then call the update() method to fill the Counter object with the new data.

The application prints ListCount in various ways. The first output is the Counter as it appears without any manipulation. The second output prints the individual unique elements in MyList along with the number of times each element appears. To obtain both the element and the number of times it appears, you must use the `items()` function as shown. Finally, the example demonstrates how to obtain an individual count from the list by using the `get()` function.

2. **Click Run Cell.**

Python outputs the results of using the `Counter` object, as shown in Figure 13-8.

Notice that the information is actually stored in the `Counter` as a key and value pair. Chapter 14 discusses this topic in greater detail. All you really need to know for now is that the element found in `MyList` becomes a key in `ListCount` that identifies the unique element name. The value contains the number of times that that element appears within `MyList`.

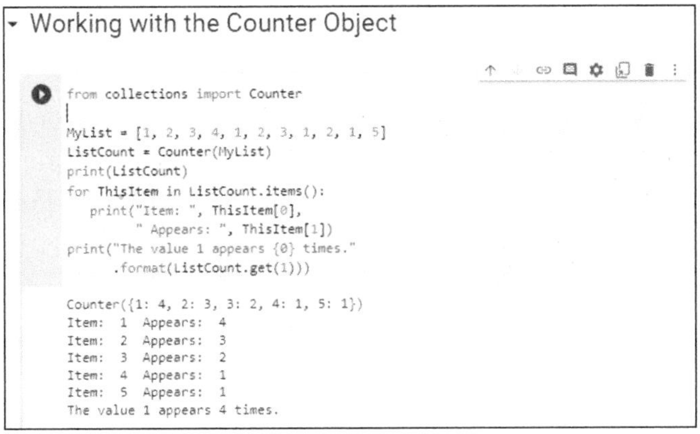

FIGURE 13-8:
The Counter is helpful in obtaining statistics about longer lists.

```
▾ Working with the Counter Object

  ⏵  from collections import Counter

      MyList = [1, 2, 3, 4, 1, 2, 3, 1, 2, 1, 5]
      ListCount = Counter(MyList)
      print(ListCount)
      for ThisItem in ListCount.items():
          print("Item: ", ThisItem[0],
                " Appears: ", ThisItem[1])
      print("The value 1 appears {0} times."
            .format(ListCount.get(1)))

      Counter({1: 4, 2: 3, 3: 2, 4: 1, 5: 1})
      Item:  1  Appears:  4
      Item:  2  Appears:  3
      Item:  3  Appears:  2
      Item:  4  Appears:  1
      Item:  5  Appears:  1
      The value 1 appears 4 times.
```

Chapter **14**

Collecting All Sorts of Data

P eople collect all sorts of things. The CDs stacked near your entertainment center, the plates that are part of a series, baseball cards, and even the pens from every restaurant you've ever visited are all collections. The collections you encounter when you write applications are the same as the collections in the real world. A *collection* is simply a grouping of like items in one place and usually organized into some easily understood form.

REMEMBER

This chapter is about collections of various sorts. The central idea behind every collection is to create an environment in which the collection is properly managed and lets you easily locate precisely what you want at any given time. A set of bookshelves works great for storing books, DVDs, and other sorts of flat items. However, you probably put your pen collection in a holder or even a display case. The difference in storage locations doesn't change the fact that both house collections. The same is true with computer collections. Yes, differences exist between a stack and a queue, but the main idea is to provide the means to manage data properly and make it easy to access when needed.

REMEMBER

You don't have to type the source code for this chapter manually. In fact, using the downloadable source is a lot easier. You can find the source for this chapter in the BPP4D3E; 14; Collection All Sorts of Data.ipynb file of the downloadable source. See the Introduction for details on how to find these source files.

Understanding Collections

In Chapter 13, you're introduced to sequences. *Collections* are simply another kind of sequence, albeit a more complex sequence than you find in either a string or list. No matter which sequence you use, they all support two functions: index() and count(). The index() function always returns the position of a specified item in the sequence. For example, you can return the position of a character in a string or the position of an object in a list. The count() function returns the number of times a specific item appears in the list. Again, the kind of specific item depends upon the kind of sequence.

You can use collections to create database-like structures using Python. Each collection type has a different purpose, and you use the various types in specific ways. The important idea to remember is that collections are simply another kind of sequence. As with every other kind of sequence, collections always support the index() and count() functions as part of their base functionality.

Python is designed to be extensible. However, it does rely on a base set of collections that you can use to create most application types. This chapter describes the most common collections (some implemented as a programming convention, like tuple and dictionary, some implemented using another class, such as stack, and some implemented directly using classes, such as queue and deque):

>> **Tuple:** A tuple is a collection used to create complex list-like sequences. An advantage of tuples is that you can nest the content of a tuple. This feature lets you create structures that can hold employee records or x-y coordinate pairs.

>> **Dictionary:** As with the real dictionaries, you create key/value pairs when using the dictionary collection (think of a word and its associated definition). A dictionary provides incredibly fast search times and makes ordering data significantly easier. Python offers a number of classes to implement the dictionary data storage collection. See https://docs.python.org/3/library/collections.html for a typical list of collections classes.

>> **Stack:** Most programming languages support stacks directly. However, Python doesn't support the stack, although there's a work-around for that. A stack is a last in/first out (LIFO) sequence. Think of a pile of pancakes: You can add new pancakes to the top and also take them off of the top. A stack is an important collection that you can simulate in Python by using a list, which is precisely what this chapter does.

>> queue: A queue is a first in/first out (FIFO) collection. You use it to track items that need to be processed in some way. Think of a queue as a line at the bank. You go into the line, wait your turn, and are eventually called to talk with a teller.

>> deque (pronounced *deck*): A double-ended queue (deque) is a queue-like structure that lets you add or remove items from either end, but not from the middle. You can use a deque as a queue or a stack or any other kind of collection to which you're adding and from which you're removing items in an orderly manner (in contrast to lists, tuples, and dictionaries, which allow randomized access and management).

Working with Tuples

As previously mentioned, a tuple is a collection used to create complex lists, in which you can embed one tuple within another. This embedding lets you create hierarchies with tuples. A hierarchy could be something as simple as the directory listing of your hard drive or an organizational chart for your company. The idea is that you can create complex data structures by using a tuple.

REMEMBER

Tuples are immutable, which means you can't change them. You can create a new tuple with the same name and modify it in some way, but you can't modify an existing tuple. Lists are mutable, which means that you can change them. So, a tuple can seem at first to be at a disadvantage, but immutability has all sorts of advantages, such as being more secure as well as faster. In addition, immutable objects are easier to use with multiple processors.

The biggest difference between a tuple and a list is that a tuple is immutable; making tuples used more often for data access, rather than data operations. Immutability also makes a tuple faster to use, consume less memory, and have fewer method calls associated with it. The following steps demonstrate how you can interact with a tuple in Python.

1. **Open a new notebook.**

    You can also use the downloadable source file, BPP4D3E; 14; Collection All Sorts of Data.ipynb.

2. **Type the following code into the notebook — pressing Enter after each line:**

    ```
    MyTuple = ("Red", "Blue", "Green")
    MyTuple
    ```

    Python creates a tuple containing three strings.

3. **Click Run Cell.**

You see the content of `MyTuple`, which is three strings, as shown in Figure 14-1. Notice that the entries use single quotes, even though you used double quotes to create the tuple. In addition, notice that a tuple uses parentheses rather than square brackets, as lists do.

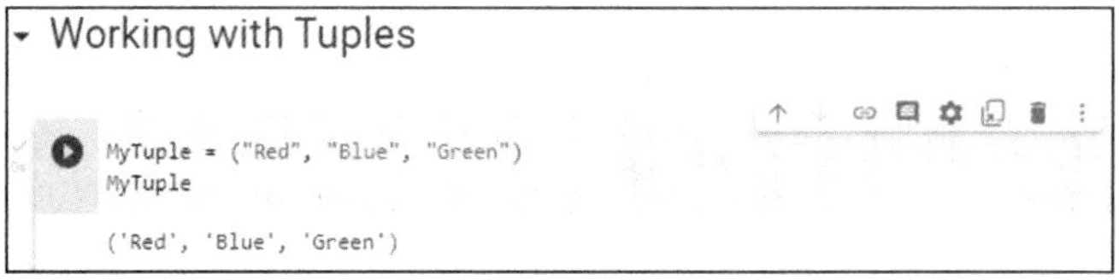

FIGURE 14-1:
Tuples use
parentheses, not
square brackets.

```
Working with Tuples

MyTuple = ("Red", "Blue", "Green")
MyTuple

('Red', 'Blue', 'Green')
```

4. **Type** print(dir(MyTuple)) **and click Run Cell.**

Python presents a list of functions that you can use with tuples as shown here:

['__add__', '__class__', '__contains__',

'__delattr__', '__dir__', '__doc__', '__eq__',

'__format__', '__ge__', '__getattribute__',

'__getitem__', '__getnewargs__', '__gt__',

'__hash__', '__init__', '__init_subclass__',

'__iter__', '__le__', '__len__', '__lt__', '__mul__',

'__ne__', '__new__', '__reduce__', '__reduce_ex__',

'__repr__', '__rmul__', '__setattr__', '__sizeof__',

'__str__', '__subclasshook__', 'count', 'index']

Notice that the list of functions appears significantly smaller than the list of functions provided with lists in Chapter 13. The `count()` and `index()` functions are present.

However, appearances can be deceiving. For example, you can add new items by using the `__add__()` function. When working with Python objects, look at all the entries before you make a decision as to functionality.

REMEMBER

5. **Type the following code into a new cell in the notebook — pressing Enter after each line:**

```
MyTuple = MyTuple.__add__(("Purple",))
MyTuple
```

This code adds a new tuple to `MyTuple` and places the result in a new copy of `MyTuple`. The old copy of `MyTuple` is destroyed after the call.

REMEMBER

The `__add__()` function accepts only tuples as input. This means that you must enclose the addition in parentheses. In addition, when creating a tuple with a single entry, you must add a comma after the entry, as shown in the example. This is an odd Python rule that you need to keep in mind or you'll see an error message similar to this one:

```
TypeError: can only concatenate tuple (not "str") to
    tuple
```

6. **Click Run Cell.**

The addition to `MyTuple` appears at the end of the list. Notice that it appears at the same level as the other entries.

7. **Type the following code into a new cell in the notebook — pressing Enter after each line:**

```
MyTuple = MyTuple.__add__(("Yellow",
                         ("Orange", "Black")))
MyTuple[4]
```

This step adds three entries: Yellow, Orange, and Black. However, Orange and Black are added as a tuple within the main tuple, which creates a hierarchy. These two entries are actually treated as a single entry within the main tuple.

TIP

You can replace the `__add__()` function with the concatenation operator. For example, if you wanted to add Magenta to the front of the tuple list, you could type `MyTuple = ("Magenta",) + MyTuple`.

8. **Click Run Cell.**

Python displays a single member of `MyTuple`, `'Yellow'`. Tuples use indexes to access individual members, just as lists do. You can also specify a range when needed. Anything you can do with a list index you can also do with a tuple index.

9. **Type MyTuple[5] and click Run Cell.**

You see a tuple that contains the tuple (`'Orange'`, `'Black'`). Of course, you might not want to use both members in tuple form.

10. **Type type(MyTuple[5]) == tuple and click Run Cell.**

TIP

Tuples do contain hierarchies on a regular basis. You can detect when an index has returned another tuple, rather than a value, by testing for type. The output is `True` in this case.

11. **Type** MyTuple[5][0] **and click Run Cell.**

At this point, you see Orange as output. Figure 14-2 shows the results of the previous commands so that you can see the progression of index usage. The indexes always appear in order of their level in the hierarchy.

TIP

Using a combination of indexes and the __add__( ) function (or the concatenation operator, +), you can create flexible applications that rely on tuples. For example, you can remove an element from a tuple by making it equal to a range of values. If you wanted to remove the tuple containing Orange and Black, you type MyTuple = MyTuple[0:5].

```
[1]  MyTuple = ("Red", "Blue", "Green")
     MyTuple

     ('Red', 'Blue', 'Green')

[2]  print(dir(MyTuple))

     ['__add__', '__class__', '__contains__', '__delattr__', '__dir__', '__doc__', '__e
     ◄                                                                              ►

[3]  MyTuple = MyTuple.__add__(("Purple",))
     MyTuple

     ('Red', 'Blue', 'Green', 'Purple')

[4]  MyTuple = MyTuple.__add__(("Yellow",
                                ("Orange", "Black")))
     MyTuple[4]

     'Yellow'

[5]  MyTuple[5]

     ('Orange', 'Black')

[6]  type(MyTuple[5]) == tuple

     True

 ▶   MyTuple[5][0]

     'Orange'
```

FIGURE 14-2:
Use indexes to gain access to the individual tuple members.

Working with Dictionaries

A Python dictionary works just the same as its real-world counterpart — you create a key and value pair. It's just like the word and definition in a dictionary. As with lists, dictionaries are mutable, which means that you can change them as needed. The main reason to use a dictionary is to make information lookup faster. The key is normally short and is always unique so that the computer doesn't spend a lot of time looking for the information you need.

The following sections demonstrate how to create and use a dictionary in various ways. When you know how to work with dictionaries, you use that knowledge to make up for deficiencies in the Python language. Most languages include the concept of a switch statement, which is essentially a menu of choices from which one choice is selected. Python doesn't include this option, so you must normally rely on if...elif statements to perform the task, but you can also use dictionaries. (Such statements work, but they aren't as clear as they could be.)

Creating and using a dictionary

Creating and using a dictionary is much like working with a list, except that you must now define a key and value pair. Here are the special rules for creating a key:

>> **The key must be unique.** When you enter a duplicate key, the information found in the second entry wins — the first entry is simply replaced with the second.

>> **The key must be immutable.** This rule means that you can use strings, numbers, or tuples for the key. You can't, however, use a list for a key.

You have no restrictions on the values you provide. A value can be any Python object, so you can use a dictionary to access an employee record or other complex data. The following steps help you understand how to use dictionaries better.

1. **Type the following code into a new cell in the notebook — pressing Enter after each line:**

   ```
   Colors = {"Sam": "Blue", "Amy": "Red",
             "Sarah": "Yellow"}
   Colors
   ```

   Python creates a dictionary containing three entries with people's favorite colors. Notice how you create the key and value pair and that you use curly braces instead of square brackets or parentheses. The key comes first, followed by a colon and then the value. Each entry is separated by a comma.

2. **Click Run Cell.**

   You see the key and value pairs, as shown in Figure 14-3. The downside is that creating the dictionary takes longer than using something like a list because the computer needs to work with additional data.

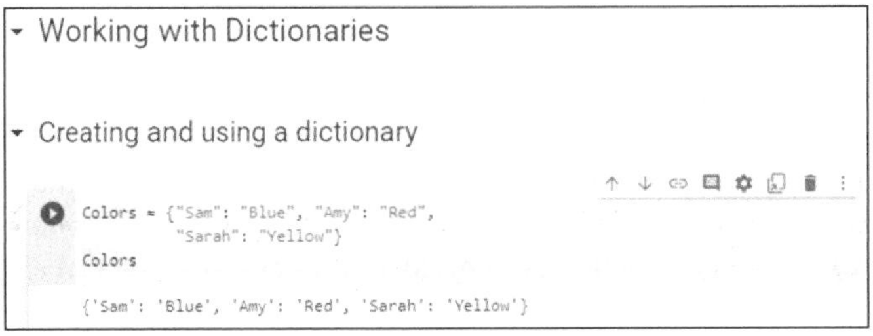

FIGURE 14-3:
A dictionary places entries in sorted order.

3. **Type** Colors["Sarah"] **and click Run Cell.**

You see the color associated with Sarah, 'Yellow'. Using a string as a key, rather than using a numeric index, makes the code easier to read and makes it self-documenting to an extent. By making your code more readable, dictionaries save you considerable time in the long run (which is why they're so popular). However, the access speed of a dictionary comes at the cost of additional creation time and a higher use of resources, so you have trade-offs to consider.

4. **Type** Colors.keys() **and click Run Cell.**

The dictionary presents a list of the keys it contains: dict_keys(['Sam', 'Amy', 'Sarah']). You can use these keys to automate access to the dictionary.

5. **Type the following code into a new cell in the notebook — pressing Enter after each line, and then click Run Cell.**

```
for Item in Colors.keys():
    print("{0} likes the color {1}."
        .format(Item, Colors[Item]))
```

REMEMBER

The example code outputs a listing of each of the usernames and the user's favorite color:

```
Sam likes the color Blue.
Amy likes the color Red.
Sarah likes the color Yellow.
```

Using dictionaries can make creating useful output a lot easier. The use of a meaningful key means that the key can easily be part of the output.

6. **Type the following code into a new cell in the notebook — pressing Enter after each line, and then click Run Cell.**

```
Colors["Sarah"] = "Purple"
Colors.update({"Harry": "Orange"})
```

```
for name, color in Colors.items():
    print("{0} likes the color {1}."
          .format(name, color))
```

The dictionary content is updated so that Sarah now likes Purple instead of Yellow. The code also adds new entry to the dictionary.

TIP

The loop used in this case also differs from the one used in Step 5. This version obtains each of the items one at a time and places the key in name and the value in color. The output will always work the same from the items() method. You need two variables, one for the key and another for the value, presented in the order shown. The reason to consider this second form is that it might be easier to read in some cases. There doesn't seem to be much of a speed difference between the two versions. Here is the updated output:

```
Sam likes the color Blue.
Amy likes the color Red.
Sarah likes the color Purple.
Harry likes the color Orange.
```

Notice that Harry is added to the dictionary. In addition, Sarah's entry is changed to the color Purple.

7. **Type the following code into a new cell in the notebook — pressing Enter after each line, and then click Run Cell.**

```
del Colors["Sam"]
for name, color in Colors.items():
    print("{0} likes the color {1}."
          .format(name, color))
```

Python removes Sam's entry from the dictionary. Here is the new output from the example:

```
Amy likes the color Red.
Sarah likes the color Purple.
Harry likes the color Orange.
```

8. **Type** len(Colors) **and click Run Cell.**

The output value of 3 verifies that the dictionary contains only three entries now, rather than four.

9. **Type the following code into a new cell in the notebook — pressing Enter after each line, and then click Run Cell.**

```
Colors.clear()
len(Colors)
```

Python reports that `Colors` has 0 entries, so the dictionary is now empty. Figure 14-4 shows the results of the previous commands so that you can see the progression of `dictionary` usage.

```
[9]  Colors["Sarah"]

     'Yellow'

[10] Colors.keys()

     dict_keys(['Sam', 'Amy', 'Sarah'])

[11] for Item in Colors.keys():
         print("{0} likes the color {1}."
             .format(Item, Colors[Item]))

     Sam likes the color Blue.
     Amy likes the color Red.
     Sarah likes the color Yellow.

[12] Colors["Sarah"] = "Purple"
     Colors.update({"Harry": "Orange"})
     for name, color in Colors.items():
         print("{0} likes the color {1}."
             .format(name, color))

     Sam likes the color Blue.
     Amy likes the color Red.
     Sarah likes the color Purple.
     Harry likes the color Orange.

[13] del Colors["Sam"]
     for name, color in Colors.items():
         print("{0} likes the color {1}."
             .format(name, color))

     Amy likes the color Red.
     Sarah likes the color Purple.
     Harry likes the color Orange.

[14] len(Colors)

     3


     Colors.clear()
     len(Colors)

     0
```

FIGURE 14-4: Dictionaries work much like lists do, but with a little extra functionality added.

Working with nested dictionaries

Unlike the dictionary on your screen (or possibly your shelf), a Python dictionary entry can contain another dictionary. It's like watching one of those Dr. Strange movies with the whole multiverse scenarios in action (see `https://www.imdb.com/title/tt9419884/` for details). Nesting dictionaries gives you all sorts of new Python powers that will amaze friends, family, and colleagues alike! Creating a nested dictionary is like creating a regular dictionary in that the keys still need to be unique, but the values are now other dictionaries. Here's how to create a nested dictionary:

1. **Type the following code into a new cell in the notebook — pressing Enter after each line:**

```
MyCompany = {"Owners": "Me",
            "Managers": {151: "Marta",
                         152: "Jerry"},
            "Programmers": {251: "Amy",
                            252: "Albert"},
            "Grunts": {351: "Gus",
                       352: "Sidney"}
           }
MyCompany
```

Python creates a nested, two-level dictionary containing four entries at the first level: Owners, Managers, Programmers, and Grunts. The second level contains an employee number, followed by a name.

2. **Click Run Cell.**

You see the key and value pairs, as shown in Figure 14-5.

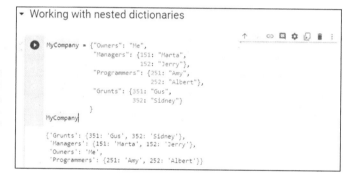

FIGURE 14-5: Nested dictionaries follow the same rules as regular dictionaries, just a little more complex.

REMEMBER

Nested dictionaries require a little extra processing if you want to fully display their content. This means using recursion or some other method to drill down into the dictionary. The next step demonstrates one technique for performing this task.

3. **Type the following code into a new cell in the notebook — pressing Enter after each line:**

```
def DisplayDict(Dict):
    for key, value in Dict.items():
        if type(value) == dict:
            print(f"{key} department includes:")
            DisplayDict(value)
```

```
        else:
            print(f"{value} is {key}")

    DisplayDict(MyCompany)
```

The code begins by calling `DisplayDict()` with MyCompany. This example uses a recursive technique in which the `value` extracted from `Dict` is first checked to determine whether it's another dictionary (type `dict`). If so, the key is actually the name of a department and is displayed as such. (Notice that this example uses an f-string, which is explained in the "Simplifying things using f-string" section of Chapter 12.) The code then recursively calls `DisplayDict()` with `value`.

After the code determines that `value` doesn't contain a dictionary, it proceeds to display the `value` with the key, the way it's done in the previous section of the chapter, except this version uses an f-string in place of the `.format()` function approach. Compare the two versions and you'll notice that the f-string approach definitely saves typing and is easier to read. Figure 14-6 shows the outputs of working with nested dictionaries.

```
def DisplayDict(Dict):
    for key, value in Dict.items():
        if type(value) == dict:
            print(f"{key} department includes:")
            DisplayDict(value)
        else:
            print(f"{value} is {key}")

DisplayDict(MyCompany)

Me is Owners
Managers department includes:
Marta is 151
Jerry is 152
Programmers department includes:
Amy is 251
Albert is 252
Grunts department includes:
Gus is 351
Sidney is 352
```

FIGURE 14-6: Recursion makes working with nested dictionaries easier.

Replacing the switch statement with a dictionary

Most programming languages provide some sort of switch statement. A switch statement provides for elegant menu type selections. The user has a number of options but is allowed to choose only one of them. The program takes some course of action based on the user selection. Here is some representative code (it won't execute) of a `switch` statement you might find in another language:

```
switch(n)
{
```

```
        case 0:
            print("You selected blue.");
            break;
        case 1:
            print("You selected yellow.");
            break;
        case 2:
            print("You selected green.");
            break;
    }
```

The application normally presents a menu-type interface, obtains the number of the selection from the user, and then chooses the correct course of action from the `switch` statement. It's straightforward and much neater than using a series of `if` statements to accomplish the same task.

Unfortunately, Python doesn't come with a switch statement. The best you can hope to do is use an `if...elif` statement for the task. However, by using a `dictionary`, you can simulate the use of a switch statement. The following steps help you create an example that will demonstrate the required technique.

1. **Type the following code into a new cell in the notebook — pressing Enter after each line:**

    ```
    def PrintBlue():
        print("You chose blue!\r\n")
    def PrintRed():
        print("You chose red!\r\n")
    def PrintOrange():
        print("You chose orange!\r\n")
    def PrintYellow():
        print("You chose yellow!\r\n")
    ```

    Before the code can do anything for you, you must define the tasks. Each of these functions defines a task associated with selecting a color option onscreen. Only one of them gets called at any given time.

2. **Type the following code into the same cell in the notebook — pressing Enter after each line:**

    ```
    ColorSelect = {
        0: PrintBlue,
        1: PrintRed,
        2: PrintOrange,
        3: PrintYellow
    }
    ```

This code is the `dictionary`. Each key is like the case part of the switch statement. The values specify what to do. In other words, this is the switch structure. The functions that you created earlier are the action part of the switch — the part that goes between the case statement and the break clause.

3. **Type the following code into the same cell in the notebook — pressing Enter after each line:**

```
Selection = 0
while (Selection != 4):
    print("0. Blue")
    print("1. Red")
    print("2. Orange")
    print("3. Yellow")
    print("4. Quit")
    Selection = int(input("Select a color option: "))
    if (Selection >= 0) and (Selection < 4):
        ColorSelect[Selection]()
```

Finally, you see the user interface part of the example. The code begins by creating an input variable, `Selection`. It then goes into a loop until the user enters a value of 4.

During each loop, the application displays a list of options and then waits for user input. When the user does provide input, the application performs a range check on it. Any value between 0 and 3 selects one of the functions defined earlier using the `dictionary` as the switching mechanism.

4. **Click Run Cell.**

Python displays a menu.

5. **Type** 0 **and press Enter.**

The application tells you that you selected blue and then displays the menu again.

6. **Type** 4 **and press Enter.**

The application ends. Figure 14-7 shows the results of using this technique.

FIGURE 14-7:
After displaying
your selection,
the application
displays the
menu again.

Creating Stacks Using Lists

A stack is a handy programming structure because you can use it to save an application execution environment (the state of variables and other attributes of the application environment at any given time) or as a means of determining an order of execution. Unfortunately, Python doesn't provide a stack as a collection. However, it does provide lists, and you can use a list as a perfectly acceptable stack. The following steps help you create an example of using a list as a stack.

1. **Type the following code into a new cell in the notebook — pressing Enter after each line:**

    ```python
    MyStack = []
    StackSize = 3
    def DisplayStack():
        print("Stack currently contains:")
        for Item in MyStack:
            print(Item)
    ```

```
def Push(Value):
    if len(MyStack) < StackSize:
        MyStack.append(Value)
        print(f"{Value} added")
    else:
        print("Stack is full!")
def Pop():
    if len(MyStack) > 0:
        Removed = MyStack.pop()
        print(f"{Removed} removed from stack")
    else:
        print("Stack is empty.")
Push(1)
Push(2)
Push(3)
DisplayStack()
input("Press any key when ready...")
Push(4)
DisplayStack()
input("Press any key when ready...")
Pop()
DisplayStack()
input("Press any key when ready...")
Pop()
Pop()
Pop()
DisplayStack()
```

In this example, the application creates a `list` and a variable to determine the maximum stack size. Stacks normally have a specific size range. This is admittedly a really small stack, but it serves well for the example's needs.

REMEMBER

Stacks work by pushing a value onto the top of the stack and popping values back off the top of the stack. The `Push()` and `Pop()` functions perform these two tasks. The code adds `DisplayStack()` to make it easier to see the stack content as needed.

The remaining code *exercises the stack* (demonstrates its functionality) by pushing values onto it and then removing them. Four main exercise sections test stack functionality.

2. **Click Run Cell.**

   Python fills the stack with information and then displays it onscreen like this:

   ```
   1 added
   2 added
   ```

```
3 added
Stack currently contains:
1
2
3
```

In this case, 3 is at the top of the stack because it's the last value added. The input() function provides a good way to momentarily stop application execution so that you can see the current stack state. The input() function argument, "Press any key when ready...", tells input() what to provide as a prompt.

3. Press Enter.

The application attempts to push another value onto the stack. However, the stack is full, so the task fails with a Stack is full! message followed by the content of the stack, which is the same as before.

4. Press Enter.

The application pops a value from the top of the stack. Remember that 3 is the top of the stack, so that's the value that is missing in the output:

```
3 removed from stack
Stack currently contains:
1
2
```

5. Press Enter.

The application tries to pop more values from the stack than it contains, resulting in an error and then a display of the now empty stack:

```
2 removed from stack
1 removed from stack
Stack is empty.
Stack currently contains:
```

Any stack implementation that you create must be able to detect both overflows (too many entries) and underflows (too few entries).

Working with queues

A queue works differently from a stack. Think of any line you've ever stood in: You go to the back of the line, and when you reach the front of the line you get to do whatever you stood in the line to do. A queue is often used for task scheduling and to maintain program flow — just as it is in the real world. The following steps help you create a queue-based application.

1. **Type the following code into a new cell in the notebook — pressing Enter after each line:**

```
import queue
MyQueue = queue.Queue(3)
print(MyQueue.empty())
input("Press any key when ready...")
MyQueue.put(1)
MyQueue.put(2)
print(MyQueue.empty())
print(MyQueue.full())
input("Press any key when ready...")
MyQueue.put(3)
print(MyQueue.full())
input("Press any key when ready...")
print(MyQueue.get())
print(MyQueue.empty())
print(MyQueue.full())
input("Press any key when ready...")
print(MyQueue.get())
print(MyQueue.get())
```

To create a queue, you must import the queue package. This package actually contains a number of queue types, but this example uses only the standard FIFO queue.

REMEMBER

When a queue is empty, the empty() function returns True. Likewise, when a queue is full, the full() function returns True. You can't iterate through a queue using a for loop as you have done with other collection types, so you must monitor empty() and full() instead.

The two functions used to work with data in a queue are put(), which adds new data, and get(), which removes data. A problem with queues is that if you try to put more items into the queue than it can hold, it simply waits until space is available to hold it.

2. **Click Run Cell.**

Python tests the state of the queue. In this case, you see an output of True, which means that the queue is empty.

3. **Press Enter.**

The application adds two new values to the queue. In doing so, the queue is no longer empty, as shown by the call to empty(), but a test of full() shows that it's not full either.

4. **Press Enter.**

The application adds another entry to the queue, which means that the queue is now full because it was set to a size of 3. This means that full() will return True because the queue is now full.

5. **Press Enter.**

To free space in the queue, the application gets one of the entries. Whenever an application gets an entry, the get() function returns that entry. Given that 1 was the first value added to the queue, the print() function will display a value of 1. In addition, both empty() and full() should now return False.

6. **Press Enter.**

The application gets the remaining two entries. You see 2 and 3 (in turn) as output.

Working with deques

A deque is simply a queue where you can remove and add items from either end. In many languages, a queue or stack starts out as a deque. Specialized code serves to limit deque functionality to what is needed to perform a particular task.

When working with a deque, you need to think of the deque as a sort of horizontal line. Certain individual functions work with the left and right ends of the deque so that you can add and remove items from either side, but nothing changes the middle. The following steps help you create an example that demonstrates deque usage.

1. **Type the following code into a new cell in the Notebook — pressing Enter after each line.**

```
import collections
MyDeque = collections.deque("abcdef", 10)
print("Starting state:")
for Item in MyDeque:
    print(Item, end=" ")
print("\r\n\r\nAppending and extending right")
MyDeque.append("h")
```

```
MyDeque.extend("ij")
for Item in MyDeque:
    print(Item, end=" ")
print("\r\nMyDeque contains {0} items."
        .format(len(MyDeque)))
print("\r\nPopping right")
print("Popping {0}".format(MyDeque.pop()))
for Item in MyDeque:
    print(Item, end=" ")
print("\r\n\r\nAppending and extending left")
MyDeque.appendleft("a")
MyDeque.extendleft("bc")
for Item in MyDeque:
    print(Item, end=" ")
print("\r\nMyDeque contains {0} items."
        .format(len(MyDeque)))
print("\r\nPopping left")
print("Popping {0}".format(MyDeque.popleft()))
for Item in MyDeque:
    print(Item, end=" ")
print("\r\n\r\nRemoving")
MyDeque.remove("a")
for Item in MyDeque:
    print(Item, end=" ")
```

The implementation of deque is found in the collections package, so you need to import it into your code. When you create a deque, you can optionally specify a starting list of *iterable items* (items that can be accessed and processed as part of a loop structure) and a maximum size, as shown.

REMEMBER

A deque differentiates between adding one item and adding a group of items. You use append() or appendleft() when adding a single item. The extend() and extendleft() functions let you add multiple items. You use the pop() or popleft() functions to remove one item at a time. The act of popping values returns the value popped, so the example prints the value onscreen. The remove() function is unique in that it always works from the left side and always removes the first instance of the requested data.

Unlike some other collections, a deque is fully iterable. This means that you can obtain a list of items by using a for loop whenever necessary.

2. **Click Run Cell.**

Python outputs the following information:

```
Starting state:
a b c d e f

Appending and extending right
a b c d e f h i j
MyDeque contains 9 items.

Popping right
Popping j
a b c d e f h i

Appending and extending left
c b a a b c d e f h
MyDeque contains 10 items.

Popping left
Popping c
b a a b c d e f h

Removing
b a b c d e f h
```

WARNING

Following the output listing closely is important. Notice how the size of the deque changes over time. After the application pops the j, the deque still contains eight items. When the application appends and extends from the left, it adds three more items. However, the resulting deque contains only ten items. When you exceed the maximum size of a deque, the extra data simply falls off the other end.

Chapter **15**

Creating and Using Classes

Classes make working with Python code more convenient by helping to make your applications easy to read, understand, and use. You use classes to create containers for your code and data, so they stay together in one piece. Outsiders see your class as a black box — data goes in and results come out.

REMEMBER

At some point, you need to start constructing classes of your own if you want to avoid the dangers of the spaghetti code that is found in older applications. *Spaghetti code* is much as the name implies — various lines of procedures are interwoven and spread out in such a way that it's hard to figure out where one piece of spaghetti begins and another ends. Trying to maintain spaghetti code is nearly impossible, and some organizations have thrown out applications because no one could figure them out.

Besides helping you understand classes as a packaging method that avoids spaghetti code, this chapter helps you create and use your own classes for the first time. You gain insights into how Python classes work toward making your applications convenient to work with. This is an introductory sort of chapter, though, and you won't become so involved in classes that your head begins to spin around on its own. This chapter is about making class development simple and manageable.

REMEMBER You don't have to type the source code for this chapter manually. In fact, using the downloadable source is a lot easier. You can find the source for this chapter in the BPP4D3E; 15; Creating and Using Classes.ipynb and BPP4D3E; 15; MyClass.ipynb files of the downloadable source. See the Introduction for details on how to find these source files.

Considering the Parts of a Class

A *class* (the blueprint used to create an object) has a specific construction. Each part of a class performs a particular task that gives the class useful characteristics. Of course, the class begins with a container that is used to hold the entire class together, so that's the part that the first section that follows discusses. The remaining sections describe the other parts of a class and help you understand how they contribute to the class as a whole.

Creating the class definition

A class need not be particularly complex. In fact, you can create just the container and one class element and call it a class. Of course, the resulting class won't do much, but you can *instantiate it* (tell Python to build an object by using your class as a blueprint) and work with it as you would any other class. The following steps help you understand the basics behind a class by creating the simplest class possible.

1. **Open a new notebook.**

    You can also use the downloadable source file, BPP4D3E; 15; Creating and Using Classes.ipynb.

2. **Type the following code into the notebook — pressing Enter after each line:**

    ```
    class MyClass:
        MyVar = 0

    MyInstance = MyClass()

    MyInstance.MyVar
    ```

    The first line defines the class container, which consists of the keyword class and the class name, which is MyClass. Every class you create must begin precisely this way. You must always include class followed by the class name.

The second line is the class suite. All the elements that comprise the class are called the *class suite*. In this case, you see a class variable named MyVar, which is set to a value of 0. Every instance of the class will have the same variable and start at the same value.

The fourth line creates an instance of MyClass named MyInstance. Of course, you'll want to verify that you really have created such an instance.

The sixth line outputs the value of MyVar found in the instance of MyInstance.

3. **Click Run Cell.**

   The output of 0, demonstrates that MyInstance does indeed have a class variable named MyVar.

4. **In a new cell, type** MyInstance.__class__ **and click Run Cell.**

   Python displays the class used to create this instance, as shown in Figure 15-1. The output tells you that this class is part of the __main__ package, which means that you typed it directly into the application code and not as part of another package.

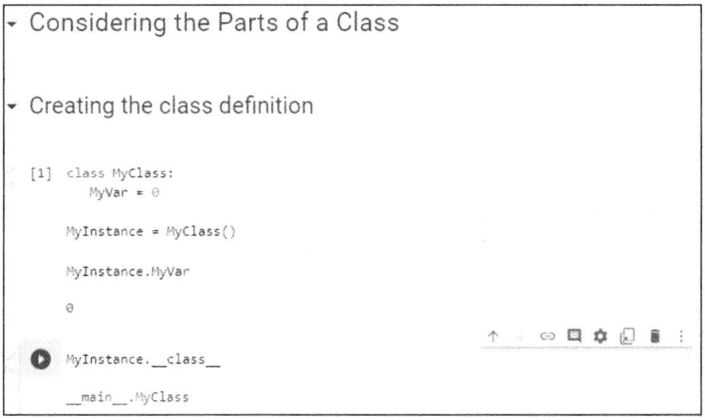

FIGURE 15-1:
The class name is also correct, so you know that this instance is created by using MyClass.

Considering the built-in class attributes

When you create a class, you can easily think that all you get is the class. However, Python adds built-in functionality to your class. For example, in the preceding section, you type __class__ and press Enter. The __class__ attribute is built in; you didn't create it. It helps to know that Python provides this functionality so that you don't have to add it. The functionality is needed often enough that every class should have it, so Python supplies it. The following steps help you work with the built-in class attributes. They assume that you followed the steps in the preceding section, "Creating the class definition."

1. **In a new cell, type** print(dir(MyInstance)) **and click Run Cell.**

   A list of attributes appears below. These attributes provide specific functionality for your class. They're also common to every other class you create, so you can count on always having this functionality in the classes you create.

'MyVar'	'__class__'	'__delattr__'
'__dict__'	'__dir__'	'__doc__'
'__eq__'	'__format__'	'__ge__'
'__getattribute__'	'__gt__'	'__hash__'
'__init__'	'__init_subclass__'	'__le__'
'__lt__'	'__module__'	'__ne__'
'__new__'	'__reduce__'	'__reduce_ex__'
'__repr__'	'__setattr__'	'__sizeof__'
'__str__'	'__subclasshook__'	'__weakref__'

   In a new cell, type help('__class__') **and press Enter.**

   Python displays information on the __class__ attribute, as partially shown in Figure 15-2. You can use the same technique for learning more about any attribute that Python adds to your class.

Working with methods

Methods are simply another kind of function that resides in classes. You create and work with methods in precisely the same way that you do functions, except that methods are always associated with a class (you don't see freestanding methods as you do functions). You can create two kinds of methods: those associated with the class itself and those associated with an instance of a class. It's important to differentiate between the two. The following sections provide the details needed to work with both.

FIGURE 15-2:
Python provides help for each of the attributes it adds to your class.

Creating class methods

A *class method* is one that you execute directly from the class without creating an instance of the class. Sometimes you need to create methods that execute from the class, such as the functions you used with the str class to modify strings. As an example, the multiple exception example in the "Nested exception handling" section of Chapter 10 uses the str.upper() function. The following steps demonstrate how to create and use a class method.

1. **Type the following code into a new cell in the notebook — pressing Enter after each line:**

```
class MyClass:
    def SayHello():
        print("Hello there!")


MyClass.SayHello()
```

The example class contains a single defined attribute, SayHello(). This method doesn't accept any arguments and doesn't return any values. It simply prints a message as output. However, the method works just fine for demonstration purposes.

2. **Click Run Cell.**

The example outputs the expected string, as shown in Figure 15-3. Notice that you didn't need to create an instance of the class — the method is available immediately for use.

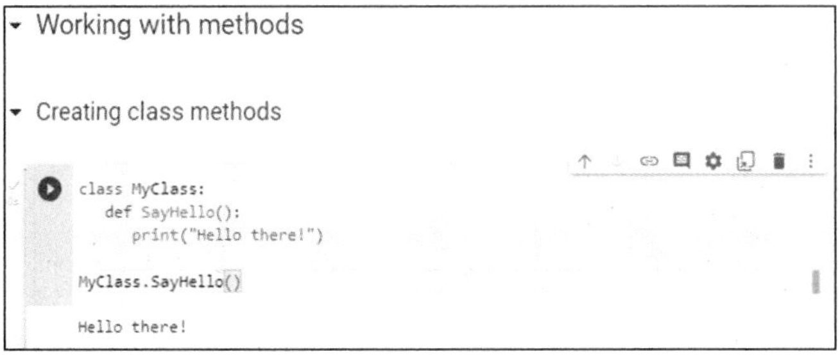

FIGURE 15-3:
The class
method
outputs a
simple message.

▾ Working with methods

▾ Creating class methods

```
class MyClass:
    def SayHello():
        print("Hello there!")

MyClass.SayHello()

Hello there!
```

REMEMBER

A class method can work only with *class data* (the data associated with the class itself, rather than a particular instance of that class). You can pass the method data as an argument, and it can return information as needed, but it can't access the instance data. As a consequence, you need to exercise care when creating class methods to ensure that they're essentially self-contained.

Creating instance methods

An *instance method* is one that is part of the individual instances. You use instance methods to manipulate the data that the class manages. As a consequence, you can't use instance methods until you instantiate an object from the class.

REMEMBER

All instance methods accept a single argument as a minimum, self. The self argument points at the particular instance that the application is using to manipulate data. Without the self argument, the method wouldn't know which instance data to use. However, self is supplied by Python, and you can't change it as part of calling the method. The following steps demonstrate how to create and use instance methods in Python.

1. **Type the following code into a new cell in the notebook — pressing Enter after each line:**

```
class MyClass:
    def SayHello(self):
        print("Hello there!")

MyInstance = MyClass()
MyInstance.SayHello()
```

The example class contains a single defined attribute, SayHello(). This method doesn't accept any special arguments and doesn't return any values. It simply prints a message as output. Notice that this instance version of SayHello() does include the self argument, which is what differentiates it from a class method.

2. **Click Run Cell.**

   You see the same message shown in Figure 15-3.

Working with constructors

A *constructor* is a special kind of method that Python calls when it instantiates an object by using the definitions found in your class. Python relies on the constructor to perform tasks such as *initializing* (assigning values to) any instance variables that the object will need when it starts. Constructors can also verify that there are enough resources for the object and perform any other start-up task you can think of.

REMEMBER

The name of a constructor is always the same, __init__(). The constructor can accept arguments when necessary to create the object. When you create a class without a constructor, Python automatically creates a default constructor for you that doesn't do anything. Every class must have a constructor, even if it simply relies on the default constructor. The following steps demonstrate how to create a constructor:

1. **Type the following code into a new cell in the notebook — pressing Enter after each line:**

```python
class MyClass:
    Greeting = ""
    def __init__(self, Name="there"):
        self.Greeting = Name + "!"
    def SayHello(self):
        print("Hello {0}".format(self.Greeting))

MyInstance = MyClass()
MyInstance.SayHello()
```

This example provides your first example of Python-style method overloading. Even though there is only one __init__() method declaration, there are actually two versions of __init__(). The first doesn't require any special input because it uses the default value for the Name of "there". The second requires a name as an input. It sets Greeting to the value of this name, plus an exclamation mark. The SayHello() method is essentially the same as previous examples in this chapter.

TECHNICAL STUFF

Python doesn't support true function overloading. Many strict adherents to strict Object-Oriented Programming (OOP) principles consider default values to be something different from function overloading. However, the use of default values obtains the same result.

2. Click Run Cell.

You see the message shown in Figure 15-3. Notice that this message provides the default, generic greeting.

3. Type the following code into a new cell in the notebook — pressing Enter after each line:

```
MyInstance2 = MyClass("Amy")
MyInstance2.SayHello()
MyInstance.Greeting = "Harry!"
MyInstance.SayHello()
```

In the first line, Python creates an instance of MyClass named MyInstance2. The instance MyInstance is completely different from the instance MyInstance2. In the second line, Python displays the message for MyInstance2, not the message for MyInstance.

The third line changes the greeting for MyInstance without changing the greeting for MyInstance2. The fourth line displays the new MyInstance message.

4. Click Run Cell.

You see the messages shown in Figure 15-4. Notice that this code provides a specific greeting for each of the instances. In addition, each instance is separate, and you were able to change the message for the first instance without affecting the second instance.

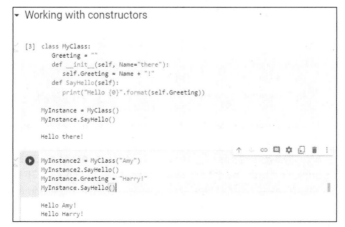

FIGURE 15-4:
Supplying the constructor with a name provides a customized output.

Working with variables

As mentioned earlier in the book, variables are storage containers that hold data. When working with classes, you need to consider how the data is stored and managed. A class can include both class variables and instance variables. The class variables are defined as part of the class itself, while instance variables are defined as part of methods. The following sections show how to use both variable types.

Creating class variables

Class variables provide global access to data that your class manipulates in some way. The following steps demonstrate how class variables work.

1. **Type the following code into a new cell in the notebook — pressing Enter after each line:**

```python
class MyClass:
    Greeting = ""
    def SayHello(self):
        print("Hello {0}".format(self.Greeting))

MyClass.Greeting = "Zelda"
MyClass.Greeting
```

   This is a version of the code found in the "Working with constructors" section, earlier in this chapter, but this version doesn't include the constructor. Normally you do include a constructor to ensure that the class variable is initialized properly. However, this series of steps shows how class variables can go wrong.

   The MyClass.Greeting = "Zelda" statement sets the value of Greeting to something other than the value that you used when you created the class. Of course, anyone could make this change. The big question is whether the change will take.

2. **Click Run Cell.**

   You see that the value of Greeting has changed, as shown in Figure 15-5.

3. **Type the following code into a new cell in the notebook — pressing Enter after each line:**

```python
MyInstance = MyClass()
MyInstance.SayHello()
```

   Python creates an instance of MyClass named MyInstance.

FIGURE 15-5:
You can change
the value of
Greeting.

```
▼ Working with variables

▼ Creating class variables

  ▶  class MyClass:
         Greeting = ""
         def SayHello(self):
             print("Hello {0}".format(self.Greeting))

     MyClass.Greeting = "Zelda"
     MyClass.Greeting

     'Zelda'
```

4. **Click Run Cell.**

   You see the message shown in Figure 15-6. The change that you made to
   Greeting has carried over to the instance of the class. It's true that the use of a
   class variable hasn't really caused a problem in this example, but you can
   imagine what would happen in a real application if someone wanted to cause
   problems.

FIGURE 15-6:
The change to
Greeting
carries over to
the instance of
the class.

```
  ▶  MyInstance = MyClass()
     MyInstance.SayHello()

     Hello Zelda
```

REMEMBER

This is just a simple example of how class variables can go wrong. The two
concepts you should take away from this example are as follows:

- Avoid class variables when you can because they're inherently unsafe.

- Always initialize class variables to a known good value in the constructor
  code.

Creating instance variables

Instance variables are always defined as part of a method. The input arguments to a
method are considered instance variables because they exist only when the method
exists. Using instance variables is usually safer than using class variables because
it's easier to maintain control over them and to ensure that the caller is providing
the correct input. The following steps show an example of using instance variables.

1. **Type the following code into a new cell in the notebook — pressing Enter
   after each line:**

   ```
   class MyClass:
       def DoAdd(self, Value1=0, Value2=0):
   ```

```
        Sum = Value1 + Value2
        print("The sum of {0} plus {1} is {2}."
              .format(Value1, Value2, Sum))

MyInstance = MyClass()
MyInstance.DoAdd(1, 4)
```

In this case, you have three instance variables. The input arguments, Value1 and Value2, have default values of 0, so DoAdd() can't fail simply because the user forgot to provide values. Of course, the user could always supply something other than numbers, so you should provide the appropriate checks as part of your code. The third instance variable is Sum, which is equal to Value1 + Value2. The code simply adds the two numbers together and displays the result.

After defining the class, the code creates an instance of MyClass named MyInstance. The last line executes DoAdd() with input values of 1 and 4.

2. **Click Run Cell.**

   You see the message shown in Figure 15-7. In this case, you see the sum of adding 1 and 4.

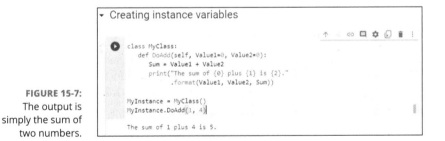

FIGURE 15-7:
The output is simply the sum of two numbers.

Using methods with variable argument lists

Sometimes you create methods that can take a variable number of arguments. Handling this sort of situation is something Python does well. Here are the two kinds of variable arguments that you can create:

» *args: Provides a list of unnamed arguments.

» **kwargs: Provides a list of named arguments.

The actual names of the arguments don't matter, but Python developers use *args and **kwargs as a convention so that other Python developers know that they're a variable list of arguments. Notice that the first variable argument has just one asterisk (*) associated with it, which means the arguments are unnamed. The second variable has two asterisks (**), which means that the arguments are named. The following steps demonstrate how to use both approaches to writing an application.

1. **Type the following code into a new cell in the notebook — pressing Enter after each line:**

```python
class MyClass:
    def PrintList1(*args):
        for Count, Item in enumerate(args):
            print("{0}. {1}".format(Count, Item))
    def PrintList2(**kwargs):
        for Name, Value in kwargs.items():
            print("{0} likes {1}".format(Name, Value))
MyClass.PrintList1("Red", "Blue", "Green")
MyClass.PrintList2(George="Red", Sue="Blue",
                  Zarah="Green")
```

For the purposes of this example, you're seeing the arguments implemented as part of a class method. However, you can use them just as easily with an instance method.

Look carefully at PrintList1() and you see a new method of using a for loop to iterate through a list. In this case, the enumerate() function outputs both a count (the loop count) and the string that was passed to the function.

The PrintList2() function accepts a dictionary input. Just as with PrintList1(), this list can be any length. However, you must process the items() found in the dictionary to obtain the individual values.

2. **Click Run Cell.**

You see the output shown in Figure 15-8. The individual lists can be of any length. In fact, in this situation, playing with the code to see what you can do with it is a good idea. For example, try mixing numbers and strings with the first list to see what happens. Try adding Boolean values as well. The point is that using this technique makes your methods incredibly flexible if all you want is a list of values as input.

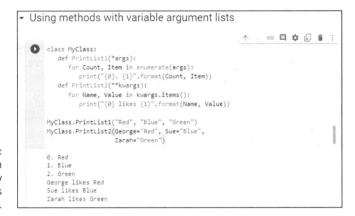

Overloading operators

In some situations, you want to be able to do something special as the result of using a standard operator such as add (+). In fact, sometimes Python doesn't provide a default behavior for operators because it has no default to implement. No matter what the reason might be, overloading operators makes it possible to assign new functionality to existing operators so that they do what you want, rather than what Python intended. The following steps demonstrate how to overload an operator and use it as part of an application.

1. **Type the following code into a new cell in the Notebook — pressing Enter after each line:**

```python
class MyClass:
    def __init__(self, *args):
        self.Input = args
    def __add__(self, Other):
        Output = MyClass()
        Output.Input = self.Input + Other.Input
        return Output
    def __str__(self):
        Output = ""
        for Item in self.Input:
            Output += Item
            Output += " "
        return Output


Value1 = MyClass("Red", "Green", "Blue")
Value2 = MyClass("Yellow", "Purple", "Cyan")
Value3 = Value1 + Value2
print("{0} + {1} = {2}"
        .format(Value1, Value2, Value3))
```

The example demonstrates a few different techniques. The constructor, __init__(), demonstrates a method for creating an instance variable attached to the self object. You can use this approach to create as many variables as needed to support the instance.

REMEMBER

When you create your own classes, no + operator is defined until you define one, in most cases. The only exception is when you inherit from an existing class that already has the + operator defined (see the "Extending Classes to Make New Classes" section, later in this chapter, for details). To add two MyClass entries together, you must define the __add__() method, which equates to the + operator.

The code used for the __add__() method may look a little odd, too, but you need to think about it one line at a time. The code begins by creating a new object, Output, from MyClass. Nothing is added to Output at this point — it's a blank object. The two objects that you want to add, self.Input and Other. Input, are actually tuples. (See "Working with Tuples," in Chapter 14, for more details about tuples.) The code places the sum of these two objects into Output.Input. The __add__() method then returns the new combined object to the caller.

Of course, you may want to know why you can't simply add the two inputs together as you would a number. The answer is that you'd end up with a tuple as an output, rather than a MyClass as an output. The type of the output would be changed, and that would also change any use of the resulting object.

To print MyClass properly, you also need to define a __str__() method. This method converts a MyClass object into a string. In this case, the output is a *space-delimited string* (in which each of the items in the string is separated from the other items by a space) containing each of the values found in self. Input. Of course, the class that you create can output any string that fully represents the object.

The main procedure creates two test objects, Value1 and Value2. It adds them together and places the result in Value3. The result is printed onscreen.

2. **Click Run Cell.**

Figure 15-9 shows the result of adding the two objects together, converting them to strings, and then printing the result. It's a lot of code for such a simple output statement, but the result definitely demonstrates that you can create classes that are self-contained and fully functional.

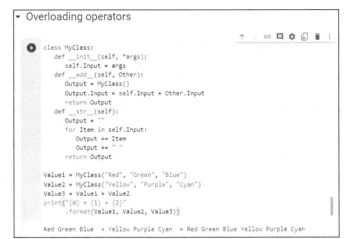

```
▼ Overloading operators

⬤  class MyClass:
        def __init__(self, *args):
            self.Input = args
        def __add__(self, Other):
            Output = MyClass()
            Output.Input = self.Input + Other.Input
            return Output
        def __str__(self):
            Output = ""
            for Item in self.Input:
                Output += Item
                Output += " "
            return Output

    Value1 = MyClass("Red", "Green", "Blue")
    Value2 = MyClass("Yellow", "Purple", "Cyan")
    Value3 = Value1 + Value2
    print("{0} + {1} = {2}"
        .format(Value1, Value2, Value3))

    Red Green Blue  + Yellow Purple Cyan  = Red Green Blue Yellow Purple Cyan
```

FIGURE 15-9:
The result of adding two MyClass objects is a third object of the same type.

Creating and Using an External Class

Sometimes you want to reuse the classes you create, which means making them external to your main application. What you end up with is your own special library that is similar to the other Python libraries found in this book. In this case, you create a class that you place into an external package and eventually access within an application.

WARNING

Because of limitations in how Colab works, the example in the following sections will work well only with Jupyter Notebook because it's hard to export .py files correctly in Colab. These sections focus on Jupyter Notebook use for this reason.

Developing the external class

Before you can do anything else, you need to create the external class, which may eventually turn into a custom library filled with multiple classes. The following sections describe how to create and save this class.

Defining the MyClass class

Listing 15-1 shows the code that you need to create the class. You can also find this code in the BPP4D3E; 15; MyClass.ipynb file found in the downloadable source, as described in the Introduction.

LISTING 15-1: Creating an External Class

```
class MyClass:
    def __init__(self, Name="Sam", Age=32):
        self.Name = Name
        self.Age = Age
    def GetName(self):
        return self.Name
    def SetName(self, Name):
        self.Name = Name
    def GetAge(self):
        return self.Age
    def SetAge(self, Age):
        self.Age = Age
    def __str__(self):
        return "{0} is aged {1}.".format(self.Name,
                                         self.Age)
```

In this case, the class begins by creating an object with two instance variables: Name and Age. If the user fails to provide these values, they default to Sam and 32.

REMEMBER

This example provides you with a new class feature. Most developers call this feature an *accessor*. Essentially, it provides access to an underlying value. There are two types of accessors: getters and setters. Both GetName() and GetAge() are *getters*. They provide read-only access to the underlying value. The SetName() and SetAge() methods are *setters*, which provide write-only access to the underlying value. Using a combination of methods like this allows you to check inputs for correct type and range, as well as verify that the caller has permission to view the information.

As with just about every other class you create, you need to define the __str__() method if you want the user to be able to print the object. In this case, the class provides formatted output that lists both of the instance variables.

Saving a class to disk

You could keep your class right in the same file as your test code, but that wouldn't reflect the real world very well. To use this class in a real-world way for the rest of the chapter, you must follow these steps:

1. **Create a new notebook called** BPP4D3E; 15; MyClass.ipynb **and add the code shown in Listing 15-1 to it.**

   You can also use the downloadable source file, BPP4D3E; 15; MyClass.ipynb.

2. **Click Run Cell.**

Python will execute the code without error when you have typed the code correctly.

3. **Choose File ⇨ Save and Checkpoint.**

Notebook saves the file.

4. **Choose File ⇨ Download As ⇨ Python (.py).**

Notebook outputs the code as a Python file.

Note that you must name the file BPP4D3E_15_MyClass.py because Python can't import external libraries with spaces in their names.

Using MyClass in an application

Most of the time, you use external classes when working with Python. It isn't very often that a class exists within the confines of the application file because the application would become large and unmanageable. In addition, reusing the class code in another application would be difficult. The following steps help you use the MyClass class that you created in the previous section.

1. **Type the following code into a new cell in the** BPP4D3E; 15; Creating and Using Classes.ipynb **notebook — pressing Enter after each line:**

```
import BPP4D3E_15_MyClass

SamsRecord = BPP4D3E_15_MyClass.MyClass()
AmysRecord = BPP4D3E_15_MyClass.MyClass("Amy", 44)

print(SamsRecord.GetAge())
SamsRecord.SetAge(33)

print(AmysRecord.GetName())
AmysRecord.SetName("Aimee")

print(SamsRecord)
print(AmysRecord)
```

The example code begins by importing the BPP4D3E_15_MyClass package. The package name is the name of the file used to store the external code, not the name of the class. A single package can contain multiple classes, so always think of the package as being the actual file that is used to hold one or more classes that you need to use with your application.

After the package is imported, the application creates two MyClass objects. Notice that you use the package name first, followed by the class name. The first object, SamsRecord, uses the default settings. The second object, AmysRecord, relies on custom settings.

Sam has become a year older. The application updates Sam's age.

Somehow, HR spelled Amy's name wrong. It turns out that *Amy* is an incorrect spelling. The application makes a correction to AmysRecord. The final step prints both records in their entirety.

2. **Click Run Cell.**

The application displays a series of messages as it puts MyClass through its paces, as shown in Figure 15-10. At this point, you know all the essentials of creating great classes.

Using MyClass in an application

```
In [14]:  import BPP4D3E_15_MyClass

          SamsRecord = BPP4D3E_15_MyClass.MyClass()
          AmysRecord = BPP4D3E_15_MyClass.MyClass("Amy", 44)

          print(SamsRecord.GetAge())
          SamsRecord.SetAge(33)

          print(AmysRecord.GetName())
          AmysRecord.SetName("Aimee")

          print(SamsRecord)
          print(AmysRecord)

          32
          Amy
          Sam is aged 33.
          Aimee is aged 44.
```

FIGURE 15-10:
The output shows that the class is fully functional.

Extending Classes to Make New Classes

As you might imagine, creating a fully functional, *production-grade class* (one that is used in a real-world application actually running on a system that is accessed by users) is time consuming because real classes perform a lot of tasks. Fortunately, Python supports a feature called *inheritance.* By using inheritance, you can obtain the features you want from a parent class when creating a child class. Overriding the features that you don't need and adding new features lets you create new classes relatively fast and with a lot less effort on your part. In addition, because the parent code is already tested, you don't have to put quite as much effort into ensuring that your new class works as expected. The following sections show how to build and use classes that inherit from each other.

Building the child class

Parent classes are normally supersets of something. In this case, you build a parent class named Animal and use it to define a child class named Chicken. Of course, you can easily add other child classes after you have Animal in place, such as a Gorilla class. However, for this example, you build just the one parent and one child class, as shown in Listing 15-2. Type this code into a new cell in the notebook.

LISTING 15-2: **Building a Parent and Child Class**

```python
class Animal:
    def __init__(self, Name="", Age=0, Type=""):
        self.Name = Name
        self.Age = Age
        self.Type = Type
    def GetName(self):
        return self.Name
    def SetName(self, Name):
        self.Name = Name
    def GetAge(self):
        return self.Age
    def SetAge(self, Age):
        self.Age = Age
    def GetType(self):
        return self.Type
    def SetType(self, Type):
        self.Type = Type
    def __str__(self):
        return "{0} is a {1} aged {2}".format(self.Name,
                                              self.Type,
                                              self.Age)
class Chicken(Animal):
    def __init__(self, Name="", Age=0):
        self.Name = Name
        self.Age = Age
        self.Type = "Chicken"
    def SetType(self, Type):
        print("Sorry, {0} will always be a {1}"
              .format(self.Name, self.Type))
    def MakeSound(self):
        print("{0} says Cluck, Cluck, Cluck!".format(self.Name))
```

The Animal class tracks three characteristics: Name, Age, and Type. A production application would probably track more characteristics, but these characteristics do everything needed for this example. The code also includes the required accessors for each of the characteristics. The __str__() method completes the picture by printing a simple message stating the animal characteristics.

The Chicken class inherits from the Animal class. Notice the use of Animal in parentheses after the Chicken class name. This addition tells Python that Chicken is a kind of Animal, something that will inherit the characteristics of Animal.

Notice that the Chicken constructor accepts only Name and Age. The user doesn't have to supply a Type value because you already know that it's a chicken. This new constructor overrides the Animal constructor. The three attributes are still in place, but Type is supplied directly in the Chicken constructor.

Someone might try something funny, such as setting a chicken up as a gorilla. With this in mind, the Chicken class also overrides the SetType() setter. If someone tries to change the Chicken type, that user gets a message rather than the attempted change. Normally, you handle this sort of problem by using an exception, but the message works better for this example by making the coding technique clearer.

Finally, the Chicken class adds a new feature, MakeSound(). Whenever you want to see the sound a chicken makes, just call MakeSound() to see it printed on the screen.

Testing class inheritance in an application

Testing the Chicken class also tests the Animal class to some extent. Some functionality is different, but some classes aren't really meant to be used. The Animal class is simply a parent for specific kinds of animals, such as Chicken. The following steps demonstrate the Chicken class so that you can see how inheritance works.

1. **Type the following code into a new cell in the notebook — pressing Enter after each line:**

```
MyChicken = Chicken("Sally", 2)
print(MyChicken)

MyChicken.SetAge(MyChicken.GetAge() + 1)
print(MyChicken)
```

```
MyChicken.SetType("Gorilla")
print(MyChicken)

MyChicken.MakeSound()
```

The example creates a chicken, MyChicken, named "Sally", who is age 2. It then starts to work with MyChicken in various ways. For example, Sally has a birthday, so the code increases Sally's age by 1. Notice how the code combines the use of a setter, SetAge( ), with a getter, GetAge( ), to perform the task. After each change, the code displays the resulting object values for you.

2. **Click Run Cell.**

    You see each of the steps used to work with MyChicken, as shown in Figure 15-11.

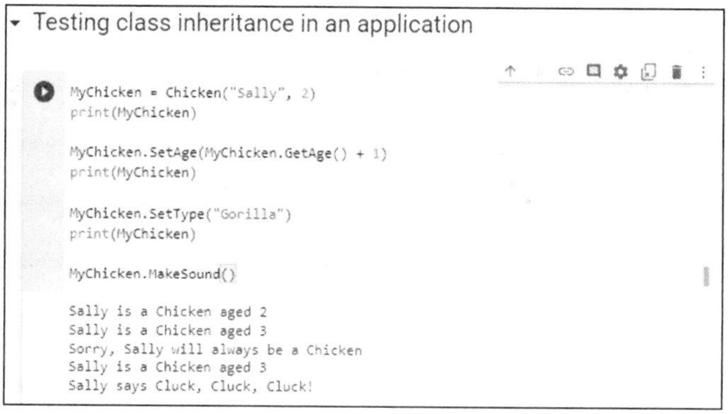

FIGURE 15-11:
Sally has a birthday and then says a few words.

4

Performing Advanced Tasks

Chapter **16**

Storing Data in Files

U ntil now, application development might seem to be all about presenting information onscreen. Actually, applications revolve around a need to work with data in some way. Data is the focus of all applications because it's the data that users are interested in. Be prepared for a huge disappointment the first time you present a treasured application to a user base and find that the only thing users worry about is whether the application will help them leave work on time after creating a presentation. The fact is, the best applications are invisible, but they present data in the most appropriate manner possible for a user's needs.

If data is the focus of applications, then storing the data in a permanent manner is equally important. For most developers, data storage revolves around permanent media such as a hard drive, Solid State Drive (SSD), Universal Serial Bus (USB) flash drive, or some other methodology. (Cloud-based solutions work fine, but you won't see them used in this book because they require different programming techniques that are beyond the book's scope.) The data in memory is temporary because it lasts only as long as the machine is running. A permanent storage device holds onto the data long after the machine is turned off or the session has ended so that it can be retrieved during the next session.

REMEMBER

In addition to permanent storage, this chapter also helps you understand the four basic operations that you can perform on files: Create, Read, Update, and Delete (CRUD). You see the CRUD acronym used quite often in database circles, but it applies equally well to any application. No matter how your application stores the data in a permanent location, it must be able to perform these four tasks in order to provide a complete solution to the user. Of course, CRUD operations must be performed in a secure, reliable, and controlled manner. This chapter also helps you set a few guidelines for how access must occur to ensure *data integrity* (a measure of how often data errors occur when performing CRUD operations).

REMEMBER

You don't have to type the source code for this chapter manually. In fact, using the downloadable source is a lot easier. You can find the source for this chapter in the `BPP4D3E; 16; Storing Data in Files.ipynb` file of the downloadable source. See the Introduction for details on how to find these source files.

Understanding How Permanent Storage Works

You don't need to understand absolutely every detail about how permanent storage works in order to use it. For example, just how the drive spins (assuming that it spins at all) is unimportant. However, most platforms adhere to a basic set of principles when it comes to permanent storage. These principles have developed over a period of time, starting with mainframe systems in the earliest days of computing. Data is generally stored in one of these ways:

» **Files:** The most common method that uses pure data representing application state information in separate containers called files, with each container having a specific filename. Files appear on local drives, on networks, and in the cloud.

» **Objects:** A method of storing serialized class instances that can appear locally with each object in a separate file or in the cloud with storage specifically designed to handle objects.

» **Blocks:** A method generally associated with the cloud, but also used on a network with Fiber Channel over Ethernet (FCoE) or Internet Small Computer Systems Interface (iSCSI), and that uses storage containers of the same size on disk within software-controlled volumes, with each of these volumes acting as a separate hard drive.

This chapter covers the use of files, not objects or blocks. In addition, it focuses on files used on a local drive, rather than networks or in the cloud. You probably know about files already because almost every useful application out there relies on them. For example, when you open a document in your word processor, you're actually opening a data file containing the words that you or someone else has typed.

Files typically have an *extension* associated with them that defines the file type. The extension is generally standardized for any given application and is separated from the filename by a period, such as MyData.txt. In this case, .txt is the file extension, and you probably have an application on your machine for opening such files. In fact, you can likely choose from a number of applications to perform the task because the .txt file extension is relatively common.

Internally, files structure the data in some specific manner to make it easy to write and read data to and from the file. Any application you write must know about the file structure in order to interact with the data the file contains. The examples in this chapter use a simple file structure to make it easy to write the code required to access them, but file structures can become quite complex.

Files would be nearly impossible to find if you placed them all in the same location on the hard drive. Consequently, files are organized into *directories.* Many computer systems also use the term *folder* for this organizational feature of permanent storage. No matter what you call it, permanent storage relies on directories to help organize the data and make individual files significantly easier to find. To find a particular file so that you can open it and interact with the data it contains, you must know which directory holds the file.

Directories are arranged in hierarchies that begin at the uppermost level of the hard drive. For example, when working with the downloadable source code for this book, you find the code for the entire book in the BPP4D3E directory within the user folder on your system when working with Jupyter Notebook or on GitHub (https://github.com/JohnPaulMueller/BPP4D3E) when working with Colab. On my Windows system, that directory hierarchy is C:\Users\John\BPP4D3E. However, my Mac and Linux systems have a different directory hierarchy to reach the same BPP4D3E directory, and the directory hierarchy on your system will be different as well.

Notice that I use a backslash (\) to separate the directory levels. Some platforms use the forward slash (/); others use the backslash. You can read about this issue on my blog at http://blog.johnmuellerbooks.com/2014/03/10/backslash-versus-forward-slash/. The book uses backslashes when appropriate and assumes that you'll make any required changes for your platform.

A final consideration for Python developers (at least for this book) is that the hierarchy of directories is called a *path.* You see the term *path* in a few places in this book because Python must be able to find any resources you want to use based on the path you provide. For example, C:\Users\John\BPP4D3E is the complete path to the source code for this chapter on my Windows system. A path that traces the entire route that Python must search is called an *absolute path.* An incomplete path that traces the route to a resource using the current directory as a starting point is called a *relative path.*

**TECHNICAL
STUFF**

To find a location using a relative path, you commonly use the current directory as the starting point. For example, BPP4D3E__pycache__ would be the relative path to the Python cache. Note that it has no drive letter or beginning backslash. However, sometimes you must add to the starting point in specific ways to define a relative path. Most platforms define these special relative path character sets:

» \: The root directory of the current drive. The drive is relative, but the path begins at the root, the uppermost part, of that drive.

» . \: The current directory. You use this shorthand for the current directory when the current directory name isn't known. For example, you could also define the location of the Python cache as . __pycache__.

» . . \: The parent directory. You use this shorthand when the parent directory name isn't known.

» . . \. . \: The parent of the parent directory. You can proceed up the hierarchy of directories as far as necessary to locate a particular starting point before you drill back down the hierarchy to a new location.

Creating Content for Permanent Storage

A file can contain structured or unstructured data. An example of *structured data* is a database in which each record has specific information in it. An employee database would include columns for name, address, employee ID, and so on. Each record would be an individual employee and each employee record would contain the name, address, and employee ID fields. An example of *unstructured data* is a word processing file whose text can contain any content in any order. There is no required order for the content of a paragraph, and sentences can contain any number of words. However, in both cases, the application must know how to perform CRUD operations with the file. This means that the content must be prepared in such a manner that the application can both write to and read from the file.

Even with word processing files, the text must follow a certain series of rules. Assume for a moment that the files are simple text. Even so, every paragraph must have some sort of delimiter telling the application to begin a new paragraph. The application reads the paragraph until it sees this delimiter, and then it begins a new paragraph. The more that the word processor offers in the way of features, the more structured the output becomes. For example, when the word processor offers a method of formatting the text, the formatting must appear as part of the output file.

REMEMBER

The cues that make content usable for permanent storage are often hidden from sight. All you see when you work with the file is the data itself. The formatting remains invisible for a number of reasons, such as these:

>> The cue is a control character, such as a carriage return or linefeed, that is normally invisible by default at the platform level.

>> The application relies on special character combinations, such as commas and double quotes, to delimit the data entries. These special character combinations are consumed by the application during reading.

>> Part of the reading process converts the character to another form, such as when a word processing file reads in content that is formatted. The formatting appears onscreen in visual form (you see the effect, not the actual formatting), but in the background the file contains special characters to denote the formatting.

>> The file is actually in an alternative format, such as eXtensible Markup Language (XML) (see `https://www.w3schools.com/xml/default.ASP` for information about XML). The alternative format is interpreted and presented onscreen in a manner the user can understand.

TECHNICAL STUFF

Other rules likely exist for formatting data. For example, Microsoft actually uses a `.zip` file to hold its latest word processing files (the `.docx`) file. The use of a compressed file catalog, such as `.zip`, makes storing a great deal of information in a small space possible. It's interesting to see how others store data because you can often find more efficient and secure means of data storage for your own applications.

Now that you have a better idea of what could happen as part of preparing content for disk storage, it's time to look at an example. In this case, the formatting strategy is quite simple. All this example does is accept input, format it for storage, and present the formatted version onscreen (rather than save it to disk just yet).

1. **Open a new notebook.**

You can also use the downloadable source file, BPP4D3E; 16; `Storing Data in Files.ipynb`.

2. **Type the following code into the notebook — pressing Enter after each line:**

```
class FormatData:
    def __init__(self, Name="", Age=0, Married=False):
        self.Name = Name
        self.Age = Age
        self.Married = Married
```

```
def __str__(self):
    OutString = "'{0}', {1}, {2}".format(
        self.Name,
        self.Age,
        self.Married)
    return OutString
```

This is a shortened class. Normally, you'd add accessors (getter and setter methods) and error-trapping code. (Remember that *getter methods* provide read-only access to class data and *setter methods* provide write-only access to class data.) However, the class works fine for the demonstration.

The main feature to look at is the __str__() function. Notice that it formats the output data in a specific way. The string value, self.Name, is enclosed in single quotes. Each of the values is also separated by a comma. This is actually a form of a standard output format, comma-separated value (CSV), that is used on a wide range of platforms because it's easy to translate and is in plain text, so nothing special is needed to work with it.

3. **Click Run Cell.**

The IDE runs the code and creates the required class for you.

4. **Type the following code into a new cell in the notebook — pressing Enter after each line:**

```
NewData = [FormatData("George", 65, True),
           FormatData("Sally", 47, False),
           FormatData("Doug", 52, True)]
for Entry in NewData:
    print(Entry)
```

Most of the time, you work with multiple records when you save data to disk. You might have multiple paragraphs in a word processed document or multiple records, as in this case. The example creates a list of records and places them in NewData. In this case, NewData represents the entire document. The representation will likely take other forms in a production application, but the idea is the same.

Any application that saves data goes through some sort of output loop. In this case, the loop simply prints the data onscreen. However, in the upcoming sections, you actually output the data to a file.

5. **Click Run Cell.**

You see the output shown in Figure 16-1. This is a representation of how the data would appear in the file. In this case, each record is separated by a carriage return and linefeed control character combination. That is, George, Sally, and Doug are all separate records in the file. Each *field* (data element) is separated by a comma. Text fields appear in quotes so that they aren't confused with other data types.

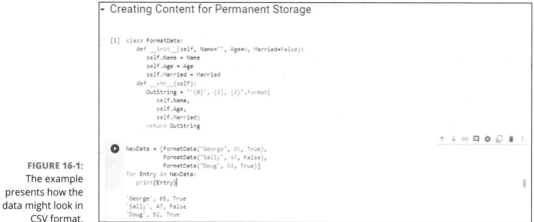

Creating a File

Any data that the user creates and wants to work with for more than one session must be put on some sort of permanent media. Creating a file and then placing the data into it is an essential part of working with Python. You can use the following steps to create code that will write data to the hard drive (albeit, only temporarily for Colab).

1. **Type the following code into a new cell in the notebook — pressing Enter after each line:**

    ```python
    import csv

    class FormatData2:
        def __init__(self, Name="", Age=0, Married=False):
            self.Name = Name
            self.Age = Age
            self.Married = Married

        def __str__(self):
            OutString = "'{0}', {1}, {2}".format(
                self.Name,
                self.Age,
    ```

```
        self.Married)
    return OutString

def SaveData(Filename = "", DataList = []):
    with open(Filename,
                "w", newline='\n') as csvfile:
        DataWriter = csv.writer(
            csvfile,
            delimiter='\n',
            quotechar=" ",
            quoting=csv.QUOTE_NONNUMERIC)
        DataWriter.writerow(DataList)
        csvfile.close()
        print("Data saved!")
```

The csv module contains everything needed to work with CSV files.

REMEMBER

Python actually supports a huge number of file types natively, and libraries that provide additional support are available. If you have a file type that you need to support using Python, you can usually find a third-party library to support it when Python doesn't support it natively. Unfortunately, no comprehensive list of supported files exists, so you need to search online to find how Python supports the file you need. The documentation divides the supported files by types and doesn't provide a comprehensive list. For example, you can find all the archive formats at https://docs.python.org/3/library/archiving.html and the miscellaneous file formats at https://docs.python.org/3/library/fileformats.html.

TIP

This example uses essentially the same text formatting code as you saw in the FormatData class, but now it adds the SaveData() method to put the formatted data on disk. Using a new class notifies everyone who views the code of the increased capability, so FormatData2 is the same class, but with more features.

Notice that the SaveData() method accepts two arguments as input: a filename used to store the data and a list of items to store. This is a class method rather than an instance method. Later in this procedure, you see how using a class method is an advantage. The DataList argument defaults to an empty list so that if the caller doesn't pass anything at all, the method won't throw an exception. Instead, it produces an empty output file. Of course, you can also add code to detect an empty list as an error, if desired.

REMEMBER

The with statement tells Python to perform a series of tasks with a specific resource — an open csvfile named Testfile.csv. The open() function accepts a number of inputs depending in how you use it. For this example, you open it in write mode (signified by the w). The newline attribute tells Python to treat the \n control character (linefeed) as a newline character.

In order to write output, you need a writer object. The `DataWriter` object is configured to use `csvfile` as the output file, to use \n as the record character, to quote records using a space, and to provide quoting only on nonnumeric values. This setup will produce some interesting results later, but for now, just assume that this is what you need to make the output usable.

Actually writing the data takes less effort than you might think. A single call to `DataWriter.writerow()` with the `DataList` as input is all you need. Always close the file when you get done using it. This action *flushes the data* (makes sure that it gets written) to the hard drive. The code ends by telling you that the data has been saved.

2. **Click Run Cell.**

   The IDE runs the code and creates the required class for you.

3. **Type the following code into a new cell in the notebook — pressing Enter after each line:**

   ```
   NewData = [FormatData2("George", 65, True),
              FormatData2("Sally", 47, False),
              FormatData2("Doug", 52, True)]
   FormatData2.SaveData("TestFile.csv", NewData)
   ```

   This example should look similar to the one you created in the "Creating Content for Permanent Storage" section, earlier in the chapter. You still create NewData as a list. However, instead of displaying the information onscreen, you send it to a file instead by calling `FormatData2.SaveData()`. This is one of those situations in which using an instance method would actually get in the way. To use an instance method, you would first need to create an instance of FormatData that wouldn't actually do anything for you.

4. **Click Run Cell.**

   The application runs, and you see a message that the data was saved as output. Of course, that doesn't tell you anything about the data. You use separate methods for viewing the data depending on whether you work with Colab or Jupyter Notebook:

   - **Colab:** Click the Files icon that appears on the left side of the browser window to display a list of files associated with this Colab session. Double-click `TestFile.csv` to see it displayed as shown in Figure 16-2. Notice that Colab assumes that every `.csv` file has a header row, so it displays the first data entry as a header.

   - **Jupyter Notebook:** Choose File ⇨ Open to display the directory listing for the current project. Click the `TestFile.csv` entry near the bottom of the page. Jupyter Notebook displays the three entries as you might expect, with no header row, as shown in Figure 16-3.

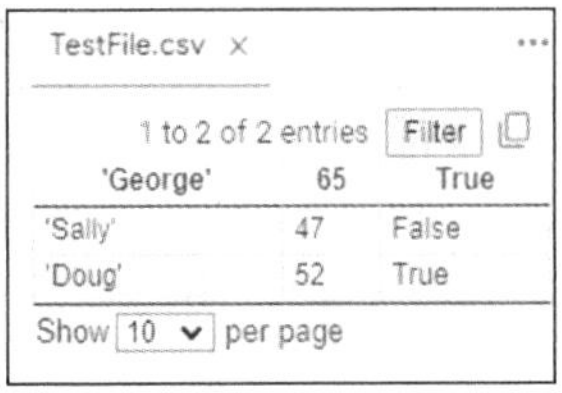

FIGURE 16-2:
Colab displays
the file content
using the first
row as a header.

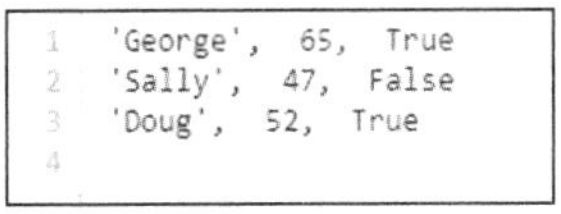

FIGURE 16-3:
Jupyter Notebook
makes no
assumption
about the
header row.

LOCAL FILE STORAGE: COLAB VERSUS JUPYTER NOTEBOOK

The files you create in Colab aren't necessarily permanent. You may find that they simply disappear between sessions when Google stops the virtual machine hosting your code. On the other hand, the files you create in Jupyter Notebook reside on your local system and will remain in place for as long as you want to keep them. You can always check the content of the directories for either IDE to determine whether your file is still in place by using the following code:

```
import os

print(os.getcwd())

DirList = os.listdir()
print(DirList)
print("TestFile.csv" in DirList)
```

The first print() output tells you where your files are stored. The second print() output provides you with a list of files in that directory. The third print() output tells you specifically whether the file you need appears in that directory. It's important to know how to check for the files you need between sessions. The only way to ensure that your files are indeed permanent when working with Colab is to save them to cloud storage, such as Google Drive. The articles at https://www.geeksforgeeks.org/uploading-files-on-google-drive-using-python/ and https://www.projectpro.io/recipes/upload-files-to-google-drive-using-python give you some ideas of how to accomplish this task.

Reading File Content

At this point, the data is on the hard drive. Of course, it's nice and safe there, but it really isn't useful because you can't see it. To see the data, you must read it into memory and then do something with it. The following steps show how to read data from the hard drive and into memory so that you can display it onscreen.

1. Type the following code into a new cell in the notebook — pressing Enter after each line:

```python
import csv

class FormatData3:
    def __init__(self, Name="", Age=0, Married=False):
        self.Name = Name
        self.Age = Age
        self.Married = Married

    def __str__(self):
        OutString = "'{0}', {1}, {2}".format(
            self.Name,
            self.Age,
            self.Married)
        return OutString

    def SaveData(Filename = "", DataList = []):
        with open(Filename,
                  "w", newline='\n') as csvfile:
            DataWriter = csv.writer(
                csvfile,
                delimiter='\n',
                quotechar=" ",
                quoting=csv.QUOTE_NONNUMERIC)
            DataWriter.writerow(DataList)
            csvfile.close()
            print("Data saved!")

    def ReadData(Filename = ""):
        with open(Filename,
                  "r", newline='\n') as csvfile:
            DataReader = csv.reader(
                csvfile,
                delimiter="\n",
                quotechar=" ",
                quoting=csv.QUOTE_NONNUMERIC)
```

```
        Output = []
        for Item in DataReader:
            Output.append(Item[0])
        csvfile.close()
        print("Data read!")
        return Output
```

Opening a file for reading is much like opening it for writing. The big difference is that you need to specify r (for read) instead of w (for write) as part of the open() method call. Otherwise, the arguments are precisely the same and work the same.

REMEMBER

It's important to remember that you're starting with a text file when working with a .csv file. Yes, it has delimiters, but it's still text. When reading the text into memory, you must rebuild the Python structure. In this case, Output is an empty list when it starts.

The file currently contains three records that are separated by the /n control character. Python reads each record in using a for loop. Notice the odd use of Item[0]. When Python reads the record, it sees the nonterminating entries (those that aren't last in the file) as actually being two list entries. The first entry contains data; the second is blank. You want only the first entry. These entries are appended to Output so that you end up with a complete list of the records that appear in the file.

As before, make sure that you close the file when you get done with it. The method prints a data read message when it finishes. It then returns Output (a list of records) to the caller.

2. **Click Run Cell.**

   The IDE runs the code and creates the required class for you.

3. **Type the following code into a new cell in the notebook — pressing Enter after each line:**

   ```
   NewData = FormatData3.ReadData("TestFile.csv")
   for Entry in NewData:
       print(Entry)
   ```

   The first step is to create a NewData object, a list, by calling FormatData. ReadData(). Notice that the use of a class method is the right choice in this case as well because it makes the code shorter and simpler. In the next step, the application uses a for loop to display the NewData content.

4. **Click Run Cell.**

   You see the output shown in Figure 16-4. Notice that this output looks similar to the output in Figure 16-1, even though the data was written to disk and read back in. This is how applications that read and write data are supposed to work. The data should appear the same after you read it in as it did when you wrote it out to disk. Otherwise, the application is a failure because it has modified the data.

FIGURE 16-4:
The application input after it has been processed.

Updating File Content

Some developers treat updating a file as something complex. It can be complex if you view it as a single task. However, updates actually consist of three activities:

1. Read the file content into memory.

2. Modify the in-memory presentation of the data.

3. Write the resulting content to permanent storage.

In most applications, you can further break down the second step of modifying the in-memory presentation of the data. An application can provide some or all of these features as part of the modification process:

>> Provide an onscreen presentation of the data.

>> Allow additions to the data list.

>> Allow deletions from the data list.

>> Make changes to existing data, which can actually be implemented by adding a new record with the changed data and deleting the old record.

So far in this chapter, you have performed all but one of the activities in these two lists. You've already read file content and written file content. In the modification list, you've added data to a list and presented the data onscreen. The only interesting activity that you haven't performed is deleting data from a list. The modification of data is often performed as a two-part process of creating a new record that starts with the data from the old record and then deleting the old record after the new record is in place in the list.

REMEMBER

Don't get into a rut by thinking that you must perform every activity mentioned in this section for every application. A monitoring program wouldn't need to display the data onscreen. In fact, doing so might be harmful (or at least inconvenient). A data logger only creates new entries — it never deletes or modifies them. An email application usually allows the addition of new records and deletion of old records, but not modification of existing records. On the other hand, a word processor implements all the features mentioned. What you implement and how you implement it depends solely on the kind of application you create.

Separating the user interface from the activities that go on behind the user interface is important. To keep things simple, this example focuses on what needs to go on behind the user interface to make updates to the file you created in the "Creating a File" section, earlier in this chapter. The following steps demonstrate how to read, modify, and write a file in order to update it. The updates consist of an addition, a deletion, and a change. To allow you to run the application more than once, the updates are actually sent to another file.

1. **Type the following code into a new cell in the notebook — pressing Enter after each line:**

```
import os.path

if not os.path.isfile("TestFile.csv"):
    print("Please run the CreateFile.py example!")
    quit()

NewData = FormatData3.ReadData("TestFile.csv")
for Entry in NewData:
    print(Entry)

print("\r\nAdding a record for Harry.")
NewRecord = "'Harry', 23, False"
NewData.append(NewRecord)
for Entry in NewData:
    print(Entry)

print("\r\nRemoving Doug's record.")
Location = NewData.index("'Doug', 52, True")
Record = NewData[Location]
NewData.remove(Record)
for Entry in NewData:
    print(Entry)
```

```
print("\r\nModifying Sally's record.")
Location = NewData.index("'Sally', 47, False")
Record = NewData[Location]
Split = Record.split(",")
NewRecord = FormatData3(Split[0].replace("'", ""),
                       int(Split[1]),
                       bool(Split[2]))
NewRecord.Married = True
NewRecord.Age = 48
NewData.append(NewRecord.__str__())
NewData.remove(Record)
for Entry in NewData:
    print(Entry)


FormatData3.SaveData("ChangedFile.csv", NewData)
```

This example has quite a bit going on. First, it checks to ensure that the TestFile.csv file is actually present for processing. This is a check that you should always perform when you expect a file to be present. In this case, you aren't creating a new file, you're updating an existing file, so the file must be present. If the file isn't present, the application ends.

The next step is to read the data into NewData. This part of the process looks much like the data reading example earlier in the chapter.

REMEMBER

You have already seen code for using list functions in Chapter 13. This example uses those functions to perform practical work. The append( ) function adds a new record to NewData. However, notice that the data is added as a string, not as a FormatData object. The data is stored as strings on disk, so that's what you get when the data is read back in. You can either add the new data as a string or create a FormatData object and then use the __str__( ) method to output the data as a string.

The next step is to remove a record from NewData. To perform this task, you must first find the record. Of course, that's easy when working with just four records (remember that NewData now has a record for Harry in it). When working with a large number of records, you must first search for the record using the index( ) function. This act provides you with a number containing the location of the record, which you can then use to retrieve the actual record. After you have the actual record, you can remove it using the remove( ) function.

Modifying Sally's record looks daunting at first, but again, most of this code is part of dealing with the string storage on disk. When you obtain the record from NewData, what you receive is a single string with all three values in it. The split( ) function produces a list containing the three entries as strings, which still won't work for the application. In addition, Sally's name is enclosed in both double and single quotes.

The simplest way to manage the record is to create a FormatData object and to convert each of the strings into the proper form. This means removing the extra quotes from the name, converting the second value to an int, and converting the third value to a bool. The FormatData class doesn't provide accessors, so the application modifies both the Married and Age fields directly. Using accessors (getter methods that provide read-only access and setter methods that provide write-only access) is a better policy.

The application then appends the new record to and removes the existing record from NewData. Notice how the code uses NewRecord.__str__() to convert the new record from a FormatData object to the required string.

The final act is to save the changed record. Normally, you'd use the same file to save the data. However, the example saves the data to a different file in order to allow examination of both the old and new data.

TIP

2. **Click Run Cell.**

You see the following output:

```
Data read!
'George', 65, True
'Sally', 47, False
'Doug', 52, True

Adding a record for Harry.
'George', 65, True
'Sally', 47, False
'Doug', 52, True
'Harry', 23, False

Removing Doug's record.
'George', 65, True
'Sally', 47, False
'Harry', 23, False

Modifying Sally's record.
'George', 65, True
'Harry', 23, False
'Sally', 48, True
Data saved!
```

Notice that the application lists the records after each change so that you can see the status of NewData. This is actually a useful troubleshooting technique for your own applications. Of course, you want to remove the display code before you release the application to production.

3. **Open the** ChangedFile.csv **file using an appropriate technique.**

You see output similar to the following:

```
'George',  65,  True
'Harry',  23,  False
'Sally',  48,  True
```

Deleting a File

The previous section of this chapter, "Updating File Content," explains how to add, delete, and update records in a file. However, at some point you may need to delete the file. The following steps describe how to delete files that you no longer need.

1. **Type the following code into a new cell in the notebook — pressing Enter after each line:**

```
import os
os.remove("ChangedFile.csv")
print("File Removed!")
```

WARNING

The task looks simple in this case, and it is. All you need to do to remove a file is call os.remove() with the appropriate filename and path (as needed, Python defaults to the current directory, so you don't need to specify a path if the file you want to remove is in the default directory). The os.remove() call will throw an exception if you try to use it to delete a non-existent file. The ease with which you can perform this task is almost scary because it's too easy. Putting safeguards in place is always a good idea. You may want to remove other items, so here are other functions you should know about:

- os.rmdir(): Removes the specified directory. The directory must be empty or Python will display an exception message.

- shutil.rmtree(): Removes the specified directory, all subdirectories, and all files. This function is especially dangerous because it removes everything without checking (Python assumes that you know what you're doing). As a result, you can easily lose data using this function.

2. **Click Run Cell.**

The application displays the File Removed! message. When you look in the directory that originally contained the ChangedFile.csv file, you see that the file is gone.

Chapter **17**

Sending an Email

This chapter helps you understand the process of sending an email using Python. More important, this chapter is generally about helping you understand what happens when you communicate outside the local PC. Even though this chapter is specifically about email, it also contains principles you can use when performing other network tasks. For example, when working with an external service, you often need to create the same sort of packaging as you do for an email. So, the information you see in this chapter can help you understand all sorts of communication needs.

To make working with email as easy as possible, this chapter uses standard mail as a real-world equivalent of email. The comparison is apt. Email was actually modeled on real-world mail. Originally, the term email was used for any sort of electronic document transmission, and some forms of it required the sender and recipient to be online at the same time. As a result, you may find some confusing references online about the origins and development of email. This chapter views email as it exists today — as a storing and forwarding mechanism for exchanging documents of various types.

The examples in this chapter rely on the availability of a Simple Mail Transfer Protocol (SMTP) server. If that sounds like Greek to you, read the sidebar entitled "Considering the SMTP server" that appears later in the chapter.

WARNING

Note that the examples in this chapter won't work with Google Colab because of limitations with the IDE and security concerns. However, if you need to send an email using Colab, you can use the example at `https://colab.research.google. com/github/j-agrawal/coding/blob/master/send_mail.ipynb`, which isn't as flexible as using the approach in this chapter but does work. The example at `https://docs.python.org/3/library/smtplib.html#smtp-example` is an even simpler method when you can send email without using the Secure Sockets Layer (SSL) encryption. If you need access to the newer STARTLS (see the differences at `https://www.sparkpost.com/resources/email-explained/ssl-tls-starttls-encyption/`) that relies on either SSL or Transport Layer Security (TLS), the discussion at `https://stackoverflow.com/questions/33857698/sending-email-from-python-using-starttls` will help you out.

REMEMBER

You don't have to type the source code for this chapter manually. In fact, using the downloadable source is a lot easier. You can find the source for this chapter in the `BPP4D3E; 17; Sending an Email.ipynb` file of the downloadable source. See the Introduction for details on how to find these source files.

Understanding What Happens When You Send Email

Email has become so reliable and so mundane that most people don't understand what a miracle it is that it works at all. Actually, the same can be said of the real mail service. When you think about it, the likelihood of one particular letter leaving one location and ending up precisely where it should at the other end seems impossible — mind-boggling, even. However, both email and its real-world equivalent have several aspects in common that improve the likelihood that they'll actually work as intended. The following sections examine what happens when you write an email, click Send, and the recipient receives it on the other end. You might be surprised at what you discover.

CONSIDERING THE SIMPLE MAIL TRANSFER PROTOCOL

When you work with email, you see a lot of references to Simple Mail Transfer Protocol (SMTP). Of course, the term looks really technical, and what happens under the covers truly *is* technical, but all you really need to know is that it works. On the other hand, understanding SMTP is little more than a "black box" that takes an email from the sender and spits it out at the other end to the recipient can be useful. Taking the term apart (in reverse order), you see these elements:

- **Protocol:** A standard set of rules. Email works by requiring rules that everyone agrees upon. Otherwise, email would become unreliable.

- **Mail transfer:** Documents are sent from one place to another, much the same as what the post office does with real mail. In email's case, the transfer process relies on short commands that your email application issues to the SMTP server. For example, the `MAIL FROM` command tells the SMTP server who is sending the email, while the `RCPT TO` command states where to send it.

- **Simple:** States that this activity goes on with the least amount of effort possible. The fewer parts to anything, the more reliable it becomes.

If you were to look at the rules for transferring the information, you would find they're anything but simple. For example, RFC1123 is a standard that specifies how Internet hosts are supposed to work (see `http://www.faqs.org/rfcs/rfc1123.html` for details). These rules are used by more than one Internet technology, which explains why most of them appear to work about the same (even though their resources and goals may be different).

Another, entirely different standard, RFC2821, describes how SMTP specifically implements the rules found in RFC1123 (see `http://www.faqs.org/rfcs/rfc2821.html` for details). The point is, a whole lot of rules are written in jargon that only a true geek could love (and even the geeks aren't sure). If you want a plain-English explanation of how email works, check out the article at `https://computer.howstuffworks.com/e-mail-messaging/email.htm`. Page 4 of this article (`https://computer.howstuffworks.com/e-mail-messaging/email3.htm`) describes the commands that SMTP uses to send information hither and thither across the Internet. In fact, if you want the shortest possible description of SMTP, page 4 is probably the right place to look.

Viewing email as you do a letter

The best way to view email is the same as how you view a letter. When you write a letter, you provide two pieces of paper as a minimum. The first contains the content of the letter, the second is an envelope. Assuming that the postal service is honest, the content is never examined by anyone other than the recipient. The same can be said of email. An email actually consists of these components:

>> **Message:** The content of the email, which is actually composed of two subparts:

- **Header:** The part of the email content that includes the subject, the list of recipients, and other features, such as the urgency of the email.

- **Body:** The part of the email content that contains the actual message. The message can be in plain text, formatted as HTML (possibly Rich Text Format, RTF, as well), and consisting of one or more documents, or it can be a combination of all these elements.

» **Envelope:** A container for the message. The envelope provides sender and recipient information, just as the envelope for a physical piece of mail provides. However, an email doesn't include a stamp.

When working with email, you create a message using an email application. As part of the email application setup, you also define account information. When you click send:

1. The email application wraps up your message, with the header first, in an envelope that includes both your sender and the recipient's information.

2. The email application uses the account information to contact the SMTP server and send the message for you.

3. The SMTP server reads only the information found in the message envelope and redirects your email to the recipient.

4. The recipient email application logs on to the local server, picks up the email, and then displays only the message part for the user.

The process is a little more complex than this explanation, but this is essentially what happens. In fact, it's much the same as the process used when working with physical letters in that the essential steps are the same. With physical mail, the email application is replaced by you on one end and the recipient at the other. The SMTP server is replaced by the post office and the employees who work there (including the postal carriers). However, someone generates a message, the message is transferred to a recipient, and the recipient receives the message in both cases.

Defining the parts of the envelope

There is a difference in how the envelope for an email is configured and how it's actually handled. When you view the envelope for an email, it looks just like a letter in that it contains the address of the sender and the address of the recipient. It may not look physically like an envelope, but the same components are there. When you visualize a physical envelope, you see certain specifics, such as the sender's name, street address, city, state, and zip code. The same is true for the recipient. These elements define, in physical terms, where the postal carrier should deliver the letter or return the letter when it can't be delivered.

However, when the SMTP server processes the envelope for an email, it must look at the specifics of the address, which is where the analogy of a physical envelope used for mail starts to break down a little. An email address contains different information from a physical address. In summary, here is what the email address contains:

- » **Host:** The host is akin to the city and state used by a physical mail envelope. A host address is the address used by the carrier or server that is physically connected to the Internet, and it handles all the traffic that the Internet consumes or provides for this particular machine. A PC can use Internet resources in a lot of ways, but the host address for all these uses is the same.

- » **Port:** The port is akin to the street address used by a physical mail envelope. It specifies which specific part of the system should receive the message. For example, an SMTP server used for outgoing messages normally relies on port 25. However, the Post Office Protocol (POP3) server used for incoming email messages usually relies on port 110. Your browser typically uses port 80 to communicate with websites. However, secure websites (those that use https as a protocol, rather than http) rely on port 443 instead. You can see a list of typical ports at `https://en.wikipedia.org/wiki/List_of_TCP_and_UDP_port_numbers`.

- » **Local hostname:** The local hostname is the human-readable form of the combination of the host and port. For example, the website `https://www.myplace.com` (not a real URL) might resolve to an address of 55.225.163.40:80 (where the first four numbers are the host address and the number after the colon is the port). Python takes care of these details behind the scenes for you, so normally you don't need to worry about them. However, it's nice to know that this information is available.

Now that you have a better idea of how the address is put together, it's time to look at it more carefully. The following sections describe the envelope of an email in more precise terms.

Host

A *host address* is the identifier for a connection to a server. Just as an address on an envelope isn't the actual location, neither is the host address the actual server. It merely specifies the location of the server.

REMEMBER

The connection used to access a combination of a host address and a port is called a *socket.* Just who came up with this odd name and why isn't important. What is important is that you can use the socket to find out all kinds of information that's useful in understanding how email works. The following steps help you see host-names and host addresses at work. More important, you begin to understand the whole idea of an email envelope and the addresses it contains.

1. **Open a new notebook.**

You can also use the downloadable source file, BPP4D3E; 17; Sending an Email.ipynb, which contains the application code.

2. **Type the following code into the notebook — pressing Enter after each line — and then click Run Cell.**

```
import socket
print(socket.gethostbyname("localhost"))
print(socket.gethostbyaddr("127.0.0.1"))
```

Before you can work with sockets, you must import the socket library. This library contains all sorts of confusing attributes, so use it with caution. However, this library also contains some interesting functions that help you see how the Internet addresses work.

The next line displays a host address as output. In this case, you should see 127.0.0.1 as output because localhost is a standard hostname. The address, 127.0.0.1, is associated with the host name, localhost.

Be prepared for a surprise. You get a tuple as output similar to this one:

```
('MAIN', [], ['127.0.0.1'])
```

However, instead of getting localhost as the name of the host, you get the name of your machine. You use localhost as a common name for the local machine, but when you specify the address, you get the machine name instead. In this case, 'MAIN' is the name of my personal machine. The name you see on your screen will correspond to your machine.

3. **In a new cell, type** print(socket.gethostbyname("www.johnmueller-books.com")) **and click Run Cell.**

You see an address for my website, which is currently:

72.167.241.46

The point is that these addresses work wherever you are and whatever you're doing — just like those you place on a physical envelope. The physical mail uses addresses that are unique across the world, just as the Internet does.

Port

A *port* is a specific entryway for a server location. The host address specifies the location, but the port defines where to get in. Even if you don't specify a port every time you use a host address, the port is implied. Access is always granted using a combination of the host address and the port. The following steps help illustrate how ports work with the host address to provide server access:

1. **Type the following code into a new cell in the notebook — pressing Enter after each line — and then click Run Cell.**

```
import socket
socket.getaddrinfo("localhost", 110)
```

Remember that a socket provides both host address and port information. You use the socket to create a connection that includes both items. The first value is the name of a host you want to obtain information about. The second value is the port on that host. In this case, you obtain the information about localhost port 110. When you run the code, you see output similar to this:

```
[(<AddressFamily.AF_INET6: 23>, 0, 0, '',
  ('::1', 110, 0, 0)),
 (<AddressFamily.AF_INET: 2>, 0, 0, '',
  ('127.0.0.1', 110))]
```

The output consists of two tuples: one for the Internet Protocol version 6 (IPv6) output and one for the Internet Protocol version 4 (IPv4) address. The address is indicated by the AddressFamily entry, which is AF_INET6 for IPv6 and AF_INET for IPv4. Each of these tuples contains five entries, four of which you really don't need to worry about because you'll likely never need them. However, the last entry, ('127.0.0.1', 110), shows the IPv4 address and port for localhost port 110.

TECHNICAL STUFF

If you really want to know more about address information content, check out the web pages at https://www.ibm.com/docs/it/i/7.1?topic=families-using-af-inet-address-family and https://www.ibm.com/docs/it/i/7.1?topic=families-using-af-inet6-address-family.

2. **In a new cell, type** socket.getaddrinfo("johnmuellerbooks.com", 80) **and click Run Cell.**

You see this output when you run the code:

```
[(<AddressFamily.AF_INET: 2>, 0, 0, '',
  ('72.167.241.46', 80))]
```

Notice that this Internet location provides only an IPv4 address, not an IPv6, address, for port 80. The socket.getaddrinfo() method provides a useful method for determining how you can access a particular location. Using IPv6 provides significant benefits over IPv4 (see https://www.mygreatlearning.com/blog/ipv4-vs-ipv6/ for details), but many Internet locations provide only IPv4 support now. (If you live in a larger city, you'll probably see both an IPv4 and an IPv6 address.)

3. **In a new cell, type** socket.getservbyport(25) **and click Run Cell.**

You see the following output:

```
'smtp'
```

The socket.getservbyport() method provides the means to determine how a particular port is used. Port 25 is always dedicated to SMTP support on any server. So, when you access 127.0.0.1:25, you're asking for the SMTP server on localhost. In short, a port provides a specific kind of access in many situations.

REMEMBER

Some people assume that the port information is always provided. However, this isn't always the case. Python will provide a default port when you don't supply one, but relying on the default port is a bad idea because you can't be certain which service will be accessed. In addition, some systems use nonstandard port assignments as a security feature. Always get into the habit of using the port number and ensuring that you have the right one for the task at hand.

Local hostname

A *hostname* is simply the human-readable form of the host address. Humans don't really understand 127.0.0.1 very well (and the IPv6 addresses make even less sense). However, humans do understand localhost just fine. There is a special server and setup to translate human-readable hostnames to host addresses, but you really don't need to worry about it for this book (or programming in general). When your application suddenly breaks for no apparent reason, it helps to know that one does exist, though.

The "Host" section, earlier in this chapter, introduces you to the hostname to a certain extent through the use of the socket.gethostbyaddr() method, whereby an address is translated into a hostname. You saw the process in reverse using the socket.gethostbyname() method. The following steps help you understand some nuances about working with the hostname:

1. **Type the following code into a new cell in the notebook — pressing Enter after each line — and then click Run Cell.**

    ```
    import socket
    socket.gethostname()
    ```

    You see the name of the local system, which is 'MAIN' on my system, but will be different on yours.

2. **In a new cell, type** socket.gethostbyname(socket.gethostname()) **and click Run Cell.**

    You see the IP address of the local system, which is '192.168.0.103' on my system. Again, your setup is likely different from mine, so the output you see will differ. This is a method you can use in your applications to determine the address of the sender when needed. Because it doesn't rely on any hard-coded value, the method works on any system.

Defining the parts of the letter

The "envelope" for an email address is what the SMTP server uses to route the email. However, the envelope doesn't include any content — that's the purpose of the letter. A lot of developers get the two elements confused because the letter contains sender and receiver information as well. This information appears in the letter just like the address information that appears in a business letter — it's for the benefit of the viewer. When you send a business letter, the postal delivery person doesn't open the envelope to see the address information inside. Only the information on the envelope matters.

TECHNICAL STUFF

It's because the information in the email letter is separate from its information in the envelope that nefarious individuals can spoof email addresses. The envelope potentially contains legitimate sender information, but the letter may not. (When you see the email in your email application, all that is present is the letter, not the envelope — the envelope has been stripped away by the email application.) For that matter, neither the sender nor the recipient information may be correct in the letter that you see onscreen in your email reader.

The letter part of an email is actually made of separate components, just as the envelope is. Here is a summary of the three components:

>> **Sender:** The sender information tells you who sent the message. It contains just the email address of the sender.

>> **Receiver:** The receiver information tells you who will receive the message. This is actually a list of recipient email addresses. Even if you want to send the message to only one person, you must supply the single email address in a list.

>> **Message:** Contains the information that you want the recipient to see. This information can include the following:

- **From:** The human-readable form of the sender.

- **To:** The human-readable form of the recipients.

- **CC:** Visible recipients who also received the message, even though they aren't the primary targets of the message.

- **BCC:** Hidden recipients who also received the message, even though they aren't the primary targets of the message.

- **Subject:** The purpose of the message.

- **Documents:** One or more documents, including the text message that appears with the email.

Emails can actually become quite complex and lengthy. Depending on the kind of email that is sent, a message could include all sorts of additional information. However, most emails contain these simple components, and this is all the information you need to send an email from your application. The following sections describe the process used to generate a letter and its components in more detail.

Defining the message

Sending an empty envelope to someone will work, but it isn't very exciting. In order to make your email message worthwhile, you need to define a message. Python supports a number of methods of creating messages. However, the easiest and most reliable way to create a message is to use the Multipurpose Internet Mail Extensions (MIME) functionality that Python provides (and no, a MIME is not a silent person with white gloves who acts out in public).

As with many email features, MIME is standardized, so it works the same no matter which platform you use. There are also numerous forms of MIME that are all part of the `email.mime` module described at `https://docs.python.org/3/library/email.mime.html`. Here are the forms that you need to consider most often when working with email:

>> **MIMEApplication:** Provides a method for sending and receiving application input and output

>> **MIMEAudio:** Contains an audio file

>> **MIMEImage:** Contains an image file

>> **MIMEMultipart:** Allows a single message to contain multiple subparts, such as including both text and graphics in a single message

>> **MIMEText:** Contains text data that can be in ASCII, HTML, or another standardized format

Although you can create any sort of an email message with Python, the easiest type to create is one that contains plain text. The lack of formatting in the content lets you focus on the technique used to create the message, rather than on the message content. The following steps help you understand how the message-creating process works, but you won't actually send the message anywhere.

1. **Type the following code into a new cell in the notebook — pressing Enter after each line.**

```
from email.mime.text import MIMEText
msg = MIMEText("Hello There")
msg['Subject'] = "A Test Message"
```

```
msg['From']='John Mueller ' + \
    '<John@JohnMuellerBooks.com>'
msg['To'] = 'John Mueller ' + \
    '<John@JohnMuellerBooks.com>'

msg.as_string()
```

REMEMBER

This is a basic plain-text message. Before you can do anything, you must import the required class, which is MIMEText. If you were creating some other sort of message, you'd need to import other classes or import the email.mime module as a whole.

The MIMEText() constructor requires message text as input. This is the body of your message, so it might be quite long. In this case, the message is relatively short — just a greeting.

At this point, you assign values to standard attributes. The example shows the three common attributes that you always define: Subject, From, and To. The two address fields, From and To, contain both a human-readable name and the email address. All you have to include is the email address.

The call to msg.as_string() displays the actual message.

2. **Click Run Cell.**

You see the output shown in Figure 17-1. This is how the message actually looks. If you have ever looked under the covers at the messages produced by your email application, the text probably looks familiar.

Defining the parts of the letter

Defining the message

```
In [8]: from email.mime.text import MIMEText
        msg = MIMEText("Hello There")
        msg['Subject'] = "A Test Message"
        msg['From']='John Mueller ' + \
            '<John@JohnMuellerBooks.com>'
        msg['To'] = 'John Mueller ' + \
            '<John@JohnMuellerBooks.com>'

        msg.as_string()

Out[8]: 'Content-Type: text/plain; charset="us-ascii"\nMIME-Version: 1.0\nContent-Trans
        fer-Encoding: 7bit\nSubject: A Test Message\nFrom: John Mueller <John@JohnMuell
        erBooks.com>\nTo: John Mueller <John@JohnMuellerBooks.com>\n\nHello There'
```

FIGURE 17-1:
Python adds some additional information required to make your message work.

The Content-Type reflects the kind of message you created, which is a plain-text message. The charset tells what kind of characters are used in the message so that the recipient knows how to handle them. The MIME-Version specifies the version of MIME used to create the message so that the recipient knows whether it can handle the content. Finally, the Context–Transfer–Encoding determines how the message is converted into a bit stream before it is sent to the recipient.

Specifying the transmission

An earlier section ("Defining the parts of the envelope") describes how the envelope is used to transfer the message from one location to another. The process of sending the message entails defining a transmission method. Python actually creates the envelope for you and performs the transmission, but you must still define the particulars of the transmission. The following steps help you understand the simplest approach to transmitting a message using Python. These steps won't result in a successful transmission unless you modify them to match your setup. Read the "Considering the SMTP server" sidebar, later in this chapter, for additional information.

1. **Open an Anaconda Prompt, type** python –m smtpd –n –c DebuggingServer localhost:1025, **and press Enter.**

Older platforms would allow you to use port 25 to transmit messages. Newer platforms display a ConnectionRefusedError instead. This is a security feature and it shows that certain platform features aren't installed by default. This command creates an SMTP server on port 1025 for you to use for this example. Don't worry when the command doesn't appear to have completed and you see just a blank line. The server is simply waiting for you to use it.

2. **Type the following code into a new cell in the notebook — pressing Enter after each line.**

```
import smtplib
s = smtplib.SMTP('localhost', 1025)

s.sendmail('SenderAddress',
           ['RecipientAddress'],
           msg.as_string())
```

The smtplib module contains everything needed to create the message envelope and send it. The first step in this process is to create a connection to the SMTP server, which you name as a string in the constructor. If the SMTP server that you provide doesn't exist, the application will fail at this point, saying that the host actively refused the connection.

WARNING

For the call to sendmail() to work, you must replace SenderAddress and RecipientAddress with real addresses. Don't include the human-readable form this time — the server requires only an address. If you don't include a real address, you'll definitely see an error message when you click Run Cell. You might also see an error if your email server is temporarily offline, there is a glitch in the network connection, or any of a number of other odd things occur. If you're sure that you typed everything correctly, try sending the message a second time before you panic. See the sidebar "Considering the SMTP server," later in this chapter, for additional details.

3. **Click Run Cell.**

   This is the step that actually creates the envelope, packages the email message, and sends it off to the recipient. Notice that you specify the sender and recipient information separately from the message, which the SMTP server doesn't read. Figure 17-2 shows typical output (viewed at the Anaconda Prompt) from this part of the example.

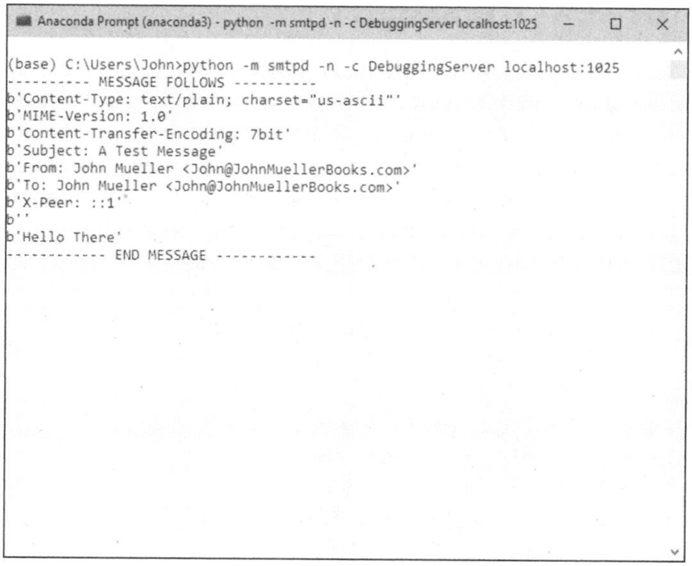

FIGURE 17-2:
You see the message transmitted by the SMTP server at the Anaconda Prompt.

Considering the message subtypes

The "Defining the message" section, earlier in this chapter, describes the major email message types, such as application and text. However, if email had to rely on just those types, transmitting coherent messages to anyone would be difficult. The problem is that the type of information isn't explicit enough. If you send someone a text message, you need to know what sort of text it is before you can process it, and guessing just isn't a good idea. A text message could be formatted as plain text, or it might actually be an HTML page. You wouldn't know from just seeing the type, so messages require a subtype. The type is text and the subtype is html when you send an HTML page to someone. The type and subtype are separated by a forward slash, so you'd see text/html if you looked at the message.

Theoretically, the number of subtypes is unlimited as long as the platform has a handler defined for that subtype. However, the reality is that everyone needs to agree on the subtypes or there won't be a handler (unless you're talking about a custom application for which the two parties have agreed to a custom subtype in advance). With this in mind, you can find a listing of standard types and subtypes at `https://www.freeformatter.com/mime-types-list.html`. The nice thing about the table on this site is that it provides you with a common file extension associated with the subtype and a reference to obtain additional information about it.

Putting everything together for text messages

Text messages represent the most efficient and least resource-intensive method of sending communication. However, text messages also convey the least amount of information. Yes, you can use emoticons to help get the point across, but the lack of formatting can become a problem in some situations. Here is what this chapter has covered, put into a single code block that you can test using the SMTP server created earlier at the Anaconda Prompt using the `python -m smtpd -n -c DebuggingServer localhost:1025` command:

```
from email.mime.text import MIMEText
import smtplib

msg = MIMEText("Hello There")
msg['Subject'] = "A Test Message"
msg['From']='SenderAddress'
msg['To'] = 'RecipientAddress'

s = smtplib.SMTP('localhost', 1025)

s.sendmail('SenderAddress',
           ['RecipientAddress'],
           msg.as_string())

print("Message Sent!")
```

If you run this code, you see the same output as that shown in Figure 17-2 at the Anaconda Prompt.

CONSIDERING THE SMTP SERVER

If you tried the example in this chapter without modifying it, you're probably scratching your head right now trying to figure out what went wrong. It's unlikely that your system has an SMTP server connected to localhost. The reason for the examples to use localhost is to provide a placeholder that you replace later with the information for your particular setup.

In order to see the example actually work, you need an SMTP server as well as a real-world email account. Of course, you could install all the software required to create such an environment on your own system, and some developers who work extensively with email applications do just that. Most platforms come with an email package that you can install, or you can use a freely available substitute such as Sendmail, an open source product available for download at https://www.proofpoint.com/us/products/email-protection/open-source-email-solution.

If you choose to use the SMTP server that your email application uses, you need to discover the SMTP server name and port. When working with a local application, such as Outlook, it's pretty easy to discover this information. For web-based email, locating it is usually a little harder, but some applications provide a special settings screen that contains the information you need. A problem occurs when your email application uses encryption to protect your messages. You need to log into the server and use the same encryption that the SMTP server does. The article at https://zetcode.com/python/smtplib/ provides some insights into how to make this work, especially if SMTP server uses the STARTTLS encryption technique. If you're using Gmail, you can find a more specific coding example at https://www.courier.com/blog/three-ways-to-send-emails-using-python-with-code-tutorials/.

No matter what sort of SMTP server you eventually find, you need to have an account on that server in most cases to use the functionality it provides. Replace the information in the examples with the information for your SMTP server, such as smtp.myisp.com, along with your email address for both sender and receiver. Otherwise, the example won't work.

Working with an HTML message

An HTML message is basically a text message with special formatting. The following steps help you create an HTML email to send off.

1. **Type the following code into a new cell in the notebook — pressing Enter after each line.**

    ```
    from email.mime.text import MIMEText
    import smtplib
    ```

```
msg = MIMEText(
    "<h1>A Heading</h1><p>Hello There!</p>","html")
msg['Subject'] = 'A Test HTML Message'
msg['From']='SenderAddress'
msg['To'] = 'RecipientAddress'

s = smtplib.SMTP('localhost', 1025)
s.sendmail('SenderAddress',
           ['RecipientAddress'],
           msg.as_string())

print("Message Sent!")
```

The example follows the same flow as the text message example in the previous section. However, notice that the message now contains HTML tags. You create an HTML body, not an entire page. This message will have an H1 header and a paragraph.

REMEMBER

The most important part of this example is the text that comes after the message. The "html" argument changes the subtype from text/plain to text/html, so the recipient knows to treat the message as HTML content. If you don't make this change, the recipient won't see the HTML output.

2. **Click Run Cell.**

The application tells you that it has sent the message to the recipient. You can see the output at the Anaconda Prompt, and it should look similar to Figure 17-2, except for the HTML formatting.

5
The Part of Tens

Chapter **18**

Ten Amazing Programming Resources

This book is a great start to your Python programming experience, but you'll want additional resources at some point. This chapter provides you with ten amazing programming resources that you can use to make your development experience better. By using these resources, you save both time and energy in creating your next dazzling Python application.

REMEMBER

Of course, this chapter is only the beginning of your Python resource experience. Reams of Python documentation are out there, along with mountains of Python code. One might be able to write an entire book (or two) devoted solely to the Python libraries. This chapter is designed to provide you with ideas of where to look for additional information that's targeted toward meeting your specific needs. Don't let this be the end of your search — consider this chapter the start of your search instead.

Working with the Python Documentation Online

An essential part of working with Python is knowing what is available in the base language and how to extend it to perform other tasks. The Python documentation at https://docs.python.org/3/ (created for the 3.*x* version of the product) contains a lot more than just the reference to the language that you receive as part of a download. (This is a multiversion site, so you can select the version of Python you want to read about in the top-left corner of the page.) You see these topics discussed as part of the documentation:

>> New features in the current version of the language

>> Access to a full-fledged tutorial

>> Complete library reference

>> Complete language reference

>> How to install and configure Python

>> How to perform specific tasks in Python

>> Help with installing Python modules from other sources (as a means of extending Python)

>> Help with distributing Python modules you create so that others can use them

>> How to extend Python using C/C++ and then embed the new features you create

>> Complete reference for C/C++ developers who want to extend their applications using Python

>> Frequently Asked Questions (FAQ) pages

REMEMBER

All this information is provided in a form that is easy to access and use. In addition to the usual table-of-contents approach to finding information, you have access to a number of indexes. For example, if you aren't interested in anything but locating a particular module, class, or method, you can use the Global Module Index.

The https://docs.python.org/3/ web page is also the place where you report problems with Python (the specific URL is https://docs.python.org/3/bugs.html). It's important to work through problems you're having with the product, but as with any other language, Python does have bugs in it. Locating and destroying the bugs will only make Python a better language.

Discovering Details Using a Tutorial

You can find various Python tutorials online, and it's usually a good idea to try more than one of them because each tutorial has something unique to offer. In addition, each tutorial has a unique method of presentation that may work better with your learning skills. Here are some tutorials you can use as starting points:

- **Learn Python:** https://www.learnpython.org/
- **Learn Python Programming:** https://www.programiz.com/python-programming
- **learnpython.org:** https://www.learnpython.org/
- **Real Python Tutorials:** https://realpython.com/
- **The Python Tutorial:** https://docs.python.org/3/tutorial/
- **Tutorials Point Python Tutorial:** https://www.tutorialspoint.com/python/index.htm
- **W3Schools Python Tutorial:** https://www.w3schools.com/python/

These tutorials present topics like:

- **Code introspection:** Provides the ability to examine classes, functions, and keywords to determine their purpose and capabilities.
- **Database access:** Most applications require some type of database interactivity to access large datasets.
- **Data science:** There are special techniques you can employ in Python to perform data science tasks, and some tutorials excel in this regard.
- **Decorator:** A method for making simple modifications to callable objects.
- **Exception handling:** An extension of the methods described in Chapter 10.
- **Generators:** Specialized functions that return iterators.
- **HR interview questions:** No one wants to go into an interview unprepared, so finding a tutorial to help you is a good idea.
- **List comprehensions:** A method to generate new lists based on existing lists.
- **Multiple function arguments:** An extension of the methods described in the "Using methods with variable argument lists" in Chapter 15.

>> **Partial functions:** A technique for creating specialized versions of simple functions that derive from more complex functions. For example, if you have a `multiply()` function that requires two arguments, a partial function named `double()` may require only one argument that it always multiplies by 2.

>> **Regular expressions:** Wildcard setups used to match patterns of characters, such as telephone numbers.

>> **Serialization:** Shows how to use a data storage methodology called JavaScript Object Notation (JSON).

>> **Sets:** Demonstrates a special kind of list that never contains duplicate entries.

Performing Web Programming by Using Python

Many developers specialize in creating online applications of various sorts using Python. The Web Programming in Python site at `https://wiki.python.org/moin/WebProgramming` helps you make the move from the desktop to online application development. It doesn't just cover one sort of online application — it covers almost all of them (an entire book free for the asking). The tutorials are divided into these three major (and many minor) areas:

>> Server
  - Developing server-side frameworks for applications
  - Creating a Common Gateway Interface (CGI) script
  - Providing server applications
  - Developing Content Management Systems (CMS)
  - Designing data access methods through web services solutions

>> Client
  - Interacting with browsers and browser-based technologies
  - Creating browser-based clients
  - Accessing data through various methodologies, including web services

>> Related
  - Creating common solutions for Python-based online computing
  - Interacting with DataBase Management Systems (DBMSs)

- Designing application templates
- Building Intranet solutions

Locating Useful (versus Useless) Modules

If you're interested in useless modules, those that apparently do nothing at all (or, at least, nothing worthwhile), you're in the wrong spot. The UsefulModules site at `https://wiki.python.org/moin/UsefulModules` provides you with all sorts of useful modules for your Python installation, grouped by category. Of special note is that graphics are categorized in a detailed manner for the following uses:

>> **Game development:** Creating game elements, including those exciting graphics everyone enjoys

>> **GUI:** Designing the user interface elements for an application

>> **ID3 handling:** Providing support for the ID3 multimedia packaging metadata normally associated with MP3, but used in other ways as well

>> **Image manipulation:** Modifying the appearance of graphics in various ways, rather than provide a particular presentation

>> **Plotting:** Displaying graphs and charts onscreen, rather than taking over the government (sorry)

>> **Presentation:** Preparing graphical information for public display, such as the creation of slides

>> **Resource Description Framework (RDF):** Defining the interconnections between data on the web, often in graphical format

Creating Applications Faster by Using an IDE

An Interactive Development Environment (IDE) helps you create applications in a specific language. The Integrated DeveLopment Environment (IDLE) editor (just type **idle** and press Enter at the Anaconda Prompt to see it) that comes with Python works well for experimentation, but you may find it limited after a while. For example, IDLE doesn't provide the advanced debugging functionality that many developers favor. In addition, you may find that you want to create graphical applications, which is difficult using IDLE.

The problem is that you can talk to 50 developers and get little consensus as to the best tool for any job, especially when discussing IDEs. Every developer has a favorite product and isn't easily swayed to try another. Developers invest many hours learning a particular IDE and extending it to meet specific requirements (when the IDE allows such tampering).

REMEMBER

An inability (at times) to change IDEs later is why it's important to try a number of different IDEs before you settle on one. (The most common reason for not wanting to change an IDE after you select one is that the project types are incompatible, which would mean having to re-create your projects every time you change editors, but there are many other reasons that you can find listed online.) The PythonEditors wiki at `https://wiki.python.org/moin/PythonEditors` provides an extensive list of IDEs that you can try. The table provides you with particulars about each editor so that you can eliminate some of the choices immediately.

Checking Your Syntax with Greater Ease

Colab and Jupyter Notebook both provide syntax highlighting to help you see keywords, variables, and other elements. These IDEs also provide some advanced error checking to point out potential errors. However, for some developers, both these IDEs can come up short because you actually have to run the cell in order to see the error information. Some developers prefer interactive syntax checking, in which the IDE flags the error immediately, even before the developer leaves the errant line of code.

The python.vim utility (`https://www.vim.org/scripts/script.php?script_id=790`) provides enhanced syntax highlighting that makes finding errors in your Python script even easier. This utility runs as a script, which makes it fast and efficient to use on any platform. In addition, you can tweak the source code as needed to meet particular needs.

Using XML to Your Advantage

The eXtensible Markup Language (XML) is used for data storage of all types in most applications of any substance today. You probably have a number of XML files on your system and don't even know it because XML data appears under a number of file extensions. For example, many `.config` files, used to hold application settings, rely on XML. In short, it's not a matter of if you'll encounter XML when writing Python applications, but when.

XML has a number of advantages over other means of storing data. For example, it's platform independent. You can use XML on any system, and the same file is readable on any other system as long as that system knows the file format. The platform independence of XML is why it appears with so many other technologies, such as web services. In addition, XML is relatively easy to learn and because it's usually text, you can usually fix problems with it without too many problems.

REMEMBER

It's important to learn about XML itself, and you can do so using an easy tutorial such as the one found on the W3Schools site at `https://www.w3schools.com/xml/default.ASP`. Some developers rush ahead and later find that they can't understand the Python-specific materials that assume they already know how to write basic XML files. The W3Schools site is nice because it breaks up the learning process into chapters so that you can work with XML a little at a time, as follows:

>> Taking a basic XML tutorial

>> Validating your XML files

>> Using XML with JavaScript (which may not seem important, but JavaScript is prominent in many online application scenarios)

>> Gaining an overview of XML-related technologies

>> Using advanced XML techniques

>> Working with XML examples that make seeing XML in action easier

After you get the fundamentals down, you need a resource that shows how to use XML with Python. One of the better places to find this information is the Tutorials on XML Processing with Python site at `https://wiki.python.org/moin/Tutorials%20on%20XML%20processing%20with%20Python`. Between these two resources, you can quickly build a knowledge of XML that will have you building Python applications that use XML in no time.

Getting Past the Common Python Newbie Errors

Absolutely everyone makes coding mistakes — even that snobby fellow down the hall who has been programming for the last 30 years (he started in kindergarten). No one likes to make mistakes and some people don't like to own up to them, but everyone does make them. So you shouldn't feel too bad when you make a mistake. Simply fix it up and get on with your life.

REMEMBER

Of course, there is a difference between making a mistake and making an avoidable, common mistake. Yes, even the professionals sometimes make the avoidable common mistakes, but it's far less likely because they have seen the mistake in the past and have trained themselves to avoid it. You can gain an advantage over your competition by avoiding the newbie mistakes that everyone has to learn about sometime. To avoid these mistakes, check out the "Common beginner mistakes in Python" article at `https://deepsource.io/blog/python-common-mistakes/`.

Understanding Unicode

Although this book tries to sidestep the thorny topic of Unicode, you'll eventually encounter it when you start writing serious applications. Unfortunately, Unicode is one of those topics that had a committee deciding what Unicode would look like, so we ended up with more than one poorly explained definition of Unicode and a multitude of standards to define it. In short, there is no one definition for Unicode.

You'll encounter a wealth of Unicode standards when you start working with more advanced Python applications, especially when you start working with multiple human languages (each of which seems to favor its own flavor of Unicode). Keeping in mind the need to discover just what Unicode is, here are some resources you should check out:

» The Updated Guide to Unicode on Python (`https://lucumr.pocoo.org/2013/7/2/the-updated-guide-to-unicode/`)

» Python Encodings and Unicode (`https://eric.themoritzfamily.com/python-encodings-and-unicode.html`)

» Unicode Tutorials and Overviews (`http://www.unicode.org/standard/tutorial-info.html`)

>> unicode_literals in Python (https://www.geeksforgeeks.org/unicode_literals-in-python/)

>> Pragmatic Unicode (https://nedbatchelder.com/text/unipain.html)

Making Your Python Application Fast

Nothing turns off a user faster than an application that performs poorly. When an application performs poorly, you can count on users not using it at all. In fact, poor performance is a significant source of application failure in enterprise environments. An organization can spend a ton of money to build an impressive application that does everything, but no one uses it because it runs too slowly or has other serious performance problems.

Numerous resources are available to help you understand performance as it applies to Python applications. However, one of the best resources out there is "A guide to analyzing Python performance," at http://pythonic.zoomquiet.top/data/20170602154836/index.html. The author takes the time to explain why something is a performance bottleneck, rather than simply tell you that it is. After you read this article, make sure to check out the "PythonSpeed Performance Tips" at https://wiki.python.org/moin/PythonSpeed/PerformanceTips as well.

Chapter **19**

Ten Ways to Make a Living with Python

You can literally write any application you want using any language you desire given enough time, patience, and effort. However, some undertakings would be so convoluted and time consuming as to make the effort a study in frustration. In short, most (possibly all) things are possible, but not everything is worth the effort. Using the right tool for the job is always a plus in a world that views time as something in short supply and not to be squandered.

Python excels at certain kinds of tasks, which means that it also lends itself to certain types of programming. Many people take this statement to mean that you'll be stuck in a data science job for the rest of your life (which is why data scientist isn't included in this chapter), but Python can do much more. For example, you may become a web developer, as described at https://www.projectpro. io/article/python-for-data-science-vs-python-for-web-development/177.

The kind of programming you can perform determines the job you get and the way in which you make your living. For example, Python probably isn't a very good choice for writing device drivers, as C/C++ are, so you probably won't find yourself working for a hardware company. Likewise, Python can work with databases, but not at the same depth that comes natively to other languages such as Structured Query Language (SQL), so you won't find yourself working on a huge corporate database project. However, you may find yourself using Python in academic settings because Python does make a great learning language. (See my blog post on the topic at `http://blog.johnmuellerbooks.com/2014/07/14/python-as-a-learning-tool/`.)

The following sections describe some of the occupations that do use Python regularly so that you know what sorts of things you might do with your new-found knowledge. Of course, a single source can't list every kind of job. Consider this an overview of some of the more common uses for Python.

Working in QA

A lot of organizations have separate Quality Assurance (QA) departments that check applications to ensure that they work as advertised. Many different test script languages are on the market, but Python makes an excellent language in this regard because it's so incredibly flexible. In addition, you can use this single language in multiple environments — both on the client and on the server. The broad reach of Python means that you can learn a single language and use it for testing anywhere you need to test something, and in any environment.

REMEMBER

In this scenario, the developer usually knows another language, such as C++, and uses Python to test the applications written in C++. However, the QA person doesn't need to know another language in all cases. In some situations, blind testing may be used to confirm that an application behaves in a practical manner or as a means for checking the functionality of an external service provider. You need to check with the organization you want to work with as to the qualifications required for a job from a language perspective.

WHY YOU NEED TO KNOW MULTIPLE PROGRAMMING LANGUAGES

Most organizations see knowledge of multiple programming languages as a big plus (some see it as a requirement). Of course, when you're an employer, it's nice to get the best deal you can when hiring a new employee. Knowing a broader range of languages means that you can work in more positions and offer greater value to an organization. Rewriting applications in another language is time consuming, error prone, and expensive, so most companies look for people who can support an application in the existing language, rather than rebuild it from scratch.

From your perspective, knowing more languages means that you'll get more interesting jobs and will be less likely to get bored doing the same old thing every day. In addition, knowing multiple languages tends to reduce frustration. Most large applications today rely on components written in a number of computer languages. To understand the application and how it functions better, you need to know every language used to construct it.

Knowing multiple languages also makes it possible to learn new languages faster. After a while, you start to see patterns in how computer languages are put together, so you spend less time with the basics and can move right on to advanced topics. The faster you can learn new technologies, the greater your opportunities to work in exciting areas of computer science. In short, knowing more languages opens a lot of doors.

Becoming the IT Staff for a Smaller Organization

A smaller organization may have only one or two IT staff, which means that you have to perform a broad range of tasks quickly and efficiently. With Python, you can write utilities and in-house applications quite swiftly. Even though Python might not answer the needs of a large organization because it's interpreted (and potentially open to theft or fiddling by unskilled employees), using it in a smaller organization makes sense because you have greater access control and need to make changes fast. In addition, the ability to use Python in a significant number of environments reduces the need to use anything but Python to meet your needs. (There is actually a compiled form of Python called *Cython*; see `https://www.infoworld.com/article/3250299/what-is-cython-python-at-the-speed-of-c.html` for details).

TIP

Some developers are unaware that Python is available in some non-obvious products. For example, even though you can't use Python scripting with Internet Information Server (IIS) right out of the box, you can add Python scripting support to this product by using the steps found in the Microsoft Knowledge Base article at `https://docs.microsoft.com/visualstudio/python/configure-web-apps-for-iis-windows`. If you aren't sure whether a particular application can use Python for scripting, make sure that you check it out online.

You can also get Python support in some products that you might think couldn't possibly support it. For example, you can use Python with Visual Studio (see `https://visualstudio.microsoft.com/vs/features/python/`) to make use of Microsoft technologies with this language. The site at `https://code.visualstudio.com/docs/languages/python` provides some additional details about Python support.

Performing Specialty Scripting for Applications

A number of products can use Python for scripting purposes. For example, Maya (`https://www.autodesk.com/products/maya/overview`) relies on Python for scripting purposes. (The video series at `https://zurbrigg.com/tutorials/beginning-python-for-maya` provides you with additional details.) By knowing which high-end products support Python, you can find a job working with that application in any business that uses it. Here are some examples of products that rely on Python for scripting needs:

>> 3ds Max

>> Abaqus

>> Blender

>> Cinema 4D

>> GIMP

>> Google App Engine

>> Houdini

>> Inkscape

>> Lightwave

>> Modo

>> MotionBuilder

>> Nuke

>> Paint Shop Pro

>> Scribus

>> Softimage

This is just the tip of the iceberg. You can also use Python with the GNU debugger to create more understandable output of complex structures, such as those found in C++ containers. Some video games also rely on Python as a scripting language. In short, you could build a career around creating application scripts using Python as the programming language.

Administering a Network

More than a few administrators use Python to perform tasks such as monitoring network health or creating utilities that automate tasks. Administrators are often short of time, so anything they can do to automate tasks is a plus. In fact, some network management software, such as Trigger (`https://trigger.readthedocs.io/en/latest/`), is actually written in Python. A lot of these tools are open source and free to download, so you can try them on your network. Also, some interesting articles discuss using Python for network administration, such as "Network Automation Using Python Programming," at `https://www.sevenmentor.com/network-automation-using-python-programming`. It's also possible to find courses on the topic, such as the one at `https://www.globalknowledge.com/us-en/course/182899/python-for-network-automation/`. The point is that knowing how to use Python on your network can ultimately decrease your workload and help you perform your tasks more easily. If you want to see some scripts that are written with network management in mind, check out 25 projects tagged "Network Management" at `http://freshmeat.sourceforge.net/tags/network-management`.

Teaching Programming Skills

Many teachers are looking for a faster, more consistent method of teaching computer technology. Raspberry Pi (`https://www.raspberrypi.org/`) is a single-board computer that makes obtaining the required equipment a lot less expensive for schools. The smallish device plugs into a television or computer monitor to provide full computing capabilities with an incredibly simple setup. Interestingly enough, Python plays a big role in making Raspberry Pi into a teaching platform for programming skills (`https://projects.raspberrypi.org/en/projects?software%5B%5D=python` and `https://realpython.com/python-raspberry-pi/`).

TIP

In reality, teachers often use Python to extend native Raspberry Pi capabilities so that it can perform all sorts of interesting tasks (`https://www.raspberrypi.org/blog/tag/python/`). The project entitled, Boris, the Twitter Dino-Bot (`https://www.raspberrypi.com/news/boris-the-twitter-dino-bot/`), is especially interesting. (There is a YouTube video about it at `https://www.youtube.com/watch?v=Q5Kc9Aqf_Zk`.) The point is that if you have a teaching goal in mind, combining Raspberry Pi with Python is a fantastic idea.

Helping People Decide on Location

A Geographic Information System (GIS) provides a means of viewing geographic information with business needs in mind. For example, you could use GIS to determine the best place to put a new business or to determine the optimum routes for shipping goods. However, GIS is used for more than simply deciding on locations — it also provides a means for communicating location information better than maps, reports, and other graphics, and a method of presenting physical locations to others. Also interesting is the fact that many GIS products use Python as their language of choice. In fact, a wealth of Python-specific information related to GIS is currently available, such as

» 15 Python Libraries for GIS and Mapping (https://gisgeography.com/python-libraries-gis-mapping/)

» Python and GIS Resources (https://www.gislounge.com/python-and-gis-resources/)

» GIS Programming and Software Development (https://www.e-education.psu.edu/geog485/node/17)

Many GIS-specific products, such as ArcGIS (https://www.esri.com/arcgis/), rely on Python to automate tasks. Entire communities develop around these software offerings, such as Python for ArcGIS (https://resources.arcgis.com/en/communities/python/). The point is that you can use your new programming skills in areas other than computing to earn an income.

Performing Data Mining

Everyone is collecting data about everyone and everything else. Trying to sift through the mountains of data collected is an impossible task without a lot of fine-tuned automation. The flexible nature of Python, combined with its terse language that makes changes extremely fast, makes it a favorite with people who perform data mining on a daily basis. In fact, you can find an online book on the topic, *A Programmer's Guide to Data Mining,* at http://guidetodatamining.com/. Python makes data mining tasks a lot easier. The purpose of data mining is to recognize trends, which means looking for patterns of various sorts. The use of artificial intelligence with Python makes such pattern recognition possible. A paper on the topic, "Practical Data Mining with Python" (https://dzone.com/refcardz/data-mining-discovering-and), helps you understand how such analysis is possible. You can use Python to create just the right tool to locate a pattern that could net sales missed by your competitor.

REMEMBER

Of course, data mining is used for more than generating sales. For example, people use data mining to perform tasks such as locating new planets around stars or other types of analysis that increase our knowledge of the universe. Python figures into this sort of data mining as well. You can likely find books and other resources dedicated to any kind of data mining that you want to perform, with many of them mentioning Python as the language of choice.

Interacting with Embedded Systems

An embedded system exists for nearly every purpose on the planet. For example, if you own a programmable thermostat for your house, you're interacting with an embedded system. Raspberry Pi (mentioned earlier in the chapter) is an example of a more complex embedded system. Many embedded systems rely on Python as their programming language. In fact, a special form of Python, Embedded Python (`https://wiki.python.org/moin/EmbeddedPython`), is sometimes used for these devices. You can even find a YouTube presentation on using Python to build an embedded system at `https://www.youtube.com/watch?v=WZoeqnsY9AY`.

TIP

Interestingly enough, you might already be interacting with a Python-driven embedded system. For example, Python is the language of choice for many car security systems (`https://www.pythoncarsecurity.com/`). The remote start feature that you might have relies on Python to get the job done. Your home automation and security system (`https://www.activestate.com/blog/how-to-automate-your-home-with-python/`) might also rely on Python.

Python is so popular for embedded systems because it doesn't require compilation. An embedded-system vendor can create an update for any embedded system and simply upload the Python file. The interpreter automatically uses this file without having to upload any new executables or jump through any of the types of hoops that other languages can require.

Carrying Out Scientific Tasks

Python seems to devote more time to scientific and numerical processing tasks than many of the computer languages out there. The number of Python's scientific and numeric processing packages is staggering (`https://wiki.python.org/moin/NumericAndScientific`). Scientists love Python because it's small, easy to learn, and yet quite precise in its treatment of data. You can produce results by using just a few lines of code. Yes, you could produce the same result using another language, but the other language might not include the prebuilt packages to perform the task, and it would most definitely require more lines of code even if it did.

REMEMBER

The two sciences that have dedicated Python packages are space sciences and life sciences. For example, there is actually a package for performing tasks related to solar physics. You can also find a package for working in genomic biology. If you're in a scientific field, the chances are good that your Python knowledge will significantly impact your ability to produce results quickly while your colleagues are still trying to figure out how to analyze the data.

Performing Real-Time Analysis of Data

Making decisions requires timely, reliable, and accurate data. Often, this data must come from a wide variety of sources, which then require a certain amount of analysis before becoming useful. A number of the people who report using Python do so in a management capacity. They use Python to probe those disparate sources of information, perform the required analysis, and then present the big picture to the manager who has asked for the information. Given that this task occurs regularly, trying to do it manually every time would be time consuming. In fact, it would simply be a waste of time. By the time the manager performed the required work, the need to make a decision might already have passed. Python makes it possible to perform tasks quickly enough for a decision to have maximum impact.

Previous sections have pointed out Python's data-mining, number-crunching, and graphics capabilities. A manager can combine all these qualities while using a language that isn't nearly as complex to learn as C++. In addition, any changes are easy to make, and the manager doesn't need to worry about learning programming skills such as compiling the application. A few changes to a line of code in an interpreted package usually serve to complete the task.

REMEMBER

As with other sorts of occupational leads in this chapter, thinking outside the box is important when getting a job. A lot of people need real-time analysis. Launching a rocket into space, controlling product flow, ensuring that packages get delivered on time, and all sorts of other occupations rely on timely, reliable, and accurate data. You might be able to create your own new job simply by employing Python to perform real-time data analysis.

IN THIS CHAPTER

» Debugging, testing, and deploying
applications

» Documenting and versioning your
application

» Writing your application code

» Working within an interactive
environment

Chapter **20**

Ten Tools That Enhance Your Python Experience

ython, like most other programming languages, has strong third-party support in the form of various tools. A *tool* is any utility that enhances the natural capabilities of Python when building an application. So, a debugger is considered a tool because it's a utility, but a library isn't. Libraries are instead used to create better applications. (You can see some of them listed in Chapter 21.)

Even making the distinction between a tool and something that isn't a tool, such as a library, doesn't reduce the list by much. Python enjoys access to a wealth of general-purpose and special tools of all sorts. In fact, the site at `https://wiki.python.org/moin/DevelopmentTools` breaks these tools down into the following 13 categories:

» AutomatedRefactoringTools

» BugTracking

» ConfigurationAndBuildTools

» DistributionUtilities

» DocumentationTools

» IntegratedDevelopmentEnvironments

- >> PythonDebuggers

- >> PythonEditors

- >> PythonShells

- >> SkeletonBuilderTools

- >> TestSoftware

- >> UsefulModules

- >> VersionControl

Interestingly enough, the lists on the Python Development Tools site might not even be complete. You can find Python tools listed in quite a few places online. One of the most interesting new tools on the market now is the dashboard, a special kind of application that makes it possible to create an interactive version of your code for nonprogrammers, as described at `https://blog.esciencecenter.nl/forget-about-jupyter-notebooks-showcase-your-research-using-dashboards-5d13451ba374`.

Given that a single chapter can't possibly cover all the tools out there, this chapter discusses a few of the more interesting tools — those that merit a little extra attention on your part. After you whet your appetite with this chapter, seeing what other sorts of tools you can find online is a good idea. You may find that the tool you thought you might have to create is already available, and in several different forms.

WARNING

All the tools in this chapter do work with Jupyter Notebook because you have control of the environment on your local system. They may not work with Google Colab because you don't have control of Google's virtual servers. The only way to ensure that a product will work with Colab using your particular browser on your particular system is to test it.

Tracking Bugs with Roundup Issue Tracker

You can use a number of bug-tracking sites with Python, such as the following: GitHub (`https://github.com/`); Google Code (`https://code.google.com/`); BitBucket (`https://bitbucket.org/`); and Launchpad (`https://launchpad.net/`). However, these public sites are generally not as convenient to use as your own specific, localized bug-tracking software. You can use a number of tracking systems on your local drive, but Roundup Issue Tracker (`https://roundup.sourceforge.io/`) is one of the better offerings. Roundup should work on any platform that supports Python, and it offers these basic features without any extra work:

>> Bug tracking

>> TODO list management

If you're willing to put a little more work into the installation, you can get additional features, and these additional features are what make the product special. However, to get them, you may need to install other products, such as a DataBase Management System (DBMS). The product instructions tell you what to install and which third-party products are compatible. After you make the additional installations, you get these upgraded features:

>> Customer help-desk support with the following features:
  - Wizard for the phone answerers
  - Network links
  - System and development issue trackers

>> Issue management for Internet Engineering Task Force (IETF) working groups

>> Sales lead tracking

>> Conference paper submission

>> Double-blind referee management

>> Blogging (extremely basic right now, but will become a stronger offering later)

Creating a Virtual Environment by Using VirtualEnv

Reasons abound to create virtual environments, but the main reason to do so with Python is to provide a safe and known testing environment. By using the same testing environment each time, you help ensure that the application has a stable environment until you have completed enough of it to test in a production-like environment. VirtualEnv (`https://pypi.python.org/pypi/virtualenv`) provides the means to create a virtual Python environment that you can use for the early testing process or to diagnose issues that could occur because of the environment. It's important to remember that there are at least three standard levels of testing that you need to perform:

>> **Bug:** Checking for errors in your application

>> **Performance:** Validating that your application meets speed, reliability, and security requirements

>> **Usability:** Verifying that your application meets user needs and will react to user input in the way the user expects

REMEMBER

Because of the manner in which most Python applications are used (see Chapter 19 for some ideas), you generally don't need to run them in a virtual environment after the application has gone to a production site. Most Python applications require access to the outside world, and the isolation of a virtual environment would prevent that access.

NEVER TEST ON A PRODUCTION SERVER

A mistake that some developers make is to test their unreleased application on the production server where the user can easily get to it. Of the many reasons not to test your application on a production server, data loss has to be the most important. If you allow users to gain access to an unreleased version of your application that contains bugs that might corrupt the database or other data sources, the data could be lost or damaged permanently.

You also need to realize that you get only one chance to make a first impression. Many software projects fail because users don't use the end result. The application is complete, but no one uses it because of the perception that the application is flawed in some way. Users have only one goal in mind: to complete their tasks and then go home. When users see that an application is costing them time, they tend not to use it.

Unreleased applications can also have security holes that nefarious individuals will use to gain access to your network. It doesn't matter how well your security software works if you leave the door open for anyone to come in. After they have come in, getting rid of them is nearly impossible, and even if you do get rid of them, the damage to your data is already done. Recovery from security breaches is notoriously difficult — and sometimes impossible. In short, never test on your production server because the costs of doing so are simply too high.

Installing Your Application by Using PyInstaller

Users don't want to spend a lot of time installing your application, no matter how much it might help them in the end. Even if you can get the user to attempt an installation, less skilled users are likely to fail. In short, you need a surefire method of getting an application from your system to the user's system. Installers, such as PyInstaller (`https://pyinstaller.org/en/stable/`), do just that. They make a nice package out of your application that the user can easily install.

Fortunately, PyInstaller works on all the platforms that Python supports, so you need just the one tool to meet every installation need you have. In addition, you can get platform-specific support when needed. For example, when working on a Windows platform, you can create code-signed executables. Mac developers will appreciate that PyInstaller provides support for bundles. In many cases, avoiding the platform-specific features is best unless you really do need them. When you use a platform-specific feature, the installation will succeed only on the target platform.

WARNING

A number of the installer tools that you find online are platform specific. For example, when you look at an installer that reportedly creates executables, you need to be careful that the executables aren't platform specific (or at least match the platform you want to use). It's important to get a product that will work everywhere it's needed so that you don't create an installation package that the user can't use. Having a language that works everywhere doesn't help when the installation package actually hinders installation.

AVOID THE ORPHANED PRODUCT

Some Python tools floating around the Internet are *orphaned,* which means that the developer is no longer actively supporting them. Developers still use the tool because they like the features it supports or how it works. However, doing so is always risky because you can't be sure that the tool will work with the latest version of Python. The best way to approach tools is to get tools that are fully supported by the vendor who created them.

If you absolutely must use an orphaned tool (such as when an orphaned tool is the only one available to perform the task), make sure that the tool still has good community support. The vendor may not be around any longer, but at least the community will provide a source of information when you need product support. Otherwise, you'll waste a lot of time trying to use an unsupported product that you might never get to work properly.

Building Developer Documentation by Using pdoc

Two kinds of documentation are associated with applications: user and developer. User documentation shows how to use the application, while developer documentation shows how the application works. A library requires only one sort of documentation, developer, while a desktop application may require only user documentation. A service might actually require both kinds of documentation depending on who uses it and how the service is put together. The majority of your documentation is likely to affect developers, and pdoc (`https://github.com/mitmproxy/pdoc`) is a simple solution for creating it.

The pdoc utility relies on the documentation that you place in your code in the form of docstrings and comments. The output is in the form of a text file or an HTML document. You can also have pdoc run in a way that provides output through a web server so that people can see the documentation directly in a browser.

WHAT IS A DOCSTRING?

This chapter talks about document strings (docstrings). A *docstring* is a special kind of comment that appears within a triple quote, like this:

```
"""This is a docstring."""
```

You associate a docstring with an object, such as packages, functions, classes, and methods. Any code object you can create in Python can have a docstring. The purpose of a docstring is to document the object. Consequently, you want to use descriptive sentences.

The easiest way to see a docstring is to follow the object's name with the special __doc__ method. For example, typing **print(MyClass.__doc__)** would display the docstring for MyClass. You can also access a docstring by using help, such as `help(MyClass)`. Good docstrings tell what the object does, rather than how it does it.

Third-party utilities can also make use of docstrings. Given the right utility, you can write the documentation for an entire library without actually having to write anything. The utility uses the docstrings within your library to create the documentation. Consequently, even though docstrings and comments are used for different purposes, they're equally important in your Python code.

Developing Application Code by Using Komodo Edit

Several chapters in this book discuss the issue of Interactive Development Environments (IDEs), but none make a specific recommendation (except for the use of Google Colab and Jupyter Notebook throughout the book). The IDE you choose depends partly on your needs as a developer, your skill level, and the kinds of applications you want to create. Some IDEs are better than others when it comes to certain kinds of application development. One of the better general-purpose IDEs for novice developers is Komodo IDE (`https://www.activestate.com/products/komodo-ide/`). You can obtain this IDE for free, and it includes a wealth of features that will make your coding experience much better than what you'll get from IDLE (included with Python). Here are some of those features:

- ❯❯ Support for multiple programming languages
- ❯❯ Automatic completion of keywords
- ❯❯ Indentation checking
- ❯❯ Project support so that applications are partially coded before you even begin
- ❯❯ Superior support

Debugging Your Application by Using pydbgr

A high-end IDE, such as Komodo IDE, comes with a complete debugger. However, if you're using something smaller, less expensive, and less capable than a high-end IDE, you might not have a debugger at all. A *debugger* helps you locate errors in your application and fix them. The better your debugger, the less effort required to locate and fix the error. When your editor doesn't include a debugger, you need an external debugger such as pydbgr (`https://github.com/rocky/python2-trepan` and `https://pypi.org/project/trepan3k/`), which is currently being updated.

REMEMBER

A reasonably good debugger includes a number of standard features, such as code colorization (the use of color to indicate things like keywords). However, pydbgr also includes a number of nonstandard features that set it apart. Here are some of the standard and nonstandard features that make pydbgr a good choice when your editor doesn't come with a debugger:

>> **Smarteval:** The eval command helps you see what will happen when you execute a line of code, before you actually execute it in the application. It helps you perform "what if" analysis to see what is going wrong with the application.

>> **Out-of-process debugging:** Normally you have to debug applications that reside on the same machine. In fact, the debugger is part of the application's process, which means that the debugger can actually interfere with the debugging process. Using out-of-process debugging means that the debugger doesn't affect the application and you don't even have to run the application on the same machine as the debugger.

>> **Thorough byte-code inspection:** Viewing how the code you write is turned into *byte code* (the code that the Python interpreter actually understands) can sometimes help you solve tough problems.

>> **Event filtering and tracing:** As your application runs in the debugger, it generates events that help the debugger understand what is going on. For example, moving to the next line of code generates an event, returning from a function call generates another event, and so on. This feature makes it possible to control just how the debugger traces through an application and which events it reacts to.

Entering an Interactive Environment by Using IPython

The Python shell works fine for many interactive tasks. However, if you have used this product, you may have already noted that the default shell has certain deficiencies. Of course, the biggest deficiency is that the Python shell is a pure text environment in which you must type commands to perform any given task. A more advanced shell, such as IPython (http://ipython.org/), can make the interactive environment friendlier by providing GUI features so that you don't have to remember the syntax for odd commands.

REMEMBER

IPython is actually more than just a simple shell. It provides an environment in which you can interact with Python in new ways, such as by displaying graphics that show the result of formulas you create using Python. In addition, IPython is designed as a kind of front end that can accommodate other languages. The

IPython application actually sends commands to the real shell in the background, so you can use shells from other languages such as Julia and Haskell. (Don't worry if you've never heard of these languages.)

One of the more exciting features of IPython is the ability to work in parallel computing environments. Normally a shell is single threaded, which means that you can't perform any sort of parallel computing. In fact, you can't even create a multithreaded environment. This feature alone makes IPython worthy of a trial.

Testing Python Applications by Using PyUnit

At some point, you need to test your applications to ensure that they work as instructed. You can test them by entering in one command at a time and verifying the result, or you can automate the process. Obviously, the automated approach is better because you really do want to get home for dinner someday and manual testing is really, really slow (especially when you make mistakes, which are guaranteed to happen). Products such as PyUnit (`https://wiki.python.org/moin/PyUnit`) make unit testing (the testing of individual features) significantly easier.

The nice part of this product is that you actually create Python code to perform the testing. Your script is simply another, specialized, application that tests the main application for problems.

REMEMBER

You may be thinking that the scripts, rather than your professionally written application, could be bug ridden. The testing script is designed to be extremely simple, which will keep scripting errors small and quite noticeable. Of course, errors can (and sometimes do) happen, so yes, when you can't find a problem with your application, you do need to check the script.

Tidying Your Code by Using Isort

It may seem like an incredibly small thing, but code can get messy, especially if you don't place all your `import` statements at the top of the file in alphabetical order. In some situations, it becomes difficult, if not impossible, to figure out what's going on with your code when it isn't kept neat. The Isort utility (`https://pycqa.github.io/isort/`) performs the seemingly small task of sorting your import statements and ensuring that they all appear at the top of the source code file. This small step can have a significant effect on your ability to understand and modify the source code.

Just knowing which modules a particular module needs can be a help in locating potential problems. For example, if you somehow get an older version of a needed module on your system, knowing which modules the application needs can make the process of finding that module easier.

In addition, knowing which modules an application needs is important when it comes time to distribute your application to users. Knowing that the user has the correct modules available helps ensure that the application will run as anticipated.

Providing Version Control by Using Mercurial

The applications you created while working through this book aren't very complex. In fact, after you finish this book and move on to more advanced training applications, you're unlikely to need version control. However, after you start working in an organizational development environment in which you create real applications that users need to have available at all times, version control becomes essential. *Version control* is simply the act of keeping track of the changes that occur in an application between application releases to the production environment. When you say you're using MyApp 1.2, you're referring to version 1.2 of the MyApp application. Versioning lets everyone know which application release is being used when bug fixes and other kinds of support take place.

Numerous version control products are available for Python. One of the more interesting offerings is Mercurial (https://www.mercurial-scm.org/). You can get a version of Mercurial for almost any platform that Python will run on, so you don't have to worry about changing products when you change platforms. (If your platform doesn't offer a binary, executable release, you can always build one from the source code provided on the download site.)

Unlike a lot of the other offerings out there, Mercurial is free. Even if you find that you need a more advanced product later, you can gain useful experience by working with Mercurial on a project or two.

The act of storing each version of an application in a separate place so that changes can be undone or redone as needed is called *source code management* or SCM. For many people, source code management seems like a hard task. Because the Mercurial environment is quite forgiving, you can learn about SCM in a friendly environment. Being able to interact with any version of the source code for a particular application is essential when you need to go back and fix problems created by a new release.

The best part about Mercurial is that it provides a great online tutorial at `https://www.mercurial-scm.org/wiki/Tutorial`. Following along on your own machine is the best way to learn about SCM, but even just reading the material is helpful. Of course, the first tutorial is all about getting a good installation of Mercurial. The tutorials then lead you through the process of creating a repository (a place where application versions are stored) and using the repository as you create your application code. By the time you finish the tutorials, you should have a great idea of how source control should work and why versioning is an important part of application development.

Chapter **21**

Ten (Plus) Libraries You Need to Know About

Python provides you with considerable power when it comes to creating average applications. However, most applications aren't average and require some sort of special processing to make them work. That's where libraries come into play. A good library will extend Python functionality so that it supports the special programming needs that you have. For example, you might need to plot statistics or interact with a scientific device. These sorts of tasks require the use of one or more libraries.

TIP

One of the best places to find a library listing online is the UsefulModules site at `https://wiki.python.org/moin/UsefulModules`. Of course, you have many other places to look for libraries as well. For example, the article entitled "Top 10 Python Libraries You Must Know In 2022" (`https://www.edureka.co/blog/python-libraries/`) provides you with a relatively complete description of the ten libraries its title refers to. If you're working on a specific platform, such as Windows, you can find platform-specific sites, such as "Unofficial Windows Binaries for Python Extension Packages" (`https://www.lfd.uci.edu/~gohlke/pythonlibs/`). The point is that you can find lists of libraries everywhere.

The purpose of this chapter isn't to add to your already overflowing list of potential library candidates. Instead, it provides you with a list of ten libraries that work on every platform and provide basic services that just about everyone will need. Think of this chapter as a source for a core group of libraries to use for your next coding adventure.

Developing a Secure Environment by Using CryptLib

Data security is an essential part of any programming effort. The reason that applications are so valued is that they make it easy to manipulate and use data of all sorts. However, the application must protect the data or the efforts to work with it are lost. It's the data that is ultimately the valuable part of a business — the application is simply a tool. Part of protecting the data is to ensure that no one can steal it or use it in a manner that the originator didn't intend, which is where cryptographic libraries such as CryptLib (`https://www.cs.auckland.ac.nz/~pgut001/cryptlib/`) come into play. One of the best parts of this particular library is that it includes bindings for:

>> C/C++

>> C# and other .NET languages

>> Delphi

>> Java

>> Python

>> Visual Basic (VB)

REMEMBER The main purpose of this library is to turn your data into something that others can't read while it sits in permanent storage. The purposeful modification of data in this manner is called *encryption*. However, when you read the data into memory, a *decryption* routine takes the mangled data and turns it back into its original form so that the application can manage it. At the center of all this is the *key*, which is used to encrypt and decrypt the data.

Interacting with Databases by Using SQLAlchemy

A *database* is essentially an organized manner of storing repetitive or structured data on disk. For example, customer *records* (individual entries in the database) are repetitive because each customer has the same sort of information requirements, such as name, address, and telephone number. The precise organization of the data (such as tabular or hierarchical) determines the sort of database you need. Some database products specialize in text organization, others in tabular information, and still others in random bits of data (such as readings taken from a scientific instrument). Databases can use a tree-like structure or a flat-file configuration to store data. You'll hear all sorts of odd terms when you start looking into DataBase Management System (DBMS) technology — most of which mean something only to a DataBase Administrator (DBA) and won't matter to you.

REMEMBER

The most common type of database is called a Relational DataBase Management System (RDBMS), which uses tables that are organized into records and fields (just like a table you might draw on a sheet of paper). Each *field* is part of a column of the same kind of information, such as the customer's name. Tables are related to each other in various ways, so creating complex relationships is possible. For example, each customer may have one or more entries in a purchase order table, and the customer table and the purchase order table are therefore related to each other.

An RDBMS relies on a special language called the Structured Query Language (SQL) to access the individual records inside. Of course, you need some means of interacting with both the RDBMS and SQL, which is where SQLAlchemy (https://www.sqlalchemy.org/) comes into play. This product reduces the amount of work needed to ask the database to perform tasks such as returning a specific customer record, creating a new customer record, updating an existing customer record, and deleting an old customer record.

Seeing the World by Using Google Maps

Geocoding (the finding of geographic coordinates, such as longitude and latitude from geographic data, such as address) has lots of uses in the world today. People use the information to do everything from finding a good restaurant to locating a lost hiker in the mountains. Getting from one place to another often revolves around geocoding today as well. Google Maps (https://pypi.org/project/googlemaps/) lets you add directional data to your applications.

In addition to getting from one point to another or finding a lost soul in the desert, Google Maps can also help in Geographic Information System (GIS) applications. The "Helping People Decide on Location" section of Chapter 19 describes this particular technology in more detail, but essentially, GIS is all about deciding on a location for something or determining why one location works better than another location for a particular task. In short, Google Maps presents your application with a look at the outside world that it can use to help your user make decisions.

Adding a Graphical User Interface by Using TkInter

Users respond to the Graphical User Interface (GUI) because it's friendlier and requires less thought than using a command-line interface. Many products out there can give your Python application a GUI. However, the most commonly used product is TkInter (`https://wiki.python.org/moin/TkInter`). Developers like it so much because TkInter keeps things simple. It's actually an interface for the Tool Command Language (Tcl)/Toolkit (Tk) found at `http://www.tcl.tk/`. A number of languages use Tcl/Tk as the basis for creating a GUI.

TIP

You might not relish the idea of adding a GUI to your application. Doing so tends to be time consuming and doesn't make the application any more functional (it also slows the application down in many cases). The point is that users like GUIs, and if you want your application to see strong use, you need to meet user requirements.

WORKING WITH DASHBOARDS

Developers are always coming up with new ways to present information. Although you can use your Notebooks for any presentation and allow traditional data manipulation using a GUI like TkInter, the resulting Notebooks don't provide an interactive experience for nonprogrammers who simply want to work with outputs. This is where a dashboard can come in handy. You export your Notebook as a .py file after adding dashboard functionality to it using standard Python programming methods. To run the dashboard, you call on the dashboard server from the command prompt or use something like a batch file and provide the .py file as input. The user will see any plots included in your Notebook with the addition of controls, such as sliders, that allow them to interact with the plot and play *what-if* scenarios that allow the user to see what happens when the data to the plot changes. You can find a number of dashboards online, including these:

- Dash (https://plotly.com/dash/)
- Panel (https://panel.holoviz.org/)
- Streamlit (https://streamlit.io/)
- voila (https://voila.readthedocs.io/en/stable/)

Providing a Nice Tabular Data Presentation by Using PrettyTable

Displaying tabular data in a manner the user can understand is important. From the examples you've seen throughout the book, you know that Python stores this type of data in a form that works best for programming needs. However, users need something that is organized in a manner that humans understand and that is visually appealing. The PrettyTable library (https://pypi.org/project/prettytable/) makes it easy to add an appealing tabular presentation to your command-line application.

Enhancing Your Application with Sound by Using PyAudio

Sound is a useful way to convey certain types of information to the user. Of course, you have to be careful in using sound because special-needs users might not be able to hear it, and for those who can, using too much sound can interfere with normal business operations. However, sometimes audio is an important means of communicating supplementary information to users who can interact with it (or of simply adding a bit of pizzazz to make your application more interesting).

One of the better platform-independent libraries to make sound work with your Python application is PyAudio (http://people.csail.mit.edu/hubert/pyaudio/). This library makes it possible to record and play back sounds as needed (such as a user recording an audio note of tasks to perform later and then playing back the list of items as needed).

TIP

Working with sound on a computer always involves trade-offs. For example, a platform-independent library can't take advantage of special features that a particular platform might possess. In addition, it might not support all the file formats that a particular platform uses. The reason to use a platform-independent library is to ensure that your application provides basic sound support on all systems that it might interact with.

Manipulating Images by Using PyQtGraph

Humans are visually oriented. If you show someone a table of information and then show the same information as a graph, the graph is always the winner when it comes to conveying information. Graphs help people see trends and understand why the data has taken the course that it has. However, getting those pixels that represent the tabular information onscreen is difficult, which is why you need a library such as PyQtGraph (https://www.pyqtgraph.org/) to make things simpler.

Even though the library is designed around engineering, mathematical, and scientific requirements, you have no reason to avoid using it for other purposes. PyQtGraph supports both 2D and 3D displays, and you can use it to generate new graphics based on numeric input. The output is completely interactive, so a user can select image areas for enhancement or other sorts of manipulation. In addition, the library comes with a wealth of useful widgets (controls, such as buttons, that you can display onscreen) to make the coding process even easier. Make sure you review the Requirements section of the PyQtGraph website for add-ins needed to use this product.

Locating Your Information by Using Whoosh

Finding your information can be difficult when the information grows to a certain size. Consider your hard drive as a large, free-form, tree-based database that lacks a useful index. Any time such a structure becomes large enough, data simply gets lost. (Just try to find those pictures you took last summer and you'll get the idea.) As a result, having some type of search capability built into your application is important so that users can find that lost file or other information. Note that a search library isn't a search engine; it provides you with the means for building your own search engine.

WARNING

A number of search libraries are available for Python. The problem with most of them is that they are hard to install or don't provide consistent platform support. In fact, some of them work on only one or two platforms. However, Whoosh (https://whoosh.readthedocs.io/en/latest/intro.html) is written in pure Python, which ensures that it works on every platform. If you find that Whoosh doesn't meet your needs, make sure the product you do get will provide the required search functionality on all the platforms you select and that the installation requirements are within reason.

Creating an Interoperable Java Environment by Using JPype

Python does provide access to a huge array of libraries, and you're really unlikely to use them all. However, you might be in a situation in which you find a Java library that is a perfect fit but can't use it from your Python application unless you're willing to jump through a whole bunch of hoops. The JPype library (`http://jpype.sourceforge.net/`) makes it possible to access most (but not all) of the Java libraries out there directly from Python. The library works by creating a bridge between the two languages at the byte-code level. Consequently, you don't have to do anything weird to get your Python application to work with Java.

WARNING

CONVERTING YOUR PYTHON APPLICATION TO JAVA

Many different ways exist to achieve interoperability between two languages. Creating a bridge between them, as JPype does, is one way. Another alternative is to convert the code created for one language into code for the other language. This is the approach used by Jython (`https://wiki.python.org/jython/`). This utility converts your Python code into Java code so that you can make full use of Java functionality in your application while maintaining the features that you like about Python.

You'll encounter trade-offs in language interoperability no matter which solution you use. In the case of JPype, you won't have access to some Java libraries. In addition, there is a speed penalty in using this approach because the JPype bridge is constantly converting calls and data. The problem with Jython is that you lose the ability to modify your code after conversion. Any changes that you make will create an incompatibility between the original Python code and its Java counterpart. In short, no perfect solutions exist for the problem of getting the best features of two languages into one application.

Accessing Local Network Resources by Using Twisted Matrix

Depending on your network setup, you may need access to files and other resources that you can't reach using the platform's native capabilities. In this case, you need a library that makes such access possible, such as Twisted Matrix (https://twisted.org/). The basic idea behind this library is to provide you with the calls needed to establish a connection, no matter what sort of protocol is in use.

The feature that makes this library so useful is its event-driven nature. This means that your application need not get hung up while waiting for the network to respond. In addition, the use of an event-driven setup makes asynchronous communication (in which a request is sent by one routine and then handled by a completely separate routine) easy to implement.

Accessing Internet Resources by Using Libraries

Although products such as Twisted Matrix can handle online communication, getting a dedicated HTTP protocol library is often a better option when working with the Internet because a dedicated library is both faster and more feature complete. When you specifically need HTTP or HTTPS support, using a library such as httplib2 (https://github.com/httplib2) is a good idea. This library is written in pure Python and makes handling HTTP-specific needs, such as setting a Keep-Alive value, relatively easy. (A *Keep-Alive* is a value that determines how long a port stays open waiting for a response so that the application doesn't have to continuously re-create the connection, wasting resources and time as a result.)

You can use httplib2 for any Internet-specific methodology — it provides full support for both the GET and POST request methods. This library also includes routines for standard Internet compression methods, such as deflate and gzip. It also supports a level of automation. For example, httplib2 adds ETags back into PUT requests when resources are already cached.

Index

(hashtag), 61
% (percent sign), 80
%% (double percent sign), 80
(#) number sign, 70
/ (forward slash), 305
: (colon), 129
[] (square brackets), 243
\ (backslash), 219, 305
{} (curly brackets), 232–233
= (assignment operator), 97

A

Abaqus, 352
about this book, 1–2
absolute path, 305
accented (special character category), 219
__add__( ) method, 292
Add New Form Field dialog box, 65
administrators, 353
%alias_magic line magic command, 86
%alias line magic command, 86
align formatting specification, 234
Amazon, Echo, 9
American Standard Code for Information Interchange
    (ASCII), 216–217
Anaconda Prompt, 205
Android tablet, 307
append( ) function, 245, 276, 317
appendleft( ) function, 276
Apple, Siri, 9
application (app)
    adding comments, 70–73
    adding documentation cells, 61–62
    browser-based, 17
    converting to Java, 376
    creating, 60–66
    CRUD acronym to describe what it does, 41
    defined, 11, 13–15
    developing code, 60–61
    as a form of communication, 11–13

interacting with form fields, 64–66
making applications fast, 347
managing data within, 108
organizing information in, 240–241
other cell content, 62–63
as procedure, 13
questions to ask when creating, 15
running, 66–68
scratch cells in, 63–64
seeing result of, 66
testing class inheritance in, 298–299, 365
using if statement in, 129–133
using indentation in, 68–70
using the if...elif statement in, 135–138
using the if...else statement in, 134
using while statement in, 152–154
viewing executed code history, 68
world's worst, 15
writing your first, 57–77
ArcGIS, 354
arguments
    creating functions with variable number of, 122–123
    defined, 120
    giving function arguments a default value, 121–122
    positional, 121
    sending by name, 121
    sending required arguments, 120–121
ArithmeticError exception, 176–177
arithmetic operators, 112
assignment operator (=), 97
assignment operators, 114–115
assumptions, in this book, 2–3
attributes
    automatically generated by Python, 210
    built-in class, 285–286
    defined, 191
audio library, 373–374
%autocall line magic command, 86
%automagic line magic command, 86
automatic indentation, 69
%autosave line magic command, 86

B

backslash (\), 219, 305
Base 2, 98
Base 8, 98
Base 10, 98
Base 16 (hex), 98
base classes, 164
bin( ) function, 99
BitBucket, 358
bitwise operators, 112, 114
black-swan events, 159
Blender, 352
blocks, data stored as, 304
body (email), 323
bold type, 74
%bookmark line magic command, 86
Boole, George, 102
Boolean algebra, 102
Boolean values, 102
bool type, 102
Boris, the Twitter Dino-Bot, 353
branches, 31
break clause, 146
breaking change, 161
break statement, 146–147
bugs, 40, 59, 158
bug-tracking sites, 358–359
built-in class attributes, 281–282
built-in exceptions, 164–165
built-in packages, 194–195
__builtins__ attribute, 210
bulleted list, adding, 75
byte code, 364

C

C# programming language, 17, 20
__cached__ attribute, 210
caller, 117, 181
capitalize( ) function, 223
car security systems, 355
catching exceptions, 157, 163–180
C/C++, 17
%cd line magic command, 86
cell magic commands, 83, 90–91

cells
  editing, 38
  moving, 39
  running all, 40
  running current, 39
  running other, 39–40
center( ) function, 226
center(width, fillchar=" ") function, 223
characters
  accented, 219
  creating strings with, 217–218
  drawing, 219
  numeric values, 216–217
  selecting, 219
  special, 218–221
  typographical, 219
chat rooms, 9
Cheat sheet, 4
checkpoints, 77
child class, 297–298
Cinema 4D, 352
Clarke, Arthur C. (science writer)
classes
  built-in class attributes, 281–282
  child class, 297–298
  creating and using, 279–299
  creating class definition, 280–281
  creating class methods, 283–284
  defined, 280
  extending classes to make new classes, 296–299
  external, 293–296
  overloading operators, 291–293
  parent class, 296–297
  production-grade class, 296–297
  saving to disk, 294–295
  testing class inheritance in application, 298–299
  tests of in application, 298–299
  working with constructors, 285–286
  working with methods, 282–284
  working with variables, 287–289
class suite, 281
class variables, 287–288
clause, 133. *See also specific clauses*
clear( ) function, 245, 248
%clear line magic command, 86

About the Author

John Mueller is a freelance author and technical editor. He has writing in his blood, having produced 122 books and more than 600 articles to date. The topics range from networking to artificial intelligence and from database management to heads-down programming. Some of his current books include discussions of data science, machine learning, and algorithms. He also writes about computer languages such as C++, C#, and Python. His technical editing skills have helped more than 70 authors refine the content of their manuscripts. John has provided technical editing services to a variety of magazines, performed various kinds of consulting, and he writes certification exams. Be sure to read John's blog at http://blog. johnmuellerbooks.com/. You can reach John on the Internet at John@ JohnMuellerBooks.com. John also has a website at http://www.johnmueller books.com/.

Dedication

This book is dedicated to Paige and Parker Groom, my inspiration for many great things and the joys of my life.

Acknowledgments

Thanks to my wife, Rebecca. Even though she is gone now, her spirit is in every book I write and in every word that appears on the page. She believed in me when no one else would.

Rod Stephens deserves thanks for his technical edit of this book. He greatly added to the accuracy and depth of the material you see here. Rod's critical thinking skills force me to truly think through all the book elements. He's also the sanity check for my work.

Matt Wagner, my agent, deserves credit for helping me get the contract in the first place and taking care of all the details that most authors don't really consider. I always appreciate his assistance. It's good to know that someone wants to help.

A number of people read all or part of this book to help me refine the approach, test the coding examples, and generally provide input that all readers wish they could have. These unpaid volunteers helped in ways too numerous to mention here. I especially appreciate the efforts of Eva Beattie, who provided general input, read the entire book, and selflessly devoted herself to this project.

Finally, I would like to thank Kelsey Baird, Susan Christophersen, and the rest of the editorial and production staff.

Publisher's Acknowledgments

Acquisitions Editor: Kelsey Baird

Project Manager and Copy Editor:
Susan Christophersen

Technical Editor: Rod Stephens

Production Editor: Mohammed Zafar Ali

Cover Image: © antoniodiaz/Shutterstock

Leverage the power

Dummies is the global leader in the reference category and one of the most trusted and highly regarded brands in the world. No longer just focused on books, customers now have access to the dummies content they need in the format they want. Together we'll craft a solution that engages your customers, stands out from the competition, and helps you meet your goals.

Advertising & Sponsorships

Connect with an engaged audience on a powerful multimedia site, and position your message alongside expert how-to content. Dummies.com is a one-stop shop for free, online information and know-how curated by a team of experts.

- Targeted ads
- Video
- Email Marketing
- Microsites
- Sweepstakes sponsorship

20 MILLION PAGE VIEWS **EVERY SINGLE MONTH**

15 MILLION UNIQUE VISITORS PER MONTH

43% OF ALL VISITORS ACCESS THE SITE **VIA THEIR MOBILE DEVICES**

700,000 NEWSLETTER SUBSCRIPTIONS **TO THE INBOXES OF** *300,000* UNIQUE **INDIVIDUALS EVERY WEEK**

# of dummies

Custom Publishing

Reach a global audience in any language by creating a solution that will differentiate you from competitors, amplify your message, and encourage customers to make a buying decision.

- Apps
- Books
- eBooks
- Video
- Audio
- Webinars

Brand Licensing & Content

Leverage the strength of the world's most popular reference brand to reach new audiences and channels of distribution.

For more information, visit **dummies.com/biz**

PERSONAL ENRICHMENT

Staying Sharp	**Facebook**	**Guitar**	**Investing**	**Beekeeping**	**Digital Photography**
9781119187790	9781119179030	9781119293354	9781119293347	9781119310068	9781119235606
USA $26.00	USA $21.99	USA $24.99	USA $22.99	USA $22.99	USA $24.99
CAN $31.99	CAN $25.99	CAN $29.99	CAN $27.99	CAN $27.99	CAN $29.99
UK £19.99	UK £16.99	UK £17.99	UK £16.99	UK £16.99	UK £17.99

Meditation	**Pregnancy**	**Samsung Galaxy S7**	**iPhone**	**Crocheting**	**Nutrition**
9781119251163	9781119235491	9781119279952	9781119283133	9781119287117	9781119130246
USA $24.99	USA $26.99	USA $24.99	USA $24.99	USA $24.99	USA $22.99
CAN $29.99	CAN $31.99	CAN $29.99	CAN $29.99	CAN $29.99	CAN $27.99
UK £17.99	UK £19.99	UK £17.99	UK £17.99	UK £16.99	UK £16.99

PROFESSIONAL DEVELOPMENT

Windows 10	**AutoCAD**	**Excel 2016**	**QuickBooks 2017**	**macOS Sierra**	**LinkedIn**	**Windows 10 All-in-One**
9781119311041	9781119255796	9781119293439	9781119281467	9781119280651	9781119251132	9781119310563
USA $24.99	USA $39.99	USA $26.99	USA $26.99	USA $29.99	USA $24.99	USA $34.00
CAN $29.99	CAN $47.99	CAN $31.99	CAN $31.99	CAN $35.99	CAN $29.99	CAN $41.99
UK £17.99	UK £27.99	UK £19.99	UK £19.99	UK £21.99	UK £17.99	UK £24.99

SharePoint 2016	**Fundamental Analysis**	**Networking**	**Office 2016**	**Office 365**	**Salesforce.com**	**Coding**
9781119181705	9781119263593	9781119257769	9781119293477	9781119265313	9781119239314	9781119293323
USA $29.99	USA $26.99	USA $29.99	USA $26.99	USA $24.99	USA $29.99	USA $29.99
CAN $35.99	CAN $31.99	CAN $35.99	CAN $31.99	CAN $29.99	CAN $35.99	CAN $35.99
UK £21.99	UK £19.99	UK £21.99	UK £19.99	UK £17.99	UK £21.99	UK £21.99

dummies.com

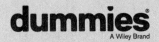

dummies
A Wiley Brand

Learning Made Easy

ACADEMIC

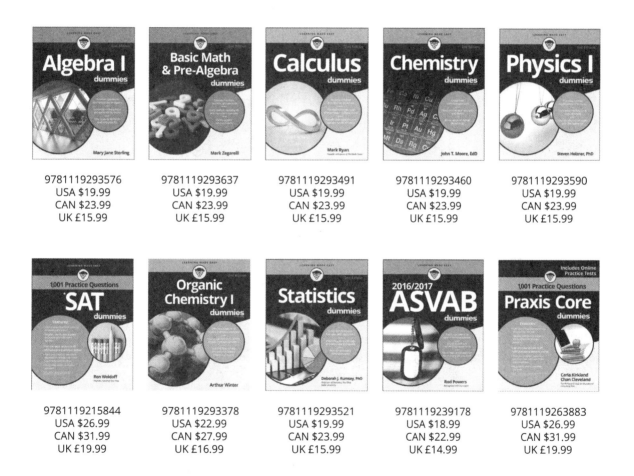

9781119293576
USA $19.99
CAN $23.99
UK £15.99

9781119293637
USA $19.99
CAN $23.99
UK £15.99

9781119293491
USA $19.99
CAN $23.99
UK £15.99

9781119293460
USA $19.99
CAN $23.99
UK £15.99

9781119293590
USA $19.99
CAN $23.99
UK £15.99

9781119215844
USA $26.99
CAN $31.99
UK £19.99

9781119293378
USA $22.99
CAN $27.99
UK £16.99

9781119293521
USA $19.99
CAN $23.99
UK £15.99

9781119239178
USA $18.99
CAN $22.99
UK £14.99

9781119263883
USA $26.99
CAN $31.99
UK £19.99

Available Everywhere Books Are Sold

dummies.com

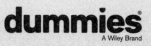

Small books for big imaginations